PARALLEL
EMPIRES

PARALLEL
EMPIRES

THE VATICAN AND THE UNITED STATES—
TWO CENTURIES OF ALLIANCE
AND CONFLICT

MASSIMO FRANCO

TRANSLATED FROM THE ITALIAN BY ROLAND FLAMINI

DOUBLEDAY

NEW YORK   LONDON   TORONTO   SYDNEY   AUCKLAND

Book design by Elizabeth Rendfleisch

Library of Congress Cataloging-in-Publication Data
Franco, Massimo.
[Imperi paralleli. English]
Parallel empires : the Vatican and the United States—
two centuries of alliance and conflict / Massimo Franco ;
translated from Italian by Roland Flamini.—1st U.S. ed.
p. cm.
Includes bibliographical references and index.
1. Catholic Church—Foreign relations—United States.
2. United States—Foreign relations—Catholic Church. I. Title.

BX1406.3.F7313 2007
327.456'34073—dc22
2007017579

ISBN 978-0-385-51893-2

To my wife, Ilaria,
and to our children,
Federica, Matteo, and Tommaso

CONTENTS

INTRODUCTION

In these early years of the third millennium, the tension-filled debate in the West over how to deal with the Islamic world centers on disagreements between the United States and Europe. But with the discussion focused on political and strategic issues, the role of a third Western protagonist has received scant attention. That protagonist is the Vatican—the Holy See—which has sometimes challenged and at other times supported the actions of the United States, emerging as a parallel empire to the one based in Washington. The Vatican has its roots in Western culture but operates outside that narrow label. Its influence is not based on military power or advanced technology, on unilateralism or on a mission of bringing democracy to the Islamic world. With its global network of priests, nuns, missionaries, and institutions the Holy See is by nature multilateralist. It uses diplomacy, moral suasion, international institutions, and other instruments of soft power.

The Vatican view is that the American response to al Qaeda terrorism, the battlefront of the third millennium, is too strident and more likely to exacerbate the problem than to solve it. While Islamic fundamentalism is the main threat to the West, Vatican officials press their arguments that historically Islam and Christian communities have generally managed to coexist in the Arab world. Today, more than two centuries of Vatican-U.S. coexistence are threatened by American behavior, and senior members of the Catholic hierarchy are concerned that Washington's actions can only lead to an increase in the Christianophobia that is one of the unintended consequences of the Iraq War. This book attempts to trace the course of the historic relationship between two Western parallel empires in times of cooperation and of dissent—pointing out a link between the old world and the new that has not previously been carefully studied; between the central government of the Roman Catholic Church, once concerned only with Europe but now an institution with global interests, and the United States, first isolationist, then the world policeman, and finally an aspiring dispenser of democracy. It's a long, tortuous story, and likely to continue as such following the death of Pope John Paul II and the election of Benedict XVI as his successor.

It is no coincidence that full relations between the Vatican and Washington, with the first exchange of ambassadors, were only established in 1984, nearly two centuries after Rome's initial approaches to the United States. The years between were marked by diplomatic and religious disputes that frustrated relations sometimes even when both states were in sync politically. The Vatican had been drawn to extend its influence to the New World by the prospect of bringing the faith to a burgeoning population of European immigrants, and at the same time converting the continent's indigenous peoples. The so-called Secret Archives of the Vatican reveal the extent of this effort, and its initial lack of success. Buried in the files are anguished reports from nineteenth-century papal emissaries on the hostile reception they received from European refugees driven to the New World by Catholic persecution. There are also stories of Catholic priests having to preach sermons in Latin or French because they spoke no English; and this behavior strengthened the perception among already settled Americans that Catholicism was a foreign religion good for Irish, Italian, and Polish immigrants but not for real Yankees.

Popes and presidents joined forces to combat Nazism and later Communism, but still America resisted recognizing the Holy See as a sovereign state. President Ronald Reagan finally agreed to send an ambassador to the Vatican, and to accept a nuncio—the Holy See's equivalent of an ambassador—in Washington to "reward" Pope John Paul II for Rome's support in the fight against what Reagan called "the evil empire." Washington considered the pope's native Poland the catalyst in the anticommunist offensive. Even so, Reagan had to pay a price for that decision. A group of conservative religious organizations brought suit against him for violating the separation of church and state. Reagan's decision had confirmed their long-held suspicion that the Vatican planned to control the United States.

Differences over strategy in the aftermath of the Islamic terrorist attacks on New York and Washington on September 11, 2001, created a rift between the United States and Europe—a process of corrosion that undermined the Western hegemony of the cold war years. But the other confrontation between the United States and the Vatican attracted less attention, partly because the Vatican was—as always—hard to read. Yet never before had the actions of Rome and Washington been so closely connected, though not always with the same aims and intentions. They are the only institutions with a truly global reach. Both proclaim their good intentions; each in its own way has taken up the contest against the rise of fundamentalism; and each shares a concern for what it sees as a decline in Western values. In recent years there has been a meeting of the minds between the Rome-based leadership of the Catholic Church and the leadership of the United States on certain basic, ethical principles rooted in a mixture of politics and religion. But, along with the rest of Europe, the Vatican has underlined its reservations about the Bush administration's approach to the ambiguous concept of a "war on terrorism."

These two parallel empires find themselves at times competing and at others cooperating in such volatile areas as the Islamic world—notably the Middle East—and in Asia. Having Christianity as a common factor does not always guarantee agreement between them on the issue of war and peace, on relations with the Islamic world, or on the definition of international order. The long, slow decline of the papacy of Pope John Paul II through his illness brought an element of uncertainty into Vatican-American relations. The pedophile priest scandal that reached its critical peak between the disastrous 9/11 attacks and the launch of the Iraq War undermined the leadership and authority of the United States Catholic bishops. But while the Vatican and the Bush administration both condemned terrorism yet differed on how to counter it, the Protestant president and the central administration of the Catholic Church found plenty of common ground in defending traditional values, notably a strong opposition to abortion, to genetic experiments, and to same-sex marriage.

Thus it was that in 2004 the Holy See revealed a marked preference for George W. Bush's reelection over his opponent, John Kerry, a Catholic. The Democratic senator's fatal flaw, in Rome's view, was his "cultural relativism," an expression dear to John Paul II, and more so to his successor Benedict XVI, who may have coined it in the first place. The latter made it his election manifesto prior to the conclave that chose him as the new pontiff on April 21, 2005.

The Vatican had already had to contend with a new development in American politics, one that appeared to change radically the traditional position of Catholics in the electorate. Bush's 2004 victory was profoundly influenced by religious issues. Moreover, in attracting the Christian vote, the Protestant candidate had received the majority of "papist" ballots. The 1960 controversy surrounding John F. Kennedy's Catholicism now seemed an anachronism. The point was not lost on the Holy See, which recognized the political impact of an ecumenical alliance and increasingly speaks of Christianity and less of Catholicism.

Parallel Empires is an attempt to explain a complex and sometimes contradictory relationship, and to examine in some depth the circumstances behind its extraordinary dynamic. In probing the relationship between these two extremities of Western civilization—the United States at one end and the papacy at the other—it is also possible to find some lateral answers to other aspects of the equation involving Europe and the very essence of the West itself. One has the impression that today's unexpected convergence of views is the result of a profound fear shared by the United States and the Vatican. America's uncertainty about its own security as a result of 9/11 finds its counterpart in the Vatican's deepening concern for the future of its ideal of Christianity, threatened by Islam's resurgence, and the dangers of the "cultural relativism" that is the battle cry of certain Christian groups in the United States and in Europe. The alliance on the ethical level between certain Protestant groups and the papacy of John Paul II previously and of Benedict XVI today is a reaction to these shadowy fears in the West.

I want to thank Bishop Sergio Pagano, prefect of the Vatican Secret Archives, the secretary general, Luca Carboni, who was my guide in the archives' labyrinths, and Barbara Jatta, of the Vatican Library, for her invaluable help in my search for old prints. I also acknowledge with thanks the cooperation of the library of *La Civiltà Cattolica* and of the

Gregorian University. But above all I am grateful to the Honorable James Nicholson, former United States ambassador to the Holy See, to senator-for-life Giulio Andreotti, and to Cardinal Pio Laghi. Without them this book would probably not even have been started. Thanks are also due to Lucio Caracciolo, whose friendly encouragement helped me to overcome my early doubts. In addition, I wish to express my gratitude to the people who, sometimes anonymously, helped me understand a long and complex relationship that seems destined to produce fresh surprises.

For this English edition I wish to acknowledge the contribution of Roland Flamini. Roland not only collaborated as a gifted translator but lent the great experience of a distinguished journalistic career and his knowledge of the subject matter to this edition. I wish to acknowledge the publisher, Bill Barry, simply by extending a big and grateful thank-you for his trust and confidence.

M. F., Rome, October 2008

PARALLEL
EMPIRES

CONCLAVE ON
AIR FORCE ONE

T HEY KNELT SIDE-BY-SIDE in Saint Peter's Basilica, a frieze of
American presidents past and present, united in a last tribute to
Pope John Paul II. The solemn funeral of a pontiff is a landmark in the
history of the Roman Catholic Church, but the presence of the three
American leaders—George W. Bush; his father, George Herbert
Walker Bush; and William Jefferson Clinton—had a historical significance of its own. It was not just that the presidents of the world's most
powerful democracy had traveled halfway round the world to honor
the head of a global faith that has never specifically recognized democracy as the only acceptable form of government, and a pontiff who in
temporal terms was Europe's only remaining absolute ruler. A seismic
gap had opened in the surface of relations between the United States
and the Vatican. On one side was the historic position of past American presidents whose successive attitudes toward the Roman hierarchy
had ranged from keeping their distance to—occasionally—cautious collaboration. On the other side was this recognition by the leadership of
the United States that in an increasingly dangerous world the common
bonds of Christianity mattered more than the differences of its com-
ponent parts. And so the cornerstone American principle of the separation of church and state had been momentarily set aside for this
symbolic act. Four decades earlier, John F. Kennedy had found himself
on Italian soil in June 1963 at the death of a previous pope, John
XXIII, and the installation of Paul VI; the president had deliberately
delayed his arrival in Rome to avoid any hint of submitting to Rome
by being seen at a pope's funeral or a new pope's installation in Saint
Peter's Basilica.

· · ·

"Here's the man who can tell us who's going to be the next pope." Bill Clinton's remark cut through the general conversation in the main cabin of Air Force One, focusing attention on the new arrival, James Nicholson, United States ambassador to the Holy See from 2001 to 2005, and after that secretary for veterans' affairs until October 2007 in the second Bush administration. Nicholson said: "I can't answer that. I don't know. Sorry, I don't have a direct line to the Holy Spirit." Even as he spoke Nicholson realized that his attempt to shrug off Clinton's implied question would not suffice. After spending nearly four years as the Bush administration's eyes and ears in the Vatican he knew he was expected to do better than that. Clinton was not going to let him off the hook that easily. "Come on, Jim," the former president urged the onetime ambassador. "What do you think is going to happen in the conclave?"

Nicholson glanced around him and quickly realized that Clinton was not the only person in the Boeing 747's salon waiting to hear what he had to say. Deployed around the comfortable space at 35,000 feet above the Atlantic were the rulers past and present of the American empire, en route to Rome for the papal funeral. Traveling with President Bush were his wife, Laura; his father, former president George H. W. Bush; and Secretary of State Condoleezza Rice. Clustered behind them was a group of distinguished Americans to complete the exceptionally large delegation going to pay the nation's last respects to the dead pontiff on behalf of the people of the United States. Nicholson, whose time in the papal state had spanned in quick succession the terrorist attack on New York and Washington of September 11, 2001, the pedophile priests scandal, and the start of the Iraq War, recounted how in his most recent reports from Rome on the papal succession the names of some cardinals came and went from the list of *papabili*—the most likely candidates—while others remained as fixed stars in the firmament. And immovable at the top of the list, Nicholson went on—pausing for dramatic effect—was Cardinal Joseph Ratzinger, perhaps partly because he was the senior member of the College of Cardinals. Clinton nodded thoughtfully, and then (as Nicholson was to recall later) strolled off to the back of the plane with studied nonchalance to join the traveling White House press corps and shoot the breeze about who was likely to be the next pope.

The flight across the Atlantic is a journey through space and time. There is the fact of traveling from one point to another; and there is the change of time zones, of having to put the human clock backward or forward, depending on the direction of the journey. The leaders, past and present, of the United States were time travelers in another sense too. Their eight-hour flight put some distance between current-day America and two centuries of prejudice and suspicion in the country about the papacy and the Roman Catholic Church. How many of those on board Air Force One grasped the wider meaning—indeed, the magnitude—of their mission? Their journey represented a reversal in historic attitudes toward the papacy that would have been unthinkable for the Founding Fathers. That the president—actually three presidents—would attend a pope's funeral was a mark of John Paul II's global impact, first, but also of his success and that of his predecessors in persuading successive administrations that papal wishes coincided with American strategic interests.

The final link between the two parallel empires of the West was about to be forged in Saint Peter's Basilica, as one "emperor" paid tribute to the other. It was to be hoped that past suspicions of popes trying to subvert American democracy, and nineteenth-century Protestant depictions of Vatican officials as diabolical agents of a foreign power, would now be consigned to the dustbin of history. More than two hundred years of long, tortuous diplomatic negotiations, of promises made and broken, of Protestant and Catholic machinations—that is, a certain type of American Protestant mentality matched against a certain type of Vatican mentality—would fade from the memory. Even the little "pre-conclave" initiated by Clinton at Nicholson's expense fed into this image of a changed world: Nicholson's diplomatic role was accepted as valid and natural. Thirty years earlier, the notion of creating such a role had stirred public protests in America.

Never before had a president of the United States attended the funeral of a pope. On this occasion, the jostling to be there was almost unseemly. Jimmy Carter, who had been the American "emperor" in 1978, the year of Pope John Paul II's election, had also wanted to attend, but was left out because the Vatican, besieged by governments wishing to be represented, had insisted that no official delegation could consist of more than five top members. With Laura Bush and Condoleezza Rice in the official party, Carter would have made a sixth.

As far as the Vatican was concerned, Carter's absence meant less than did the formidable, highest-level American presence. Senior prelates had anticipated a qualitative leap over the usual United States funeral delegation, but this turnout was beyond their expectations. The first hint had come when in the immediate aftermath of the pope's death a senior cardinal in Rome had received a phone call in the middle of the night from an old Washington friend expressing his sorrow and the sorrow of all Americans. The friend was former president George H. W. Bush. But such changes are not sudden, and this one had been maturing for some time, and certainly throughout the long pontificate that had just come to a close. The irony is that had the pope passed away two years earlier amid the flurry of forceful Vatican challenges to the invasion of Iraq, publicly denounced every Sunday by the pope himself from the window of his study overlooking Saint Peter's Square, and with the pedophile priests scandal raging at its most virulent, the American delegation to the funeral most likely would have been less exalted. But as John Paul's life passed very slowly into death, resentment and alienation gave way to compassion, and, for the American leadership, Rome seemed somehow the only place to be.

President George W. Bush had watched in amazement the extraordinary images of a vast, unending river of humanity shuffling patiently forward for a last glimpse of the dead pope lying in state in Saint Peter's Basilica, free of any incidents and apparently unconcerned about any terrorist threat. In the United States, it was wall-to-wall coverage on the television networks, with interview after interview with Americans of every race and creed from among the waiting crowd in Saint Peter's Square. The president's inner circle recognized it as a Christian event—not Catholic or Protestant, but Christian—a welcome phenomenon in a Europe they regarded as a secularist desert.

Hence the kneeling leader, symbol of a fusion back home between Catholic conservatives and the Evangelical churches that had once been mortal enemies. The *Economist* magazine captured this development when it labeled the U.S. Supreme Court "the papal court." With the appointment of John Roberts as Chief Justice and of Samuel Alito as the newest Associate Justice to replace Sandra Day O'Connor, five out of the nine members of the bench were now Roman Catholics. Yet in 1853, the first Vatican "secret agent" (actually an apostolic—or papal—visitor) sent to the United States to get the measure of the place reported to his superiors in Rome that, surprisingly, the chief justice of the Supreme Court was a Catholic. At the time, however, that fact was a temporary anomaly rather than an indication of any progress made by American Roman Catholics on the long road of their integration—an anomaly bobbing precariously in a sea of prejudice that would cause the pope's visitor, Gaetano Bedini, to have to leave America in a hurry.

THE CARDINAL WHO
HUNTED HERETICS

AMERICA IN THE VATICAN ARCHIVES

Not long ago there arrived from the United States of America an article published in the newspaper *The Express* in which we read that leading anarchist fugitives from Italy and Europe who have sought refuge there tried to lend credibility to their lies against the Pontifical Nuncio Mons. G. Bedini by naming fifty individuals whom they claim were persecuted, tortured, and finally executed by the Nuncio's orders during the period when he was governor of the four Pontifical Legations (districts) as Special Commissioner. In addition, they listed their ages and the date of their sentencing, hoping this mass of evidence would convince that distant people that the Nuncio was, and is bloodthirsty, cruel, and vindictive, thereby bringing upon him universal disrespect and contempt and paralyzing his mission.

THE YELLOWING PAGE from *Vero Amico* Supplement Number 12 in the files of the Vatican Secret Archives belongs to an America and a papacy that are no more. But in 1853 it reflected two worlds, one so culturally and geographically distant as to be almost incomprehensible, and the other on the verge of an abyss.

The Vatican state was still recovering from the short-lived revolutionary Republic of Rome. Five years earlier that government had forced Pope Pius IX to flee to Gaeta, until he was restored to power by the combined armies of Austria, France, and Naples. America was an exotic place, and among that "distant people" were political refugees from the brutal suppression that had followed the papal restoration. Even without the additional element of failed Italian revolutionaries, to many Americans the pope was an insidious enemy, feared for his unchecked power and for the papacy's sinister secretiveness. He was someone to be kept at a distance from the paradise of the New World, to avoid contamination with the oppressive practices remembered from the old one. Documents conserved for over two centuries in the Vatican Secret Archives, which make up the cumulative memory of the papacy, tell the story of a religious war not with the Muslim "infidel" but against the *protestantici,* as the Vatican in those days called the *protestanti,* the Protestants, many of whom had carried in their baggage to America the residual hate for the Catholic Church that had driven them out of Europe in the first place. This was particularly true of citizens who had sought refuge from religious persecution and from bloody conflicts fought in the name of the Church and of the Protestant Reformation.

The visit to the United States of Monsignor Gaetano Bedini, titular archbishop of Thebes and apostolic nuncio in Rio de Janeiro at the imperial court of Pedro II of Brazil, became a sort of metaphor for the divergences and lack of understanding between the two "Wests" on opposite sides of the Atlantic. The prelate was sent by Pius IX to establish a diplomatic mission in Washington, but the White House and American public opinion, and even some of the American Catholic bishops, saw the prelate's assignment as an assault on the constitutional separation of church and state that would in turn upset the delicate religious balance, jealously protected by the United States as a key element in uniting their young immigrant society. The reports from America in the Vatican Archives resonate with the vehement antipapist rhetoric of the refugees from the Roman Republic and the German-language newspapers of Lutheran immigrants in America, and provide a taste of what Bedini was up against.

THE BEDINI REPORT

THE MOST COMPLETE description of the situation comes from Bedini himself. His report of what degenerated into a nightmare visit is preserved in the Vatican Archives in a light blue folder secured with tape in the Cardinals and Curia Officials files of the Secretariat of State.

The thick notebook with its marbleized cover could well have contained a high school assignment; instead its contents are of historical significance. The language is dry and stiffly formal as befits a diplomatic report, but every page betrays the fear and dismay of someone who has come face-to-face with an alien, baffling, and even menacing world. Bedini describes America in the mid-nineteenth century for the benefit of Curia officials. In page after page written in black ink the prelate writes of courteous, respectable middle-class Protestants and a dirty and often malodorous Catholic underclass. He also reports a passionate anti-papist sentiment he had never before experienced.

What jumps out at the reader is that Bedini is observing a world he doesn't understand. "My mission encountered vigorous opposition from refugee revolutionaries from Europe led and incited by an apostate." He does not reveal the identity of the "apostate," but more on him later. Bedini goes on to refer to himself in the third person, expressing relief that he survived every attack. "Answering every calumny with silence, the Nuncio earned more admiration from the Catholics." He spoke of the "Catholic Religion" making "admirable progress" in America.

> The population of the (United States) is about twenty-four million. Two million are Catholics, and of the remaining twenty-two a good seventeen million can be said to have no real religion at all. Therefore, the activists who challenge the two million Catholics are about five million. The seventeen million are almost pagan, or at least indifferent to religion, and are little cause for concern: they do not share the anti-Catholic prejudice of the Protestants.

Possibly to tell his superiors something they would like to hear, he said the Protestant faith was "reduced to nothing . . . a sentiment shared even by those who practice it." Being a Vatican official who had experienced the dangers facing the established order from the new revolutionary fervor in Europe, he quotes a Protestant senator who expresses his fear that the same desire for liberty was spreading in his country, and Bedini states that "the Catholic Religion is the foundation for real authority, and indispensable for any government." He had transferred his own fears to the senator to describe a country that he perceived to be on the brink of anarchy.

Bedini was shocked by the way in America "the vote, public sympathy, indeed, popular whim is everything: there is a willingness to sacrifice any conviction to win an election, or to gain favor with the press. The power of the street is more exigent than the oldest, the most powerful, and even the most tyrannical monarchy. That is the conclusion one reaches in the land of liberty."

Popular whim. Power of the street. It's the language of a member of a ruling class living in the past, a denizen of a system of authoritarian power shaken out of his sheltered life by this sudden encounter with the brash novelty of popular suffrage. In the Old Continent the top echelons of the Church identified with, and generally were drawn from, elite society and identified with the monarchical system. In the United States, on the other hand, the Catholics were "the Irish, who perform the most menial work, live in abject poverty, and retain for the longest time the meanest and sometimes repellant appearance. One cannot help but come to the conclusion that Catholicism is the religion of the poor." The nuncio's disdain was clear, as was his envy for the privileged position and prosperity of American Protestants who had a lock on public sector employment and held the most prestigious and remunerative positions. "Catholicism is not popular," Bedini concluded to the Vatican, "in the sense that it is not attractive to the general public; and in that republic everything depends on public opinion, which means the uninformed majority led by a clever, very active minority who are never, never the most virtuous."

"KILL THAT BUTCHERING PRIEST!"

BEDINI'S VISIT BEGAN in New York on June 30, 1853, accompanied by Monsignor Ernest Cologneri from the apostolic legation in Mexico, and his private secretary, an English priest named John Virtue. At first the nuncio's presence attracted little attention. The Vatican had sent letters of accreditation to Washington in advance to secure the prelate access to President Franklin Pierce and William L. Marcy, the secretary of state, and there had been no objection from either official. But the indifferent calm was to turn into a rolling storm of protest that would pursue the visiting prelate along every stage of his three-month journey, turning it into his personal via crucis.

Bedini's American nemesis was Alessandro Gavazzi, a member of the Barnabite order, who had sought refuge in America three months earlier. Gavazzi is the "apostate" mentioned in Bedini's report. He dogged the Vatican diplomat from one city to the next, inciting Protestants against him with stories of the nuncio's alleged crimes in Italy, at one point even coming close to being responsible for Bedini's being stabbed to death.

Bedini's past was perfect fodder for anti-papist hate. In 1849, when the newly formed Roman Republic stripped the pontiff of his temporal power, Bedini had followed Pius IX into exile in Gaeta. The *Dizionario Biografico degli Italiani,* the Italian biographical dictionary, says, "[Bedini] did not hide his reactionary tendencies, and supported the restoration of papal authority." Pope Pius IX sent him to Bologna on a secret mission to try to persuade Swiss army units there to join forces with papal troops to liberate Rome. He was unsuccessful, but meanwhile Austrian troops had taken part in sweeping away the republic, and Bedini returned to the Vatican in their wake. He claimed credit for restoring the Holy See to power, but it was the Austrians who were in control of the situation, and not the archbishop. When the Austrians arrested the Barnabite father Ugo Bassi, who was said to be Giuseppe Garibaldi's priest, Bedini either made no effort to halt his execution or failed in the attempt. It was probably the latter because, as the liberal politician Marco Minghetti said dismissively, Bedini had as much influence "as my left boot." Whatever the reason, Italian refugees from the Papal States who had come to America, with Gavazzi, another Barnabite priest, in the forefront, used the story to discredit and threaten the nuncio.

Bedini visited Washington, Baltimore, a Native American community, and Philadelphia, where in 1844 Protestants had burned down a number of Catholic churches, with the loss of several lives. When he arrived in Detroit on board the steamer USS *Michigan,* the *Detroit Tribunal* newspaper reported that a Vatican official with no diplomatic status was traveling round the United States at the taxpayers' expense.

The *Michigan's* skipper, Captain Bigelow—who was acting under orders from the administration—came under heavy critical fire for giving Bedini and his party free passage. Bedini's defenders saw nothing wrong with the Vatican representative, technically a guest of the United States government, having the courtesy of a steamer at his disposal, but the predominantly Protestant public took a different view.

As Bedini was leaving Detroit, the story of his alleged role in Ugo Bassi's execution surfaced in the midwestern city. As the nuncio boarded a train, Gavazzi and some of his friends entered the same car. By Bedini's own account the train ride passed without incident, but the tension can only be imagined. Gavazzi had been busy venomously undermining Bedini's reputation, and to a section of the American press the papal representative was now known as "the Bloody Butcher of Bologna." His mission, warned the *New York Observer* on August 23, 1853, was "to find the best way of riveting Italian chains upon us which will bind us as slaves to the throne of the fiercest tyrant the earth knows."

Some newspapers came to Bedini's defense, but Gavazzi's campaign dominated the media. The wayward priest rushed from city to city or used the diabolic new system of communication, the telegraph, to spin more wild tales, and to send instructions to his contacts, his agents. The German-language paper *Flugblatter* in Milwaukee, and the *Milwaukee Sentinel* described Bedini as an assassin and antirepublican. It was fortunate that Bedini chose that moment to visit Canada, for the malicious propaganda was mounting against him. Perhaps he looked for a cooling-off period outside of the United States.

Not that Canada was free from anti-papist sentiment. In January 1836 the alleged misadventures of a young novice in the Hotel de Dieu nunnery in Montreal had become a best seller on both sides of the border. In her book, *The Awful Disclosures of Maria Monk, or, The Hidden Secrets of a Nun's Life in a Convent Exposed*, Monk claimed to have witnessed a number of horrific crimes and incidents of sexual abuse in the convent, and when she herself became pregnant by a priest from a nearby seminary, she fled to the United States. The book's publication caused an enormous public outcry that fed on anti-Catholic sentiment. Its release was much anticipated, having been announced some months prior in the *American Protestant Vindicator*, a stridently anti-immigrant and anti-Catholic nativist newspaper. An on-the-spot inquiry by a Protestant editor turned up no evidence to support Maria Monk's claims, or even to indicate that she had ever been inside the convent, but American Protestants refused to accept the results.

In Canada Bedini received a letter from a priest in New Jersey warning him of a plot on his life. The informer told the prelate that Italian revolutionaries were conspiring to attack him with knives outside the archbishop's residence in New York when he returned to the city. One of the plotters, a "Signor Sassi," struck with horror at the plan, informed Archbishop John Hughes of New York. Within a week Sassi was stabbed at night in New York and died in a hospital a few days later from his wounds. Bedini was leaving Canada and returning to America via Boston. To the Vatican Bedini admitted that he was tempted to quit the United States altogether "when the young Italian who had revealed to me the plot against my life by the Italian revolutionaries in New York was himself assassinated. Until that happened I was not too certain of his credibility, but (his death) brought home my own danger, and my return to the United States was in doubt. But as I was considering leaving the United States I received a letter from (the archbishop of New York)." The atmosphere was now very tense. But Hughes's letter urged him not to abandon America but to be assured of "the protection and love of Catholics."

"THE GERMAN SCOUNDRELS OF CINCINNATI"

THE VATICAN DIPLOMAT continued to crisscross the length and breadth of the country, greeted everywhere with a bizarre mixture of applause, deference, tumult, and hostility. Pittsburgh, Louisville, Cincinnati. In the latter city in the second half of December 1853 anti-papist sentiment loomed like a permanent dark cloud over the Catholic mission. In 1847 a fifth of Cincinnati's 90,000 inhabitants were German immigrants, and of the city's seventy-six churches, eight were Lutheran and another eight Catholic. But by 1853 the influx of immigrants from Germany had swelled the size of the German community to one-third of the city's population, which then stood at 120,000. The "Forty-Eighters," European liberal revolutionaries, vanquished and hostile to

Rome, found a haven there, strengthened further by the establishment of their powerful newspaper the *Hochwachter.* On the national stage the "Know-Nothing" movement was gaining ground. Formed as a popular reaction to the large increase in the number of immigrants—mostly Irish Catholics—entering the United States and the suspicion of a "Roman" plot to infiltrate the government, the "American Party" (its official name) acquired its nickname from the fact that, as a semisecret organization, its members were supposed to reply to questions about its activities with "I know nothing."

In the eyes of Cincinnati Protestants, Bedini "represented everything that is reactionary." On the day of his arrival in the city the *Hochwachter* published the following blistering article:

> Reader. Dost thou know who Bedini is? Lo! The skin will not leave his hands which at his command was flayed from Ugo Bassi! Lo! A murderer, a butcher of men . . . The Church celebrates its bloody horrible mysteries. His slaying of Ugo Bassi, that priest of liberty, and letting him die in agony—that was not his only and worst deed . . . Bedini is the Italian tiger; he is the hyena of Italy. Reader . . . the sons of Italy are too thinly scattered among us to punish the bloodhound of Bologna for his dark and bloody deeds. The Yankee neither possesses feelings nor principles . . . do not count upon the Yankee for your revenge. Do not count upon the sons of the Green Isle, the vulgar Irish. They are not able to look through the gown of their priest. Germans, you are called for! Down with Bedini!

Behind the protest were members of the Society of the Free Men, newly arrived German radicals who embraced the notion that there could be no real freedom until Catholicism was abolished. The German newspaper decided to organize its own counterdemonstration to challenge the civic welcome for the visiting Vatican diplomat. On the evening of Christmas Day, a group of about five hundred men, some of them armed with weapons, followed by about a hundred women, marched on the cathedral. They carried placards saying, DOWN WITH BEDINI, NO PRIESTS, NO KINGS, DOWN WITH THE BUTCHERS OF ROME, DOWN WITH THE PAPACY. The cardinal left an account of his run-in with "the German scoundrels," as he called them, in his report to the

Vatican. He left Cincinnati with images of the protest still vivid in his memory, and the shouted insults still ringing in his ears. In Cincinnati, he said in his report,

> the demagogic rage of Europe resurfaced with a vengeance. The German revolutionary sentiment, which I have described elsewhere, launched their attack against this "tyrant of Italian patriots," and the effect was truly tremendous. I provided details in my dispatches, so I will not repeat them here. The fact is that the language of the (American) bishops began to change. Before Cincinnati they urged me not to be afraid, to go forward and not go back: afterwards, I began to hear repeated suggestions that it would be better if I returned to Europe.

What had begun six months earlier as a diplomatic visit to test the ground, and to explore both the prospects for, and reaction to bilateral relations between the United States and the Vatican had by the beginning of 1854 been reduced to a panic-stricken rush to the Atlantic coast and the hope of embarkation on a departing ship. Quitting Cincinnati for stops in Kentucky and eventually Baltimore had brought no respite from the newspaper attacks on "the Butcher of Bologna," or the public burning of images of Bedini and Pius IX. The fact that the United States Senate was at the time addressing the issue of diplomatic relations with the Vatican fanned the flames of hatred and protest.

On January 11, Bedini arrived in Washington. On January 19, he dined with President Pierce. The warm welcome from the Catholic community, which fêted him, and his meetings with members of the diplomatic corps in the capital helped restore some of his shattered composure. But there was one other question that had from the start loomed over his trip, and that was the question of his status: should he be treated as the diplomat that he actually was, with all the consideration due to his position, or simply as a private citizen? The Vatican was aware of his predicament, as well as his problems with demonstrators verging on physical violence, and repeatedly asked for clarification from Lewis Cass, the United States minister (one step down from ambassador) to the Holy See in Rome.

In reality, the lack of clarity was partly the Vatican's fault. Bedini was nuncio, the pope's ambassador, but to the imperial court of Brazil, not to the United States. How should the White House treat him? Public opinion was also equivocal. The Catholic community had at first received him enthusiastically. Several mayors had welcomed the man sent by the pope. As the press campaign against him grew more virulent the welcome slowly changed to maintaining a cautious distance. Within the American Catholic episcopate there were those who from the start had regarded the man from the Roman Curia as an intruder and a busybody and wondered what exactly he was doing in the United States, and their attitude ranged from embarrassment to indifference. The Bedini mission foreshadowed all the difficulties and misunderstandings that were destined to beset relations between America and the Vatican for decades. The prelate could rage—as he did in his report—against "the brute Gavazzi who hopped from one city to another, sometimes ahead of me, and sometimes following me, but always intent on spreading venom (against me)," but his problem was a political one.

JUST A DISTINGUISHED VISITOR

BEDINI'S FINAL CONCLUSION was that the root of his troubles went all the way back to the White House itself. The American authorities from President Pierce on down simply refused to go out on a political limb and officially define his status. On the one hand, Pierce was anxious not to undermine Washington's friendly relations with the Papal States that had helped open up Europe to American trade. On the other hand, Bedini's visit had incited such a passionate intensity of public opposition from the country's political and religious refugees that the U.S. administration saw that the people didn't desire any closer arrangement between the United States and Rome; and in the final analysis all politics are local. "Are the Catholics of North America, home of liberty and democracy, satisfied with the existence of (an American) legation in Rome, which is not reciprocated in Washington?" Bedini asked in his report. "Not really," was his own answer. But after his visit his impression was that reciprocity would be difficult to establish.

The only thing that was humiliating to my dignity as nuncio was not the persecution of those sad people—every honest person has the right to revel in his own convictions—but the inaction of the authorities, the government's continued indifference. It was repeatedly made plain to me by the Secretary of State, and by the President himself, that I had no diplomatic status. I was told: "You are Nuncio to Brazil, not the United States, and as such we regard you as a distinguished visitor."

A distinguished visitor. That was his status as far as the administration was concerned. An important guest, but without any special rights, or immunity. That courteous description acknowledged no special link between the United States and the Holy See, whose envoy he was, and made him a lightning rod for public prejudice, a prejudice that would remain for more than a century. "I think it superfluous to waste time demonstrating the error of this approach, which neither the French ambassador (in Washington), nor other distinguished members of the diplomatic corps, nor the Attorney General—who was expressly consulted—could rectify," he wrote.

After the incidents in Cincinnati, the nuncio's presence had become awkward for the administration. Far from "a distinguished guest," the nuncio had become an unwelcome one, urged by the American Catholic episcopate with increasing concern not to make any more public appearances. Catholicism was growing in the United States, but it was still weak. Bedini described Protestantism in America as being "in great decline," but in reality Protestantism was more firmly rooted in the culture, economy, and psychology of the young American nation than Catholicism was. While celebrating Mass in the Visitation Convent's chapel at Georgetown, in Washington, DC, he was shocked by one of several episodes. "A Protestant lady had anxiously entered the church," Bedini tells in his secret report. "She said that she wanted to check if the Papal Nuncio had actually horns on his head."

ESCAPE TO NEW YORK

HIS DEPARTURE FROM Washington at the end of January was shrouded in mystery. Some said that he had gone back to Philadelphia; others that he had headed directly for New York, more than ever eager to depart. On his last days in America he kept a low profile, holed up at the residence of the parish priest of Saint Patrick's Cathedral. When he regained some of his nerve he went shopping in Manhattan for souvenirs to take back to Rome. Even his low-key presence worried the authorities. The mayor and the New York police had received information that nativists were planning to picket the ocean liner *Baltic* when the cardinal embarked for his journey home, and the police advised that it would be wiser for him to make his departure in secret. The Vatican diplomat spent his last hours on American soil imparting his blessing and distributing holy pictures of the Madonna of Rimini, an image of a black Blessed Virgin that is revered in the east coast Italian city of Rimini. His greatest disappointment was that in the end the American Catholic bishops had not come to his defense, but on the contrary had abandoned him to his plight as an undesirable. His other regret was the United States government's failure to take any action to halt the insults he had endured. To the end, however, he continued to show his gratitude toward those Catholics who showed him kindness. "Ancore une fois, cher Monseigneur, adieu, adieu, adieu!" he wrote to the archbishop of New York on February 3, 1854. "Once again, dear monsignor, farewell, farewell, farewell!" At dawn the following day, Bedini and his secretary prepared to leave New York, "like two condemned men whom the authorities were trying to smuggle out to avoid a lynch mob," a witness wrote.

On February 4, a rumor spread that an important visitor was on the point of leaving New York from the Staten Island dock. Bedini's enemies, thinking it was "the distinguished visitor" rushed to the embarkation point—but it was a red herring. The two "condemned men" were hidden at another dock from where they boarded the tug *Active,* which in the afternoon transferred Bedini and his terrified traveling companion to the three-masted passenger ship SS *Atlantic* bound for Liverpool, England. Before sailing into the New York roads the *Atlantic* fired a gun in salute to the diplomat and sounded its siren. In his meticulous reconstruction of the Bedini mission, the Reverend James Connelly points out that never in the history of the United States had the ambassador of a friendly country been forced to leave America in such an ignominious fashion. The shock took a long time for Rome to absorb, and the details, stored in the Vatican's archives, are still shocking. Yet, though the plan to establish a papal embassy in Washington had failed miserably, the trip did have positive consequences.

Bedini went on to raise the funds to start the Pontifical North American College in Rome. Pius IX gave the project his enthusiastic support and donated a building on via dell'Umiltá as its permanent home; but the United States bishops, jealous of any invasion of their autonomy, did not share the pope's enthusiasm. The American episcopate regarded the Holy See's intention to open a seminary for young Americans in Rome as an insult to the work already being done in training priests in the United States. In other words, the issue of the North American College revived the clash between two different visions and two Catholic cultures. Here again were the same jealousy and same sense of independence that had undermined Bedini's mission, and would scar for decades relations between the United States and the Holy See. Meanwhile, the Bedini report had at least provided the basis for a fresh Vatican approach that would take into account the individualism and anti-centralism of American religious sentiment, and help Catholicism to deepen its roots, to grow, and to scratch away at the prejudice so as to compete with the country's many variations of Protestantism.

"I ARRIVED A DECADE TOO EARLY"

POOR CARDINAL BEDINI knew that his mission in the land of multiple religions had not gone according to plan because there was no plan. This was one instance when the Vatican had clearly miscalculated. The time for diplomatic relations was not ripe; in fact it was an unripe fruit and a bitter one at that. Even without the trauma of clashing with the *protestantici,* the Protestants, and the disruptive role of Gavazzi and the "German scoundrels," the United States would have been a hard nut to crack. This was not some exotic country where Catholicism could be introduced virtually unopposed from the ground up. It was a country that had historically given refuge to enemies of the papacy, who brought with them their hatred of the Church of Rome, and hopes of constructing a life outside its sphere of influence. Bedini had understood, perhaps vaguely, that his diplomatic initiative had failed for historical reasons that went beyond President Pierce's lack of response. American officials had not been hostile to Bedini. Rather, they had treated him as someone who did not—and perhaps could not—grasp the complex realities of their society.

While he was lying low in the residence of the parish priest of Saint Patrick's waiting to make his getaway from the New World, Bedini met Edward Purcell, brother of John Baptist Purcell, the archbishop of Cincinnati, who had become one of his closest American friends. "Perhaps I came to this country too early," was Bedini's weary comment. "I am here ten years too soon." Ten years? He was erring hugely on the optimistic side. It would take far longer for anti-papist sentiment to fade away, and for the successor of Peter in Rome to be seen as anything but a tyrannical figure.

PRESIDENT WASHINGTON, PIUS VI REQUESTS . . .

JOHN ADAMS'S PROPHECY

IT WAS NO ACCIDENT that America had kept "the tyrant" at bay for almost a century. "Congress will probably never send a Minister to His Holiness who can do them no service, upon condition of receiving the Catholic Legate or Nuncio; or, in other words, an ecclesiastical tyrant, whom, it is hoped, the United States will be too wise ever to admit into their territories." So wrote John Adams to the Continental Congress in 1779. No minced words here; no diplomatic double-talk. Here the future president of the United States laid it on the line. Here was evidence of a new culture, a new approach to geopolitics. America would not, could not, associate itself with a state that had the stench of incense, the odor of authoritarianism, and more than a whiff of obscurantism—a potent blend, in short, of the faults of Old Europe, the old world.

Adams was laying the foundation of America's relations with the Vatican; and for two centuries that policy—the Protestant Founding Fathers' intended tombstone of the papacy in America, reflecting precisely their love of freedom and independence, reinforced with an undercurrent of anti-Catholicism as old as the oldest settlements—Adams's policy, would be periodically embellished or tweaked, but never removed. That it should be Adams who put such a view in place was no accident. The second president of the United States (1797–1801), and the first to live in the White House, he was the son of a deacon in Braintree, Massachusetts. His Puritan great-great-grandfather had immigrated to the New Continent in 1640 to escape religious persecution.

Contemporaneously, in March 1634 another small group of English settlers, including three Jesuits, had set foot in Chesapeake Bay, in what they called Maryland. Besides the three priests, the new arrivals consisted of seventeen landowners, mainly Catholics, and two hundred farmworkers, mainly Protestants. The members of this mixed community led by George Calvert were conscious of the fact that religious freedom in their new surroundings meant coexistence with other faiths, and that Catholicism would not—could not—be the religion of the state, as it had once been in the Old Country. If they hoped to survive in this new and essentially hostile world, their first loyalty had to be to the king, not the pope; and religion had to remain a private matter. As Thomas Spalding explains in his detailed history of the Baltimore diocese, the first one established in the New World, the main danger to Roman Catholics was not from the Native Americans whom they called Indians, but from other English settlers of different Christian persuasions. And that antagonism was to remain a fact of life for American Catholics for more than three centuries.

Along with their few possessions and their hopes, these settlers brought with them a heavy burden of bitter memories of a Europe divided by a pitiless and bloody religious conflict. The memory of the birth of Protestantism at the Diet of Worms of 1521 when a group of German princes refused to declare allegiance to the Catholic monarchy and to the pope; of the Edict of Nantes of 1598 offering protection to the Protestants in France—and then the expulsion of the Huguenots by King Louis XIV in 1685.

The Flemish painter Adriaen Pietersz van de Venne's 1614 work *Fishing for Souls* depicts the European divide. Deployed on one bank of the river is James I of England surrounded by Protestant pastors, their austere black garb relieved only by white lace collars and cuffs; on the other bank is Archduke Albrecht of Austria, the cardinal archbishop of Toledo. They are observing a contest between a boatload of priests and another of Lutheran pastors each striving to convert men and women who are swimming in the water. The two groups scarcely look at each other. There is no joy in the twilight of that Flemish painting, only alienation to the point of hatred; and the same alienation was borne across the ocean by the German souls, and the French and the English who fled to the New World, convinced by their own experience that Catholicism and liberty were incompatible.

Throughout the colonial period the Catholics in Baltimore never numbered more than 12 percent of the total population, yet as time went by the laws against the "papists" became progressively tighter, with regard to not just worship, but also their economic condition. The clergy were a favorite target. Land acquired from the Indians by the Jesuits and held in the name of the Society of Jesus contravened a law "imported" from England barring religious communities from owning property. The owner was required to be an individual, preferably a layman. Politically, the Catholic minority was also regarded as a kind of fifth column for England's enemies in Catholic Europe. Every new conflict between England and a nation of the Catholic faith in the Old World was the signal for a wave of fresh reprisals in the new one. Spalding notes that hostility toward papists was at its most intense during the French and Indian wars between 1754 and 1763; but it would not be the last hostility, and American Catholics, who were adept at recognizing the warning signs, discouraged efforts by the Vatican to send a bishop and to increase Rome's influence. The only way for the Catholic community to grow without provoking opposition was to do so internally, without outside interference. And the only antidote against suspicion and resentment was to be staunch patriots and supporters of the American cause. In 1773 Charles Carroll of Carrollton was responsible for committing Maryland's Catholic community to the anticolonial cause. In 1776 he represented that state in the Continental Congress and was the only Catholic among the signers of the Declaration of Independence.

FATHER CARROLL AND THE INTERFERING WAYS OF PROPAGANDA FIDE

CARROLL PUT FORWARD the name of his Jesuit kinsman John to accompany a committee composed of Benjamin Franklin, Samuel Chase, and Carroll himself to seek the neutrality of Canada during the War of Independence. It was too late to discuss the question of union with the Canadians, or even of neutrality, but in the course of the mission John Carroll developed a friendship with Benjamin Franklin that was to prove decisive for the latter's own future and the future relations between the United States and the Vatican. Carroll tried to steer clear of politics: he was an American priest to the marrow and knew that the residual distrust between Catholics and Protestants could easily resurface. The main problem confronting him at the time was how to protect the property of the Society of Jesus from confiscation by the Vatican because in 1773 the Jesuit order had been dissolved by Pope Clement XIV. The main threat came from the Congregation of Propaganda Fide in Rome, a sort of global holdings organization for ecclesiastical property. In reality, Propaganda Fide was attempting to place land owned by the Church across the Atlantic under its protective umbrella, but Carroll knew well that the Vatican's involvement would not sit well in the United States. "In these United States our religious system has undergone a revolution if possible more extraordinary than the political one," he wrote to Charles Plowden, an English friend and an ex-Jesuit. All faiths were regarded as being on the same plane, and it was important to avoid "causing jealousy by being dependent on a foreign jurisdiction . . . that will never be tolerated here." In Pennsylvania, Delaware, Maryland, and Virginia every citizen enjoyed the same civil rights, without exception or distinction, "and these (rights) extend to religion . . . This is a blessing and an advantage, which we must take great care to preserve and to develop," Carroll wrote.

Propaganda Fide had its own agenda. With little regard for the particular concerns of the New World, the group transmitted a request to the Congress for permission to send to America an apostolic vicar nominated by the pope. A furious Carroll told Plowden that no representative of Propaganda Fide would ever be admitted into the United States. The Catholic clergy in America was determined that "the only link that there can be with Rome is to acknowledge the pope as the spiritual leader of the Church." No Vatican congregation would ever be permitted to exert its spiritual authority. No bishop assigned by Rome would ever be accepted. "If there's going to be a bishop, let him be an American, and Rome must never intrude. We will be free of their machinations." The Vatican failed to appreciate that the Catholic Church in the United States required a different approach, or, it would seem, to care that it did. Without bothering to keep the fragile American episcopate in the loop, the Holy See used diplomatic channels to try to establish contact with the government in Washington. So while

Carroll wrote furious letters to his friends, the papal court made use of the good offices of the French to transmit to the American authorities its desire to send an apostolic vicar. When the nuncio in Paris contacted Benjamin Franklin with this proposal, the Congress instructed the latter to reply that as a spiritual matter, the request was outside the competence of the Congress, which could, therefore, neither agree to it nor refuse it.

The Holy See then realized that it would have to deal with the Catholic clergy in America after all. Searching for a local representative who had rapport with Washington, the choice fell naturally on John Carroll, and in June 1784 the Vatican secretary of state, Cardinal Leonardo Antonelli, appointed him "Superior of the Mission in the Thirteen United States." Carroll's reply to Rome was that he was not sure that the United States was ready to accept a bishop of the Holy Roman Church. There were, he reported to Rome, 15,800 Catholics in Maryland, 7,000 in Pennsylvania, and about 1,500 in New York, with nineteen priests serving in the Maryland area, five in Pennsylvania, and none in New York. The Vatican's reputation at that time was particularly negative. Ex-Jesuits in America who had converted to Protestantism fanned the flames of prejudice with stories about Rome, some false, some true. To justify their rejection of their former calling they said the pontiff presided over a repressive regime that was totally alien to the American love of liberty.

Carroll's hope was that the United States would become a beacon of religious tolerance for the entire world, but he recognized that it was a long and uncertain road. The Mass in Latin was unpopular among American Catholics: for the most part they were praying in a strange tongue that they did not understand, and one that they associated with a world they, or their recent ancestors, had left behind. It also implied the imposition of a spirituality by the Holy See, and not one accepted out of choice. Carroll was well ahead of his time in advocating the use of the vernacular in the liturgy not as "something to be desired, but demanded," as he put it.

There was still no agreement on the question of ecclesiastical ownership of property, where an Anglo-Saxon, Protestant establishment refused to negotiate with what was labeled "the dead hand of the church." The other open issue was taxation. Carroll complained that

Catholics, Presbyterians, Methodists, Quakers, and Anabaptists were being pressed financially, while state support gave the Episcopal Church a crushing advantage. Month after month his measured, cautious approach to problems was meeting with increasingly radical views, and the time seemed ripe for a papal decision on the appointment of someone to exercise authority in the American Catholic Church, in other words, a bishop.

PIUS VI AND GEORGE WASHINGTON

"IT WAS 1788 and the pope, Pius VI, dispatched an emissary to Paris to meet with the diplomat just posted there from the new republic in North America, the United States. The diplomat was Benjamin Franklin, and the pope's request of him was short and simple: Would it be okay with President George Washington if the pope named a bishop in the new land?" Franklin dutifully queried President Washington, and "the word came back to tell the Pope he can appoint any bishop he wants for the United States, since that was what the revolution in the colonies was all about—freedom, to include religious freedom. The Pope promptly elevated Jesuit Father John Carroll to become America's first Catholic bishop." That account of how it went is by James Nicholson, the former United States ambassador to the Holy See. It was written as an insert to the Italian review *30Giorni*, edited by Giulio Andreotti, an Italian senator for life, and Italy's Christian Democrat prime minister several times over. Nicholson does not describe the long, complex and laborious process that eventually led to the Carroll appointment. It was the priests in Maryland—Carroll included—who petitioned Rome on March 12, 1788, for a bishop for the United States. Cardinal Antonelli replied that the priests of the mission were allowed to select the city and, for this one case only, to name their candidate for submission to the pope. Twenty-four out of twenty-five priests at the meeting (in other words, everyone except Carroll himself) voted in favor of Carroll's elevation.

Baltimore was chosen as the first see because it was the only city where the Catholic community was large enough and forceful enough to have an impact on public opinion, and could form a bridgehead for further expansion of the Church in the United States. There was no acknowledgment from the government of the Vatican's role in Carroll's appointment. No particular interest was expressed in conferring diplomatic status on any Vatican prelate. The American government's green light for the appointment of a bishop was a small, and in the eyes of the United States harmless, gesture toward this strange, minuscule independent territory that represented all that was contrary to the American concept of liberty, and yet seemed anxious to establish a foothold in a distant Protestant land. The American leadership could, however, see the advantage of establishing a commercial office in Rome. "In the eighteenth century, the U.S. mission to the Holy See (the Papal States) was put in primarily to protect U.S. merchant interests," Nicholson points out. The port of Civitavecchia, on Italy's west coast, and Ancona, in the Adriatic, were both located in the Papal States, and both were desirable maritime entry points for American goods destined for eastern Europe. In December 1784 the papal nuncio in Paris had advised his United States counterpart that both Civitavecchia and Ancona were open to American shipping.

But there was no talk of establishing diplomatic relations. And reading Carroll's correspondence to his Jesuit friends, with its frequent outbursts against the Vatican's maneuvers, it is easy to see why. Pius VI could write to George Washington as one head of state to another, but the general view (to the extent that there was any view at all) was different. The Vatican was a foreign country, one that was not liked in the New World, and the idea of a black-robed ambassador aroused suspicion and reserve. Carroll's appointment itself was something of an anomaly, a transplanted European idea. The document of his appointment dated November 6, 1789, had to be created from scratch to fit the new situation because the standard text could not be used. Carroll had to find another bishop to perform the consecration. He received invitations to hold the ceremony in Dublin, Quebec, and Paris, but friendship and an old affection for England won out, and he opted for Mr. Weld's chapel at Lulworth Castle in Dorset, England, where his friend Charles Plowden was the resident priest. It was not the best of times to feel nostalgic about Europe: the French Revolution had shaken to its foundations the traditional relationship between church and state.

"A NEW EMPIRE IN THE WEST"

WHEN CARROLL ARRIVED in London on July 22, 1790, he found English Catholics bitterly divided over the last vestiges of discriminatory legislation before their eventual emancipation. The Act of Uniformity, the Penal Laws, and other statutes placed heavy burdens on Catholics requiring them to abjure the authority of the pope and the doctrine of transubstantiation. Special dispensation was available to take the prescribed oaths without the risk of perjury, but many fought the discriminatory laws as violations of freedom of worship. Bishop Charles Walmesley, a prominent Benedictine and an outspoken opponent of anti-Catholic legislation, officiated at Carroll's consecration, and Carroll's friend Plowden—another staunch defender of Catholic rights—delivered the homily. In his own address Carroll paid tribute to Lord Robert Petre, who played a role in the struggle for Catholic emancipation. Religious tolerance in the United States, he said, served as an example for Great Britain. Plowden called America a beacon for the future of the Catholic Church. The American Revolution had fragmented the great British Empire, but Divine Providence had created a new empire in the West, Plowden declared, where the faith brought by Saint Augustine of Canterbury to the English-speaking people could be reborn.

Such constraints were, of course, hardly reserved for English-speaking Catholics. The New World was destined to become a haven for men and women of every religion fleeing from persecution in many other countries besides England. Nor, in the closing years of the Age of Reason, had that persecution become a thing of the past. A few weeks before his return to America, Bishop Carroll received a visit from Abbe François-Charles Nagot, of the Society of Sainte-Sulpice, who wished to open a seminary in Baltimore. He told Carroll that his superior, Abbe Emery, had predicted that the French Revolution would eradicate religion in France, and the Civil Constitution of the Clergy of 1790, which destroyed the monastic orders, had proved him right. Thousands of French priests were forced to leave the country, and the emergent church in America could have made use of these forced migrations. Not that this "discovery of America" was in any way an official Vatican strategy. Rather, it was driven by desperation.

There were only about 25,000 Catholics in America out of a population of 4 million—or about 0.8 percent—but the number of clergy was sparse even for that small community; so any new arrivals were welcomed.

New arrivals had to adapt to changes in the liturgy necessitated by the circumstances and challenges of the New World, and even adjustments to what the Vatican would regard as orthodoxy. "America is considered a land of nonbelievers, where there is no resident clergy, only missionaries," John M. Cranche, the vice president of Sainte Marie College in Baltimore, told Alexis de Tocqueville, who recorded the conversation in *Democracy in America,* his seminal book on the society in the early United States. Cranche told de Tocqueville that while public opinion harbored a strong anti-Catholic prejudice, Protestant children who attended Catholic schools were altered by the experience, which was strong enough to remove the prejudice, "but not to convert them." In that respect, marriages between a Protestant and a Catholic tended to produce more satisfactory results. "Such marriages are prohibited in Europe, but we encourage them," Cranche said. "We have noted that when the Catholic spouse is the mother, the children always become [Catholics], and often the father as well." Cranche said he was optimistic. "I believe that America is destined to become the core of Catholicism," he told the curious and at the same time skeptical French traveler. "(Catholicism) is spreading without the help of the civil power and without causing resentment, solely with the strength of the faith itself and totally independent of the state." If this was a somewhat rosier picture than was called for by reality it reflected the American pragmatic approach to the tumultuous state of society in the New World.

AN AMERICAN CONSUL IN THE VATICAN

IN THE AREA of diplomatic exchanges some slight progress was made, mainly prompted by commercial considerations. The United States accepted the Holy See's invitation to send a representative to Rome. Nothing too high level; perhaps a chargé d'affaires, or a consul. Even so, the American approach remained cautious and watchful for any whiff of an infringement of the separation of church and state. Ironically, it was John Adams, once the strongest opponent of any diplomatic contact with "the tyrant" in Rome, but now the U.S. president, who in June 1797 appointed Giovanni Sartori as the first consular representative of the United States to Rome. Sartori was the first of eleven successive consular officers to serve in the Holy See until 1867 when the United States suspended its mission, three years before the Papal States were overrun by monarchist troops and the Italian nation was established. But both sides walked on eggshells. Every step forward was taken gingerly, accompanied by mutual assurances of noninterference; and the relationship was lopsided, with the Holy See pressing for closer ties and the United States holding back, hesitating, delaying.

In spite of their consular rank, successive American representatives received what one of them described as "unusual privileges and favors" from the Vatican. In official ceremonies they were treated the same as the ambassadors of other countries. The special consideration was a calculated move designed to send the message that the Vatican wanted full diplomatic relations with the United States. When Sartori arrived in Rome in 1826, the Holy See appointed a consul to New York, Count Ferdinando Lucchesi, and no fewer than twenty-one vice consuls in cities such as Baltimore, Philadelphia, New Orleans, Charleston, Norfolk, Savannah, Cincinnati, and Boston. On June 1, 1847, the Vatican again put forward the proposal to raise the level of diplomatic relations. Nicholas Browne, the United States consul in Rome, reported to Secretary of State James Buchanan that Pope Pius IX had "expressed the desire that diplomatic relations be established between the two governments." The report was sent to President James Polk, and in his December 1847 address to Congress Polk mentioned almost as an aside that he felt the recent events in the Papal States warranted the broadening of relations.

On March 21, 1848, the United States Senate debated an appropriations bill providing funding for Polk's chargé d'affaires at the papal court. The outcome was that the secretary of the American legation in Paris, Jacob L. Martin, was sent to Rome. It was a small step up from consul, but a significant one. At the time Pius IX was perceived as a protector of popular movements against established governments, exercising a "temporal moral power," said Senator Lewis Cass, who argued in favor of sending a full ambassador to the Papal States. In his speech on the Senate floor, Cass proclaimed, "The eyes of Christendom are upon its sovereign. He has given the first blow to despotism—the first impetus to freedom. Much is expected of him . . . The diplomacy of Europe will find full employment at his court, and its ablest professors will be there. Our government ought to be represented there also." As Felice Cicognani, the United States consul in Rome in 1831, had told Washington, then anxious to learn what was going on in the Old World, the city was "a good listening post." In support of Cass, Senator Edward Hannigan of Indiana voiced the same sentiment. The United States needed relations because Rome served as an "emporium of the intelligence of Europe."

Even so, the strategic argument in favor of formal relations was secondary: the main question that occupied the senators was whether there were commercial benefits to be had from expanded contact with the Papal States. Whereas other senators maintained that Rome was of no particular significance from a commercial standpoint, Senator John Dix of New York argued that, while the economic situation in the Papal States was depressed, if Pius IX's political and social reforms took root, "I know of no state of the same magnitude which may hope for a high prosperity."

POPE AND DIPLOMAT HAND IN HAND

IT SUITED BOTH sides to place the issue of religion in the background, at least for the moment. Pope Pius IX was viewed in a benign light by the American leadership; and the pope used the occasion of his first meeting with Jacob Martin to express his satisfaction with the United States. He said he was pleased to have concluded an agreement with "such a great nation, especially one in which the Catholic Church has nothing to fear from the government, nor the government from the Catholic Church." This was more a diplomatic nicety than an actual fact because religious tension was high in the United States. For the Vatican, America was "a Protestant state dear to the pontiff"; for the Americans, the Vatican was a country removed from their reality, and hard to read. Martin had arrived in Rome from Paris on August 2, 1848, and took lodgings in the Hotel Serny at 3, Piazza di Spagna. On August 19, he had his first papal audience as the representative of the United States to the Holy See. According to a reconstruction of that first encounter by Carlo De Lucia in *L'Osservatore Romano*, Pius IX "pushed protocol to the limit and they [the pope and Martin] talked at length, walking up and down in the great audience chamber, with the pope holding the diplomat's hand in his own."

While this was not such an unusual gesture, it underlined the pope's satisfaction. Martin was, after all, a seasoned member of his profession, who had even briefly directed the affairs of the State Department. He had also headed the American legation in Paris. His audience with the pope had begun in French, which the pope spoke "passably well," as Martin wrote to Buchanan the following day. "But after a while Pius IX asked to continue the conversation in Italian." Cordial as it was, the meeting could not altogether ignore the existing problems surrounding that first mission. Martin had received confidential instructions setting out the lines of demarcation of his assignment. As narrated in *L'Osservatore Romano*,

> Buchanan cautioned Martin never to forget that his diplomatic mission in Rome was to the government of the Papal States and to the pope as the head of those states, and not as head of the Roman Catholic Church . . . To avoid misunderstandings, Buchanan recommended that Martin should also make the papal government aware of this distinction between the spiritual and temporal power.

CASS'S THEORY

THAT SAME POINT has been repeated to successive representatives by the U.S. secretary of state. In his brief account of relations between the United States and the Holy See, former U.S. ambassador James Nicholson wrote that to this day a fundamental distinction is made between the Holy See and the Roman Catholic Church to avoid confusion and to ward off possible negative reactions in the United States; and this same point was first articulated in the 1848 Senate debate by

Senator Cass in support of diplomatic relations. To those senators who were withholding support for religious reasons, Cass argued that diplomatic representation in Rome had nothing to do with the pope's role as head of the Catholic Church. Cass pointed out that the United States would be sending an envoy to the pope in his position as sovereign, but not in his role as spiritual head of the Roman Catholic Church. It was one thing to advance the argument, another to sell it to a hostile public. Meanwhile, in 1848 a wave of nationalism spread through Europe, including the Papal States, and ironically the revolutionaries of the emergent (and, as it turned out, short-lived) Roman Republic drew inspiration from the American struggle for freedom from British colonialism. By the time Martin (who died in Rome in March 1848) was succeeded by Senator Cass's son Lewis Cass Jr. the pope had fled the revolutionary ferment in his capital for the safety of Gaeta. Pius IX's reputation as a reformer rapidly disappeared, giving way to a hard-line despotism. To the Protestants and nonconformists he became "the tyrant of Rome," and the title was no myth.

All the American Protestant establishment's old prejudices and objections against the Vatican quickly resurfaced. The diplomatic mission had been decided, but in spite of continued pressure from the pope there was no question of exchanging ambassadors: the timing was not right. Some of the reasons put forward for halting the advance of the diplomatic process were clearly stalling maneuvers. American officials suggested that there would be less opposition if the Vatican diplomats wore ordinary clothes instead of clerical garb. The combination of priest and diplomat probably took some getting used to, but the real reason was surely the very nature of the Vatican state. James Connelly wrote that the United States Congress could have accepted a Vatican prelate as ambassador, but not official dealings at that level with a reactionary Vatican state. Anti-Catholicism was the fundamental reason for the United States' refusal to establish full diplomatic relations with the Vatican, Connelly says. Rejection was made brutally clear in the response to Monsignor Gaetano Bedini's mission to Washington. Even so, that was just the beginning. The road to eventual understanding would be strewn with many more blunders and setbacks as successive popes attempted in vain to close the cultural gap.

PAPAL BLUNDERS

THE AMERICAN MISCALCULATION

THE MAIN REASON that Gaetano Bedini's mission to the United States was such a diplomatic disaster was rooted in the Vatican's refusal to accept that to Americans the separation of church and state, of politics and religion, was, well, holy writ. To the prelates in Rome the division seemed excessive, even impractical. They failed to see this U.S. doctrine as a reason for taking a different approach to American Catholics than they would with Europeans. Yet the difference was fundamental, and as a result of not appreciating that difference the Vatican took a series of false steps, with results for the Vatican ranging from damaging to merely embarrassing. There was, for example, the occasion when Pope Pius IX visited the USS *Constitution* in Gaeta harbor, in 1849. During the pope's brief exile in Gaeta under the protection of Ferdinand II, king of the Two Sicilies, the latter had had occasion to receive John Rowan, the U.S. chargé d'affaires in Naples. During the meeting the king in effect invited himself on board the USS *Constitution,* an American frigate, then expected in Naples waters. The American diplomat had little choice but to welcome the king, and even extended an invitation to the pontiff.

In James Nicholson's account of the incident, the *Constitution*'s captain, John Gwinn, received both rulers as guests on board his ship in spite of specific orders from Washington to the contrary. Both the pope and Ferdinand II were engaged in suppressing revolutions in their respective territories, and Gwinn had been told that the United States wanted to maintain strict neutrality. Instead, Pope Pius was given a free run of the ship, and in the three hours that he was on board, blessed the sailors and gave rosaries to Catholic members of the crew just as he would have done at a papal audience with pilgrims. The pope also felt briefly seasick and withdrew to the captain's cabin to recover; and—according to Nicholson—on his departure Pius IX was accorded the honor of a twenty-one-gun salute as he went over the side. Gwinn was ordered before a court-martial for disobeying orders and allowing on American territory a ruler who opposed democracy. The officer died of a stroke before the hearing. Pius IX, on the other hand, returned to Rome the following year and reigned for longer than almost every other pontiff in history.

WHEN PIUS IX SUPPORTED THE SOUTH

BEING ONE OF the longest-living popes in history also meant, peripherally, that Pius IX accumulated the most criticism from the United States. The American mission to the Vatican remained in place, tolerated by Congress. In 1854 the rank of the resident American representative was raised to minister, one level below ambassador. There are indications that Rome was not a coveted post in the American Foreign Service. The occupant was under constant congressional scrutiny to ensure that he did not step outside the limitations of his very narrow brief in dealing with the Vatican. Any hint of additional concessions had to be scrupulously avoided. At home the strong anti-Catholic sentiment that was wrecking the Bedini mission had not subsided. On November 16, 1853, the *New York Tribune* reported a vitriolic sermon by Gavazzi, Bedini's nemesis, at the Broadway Tabernacle. The Italian political refugee called on Americans to deny Catholics the same rights as Protestants because Catholics, he said, didn't understand free institutions. "Black slaves and Roman Catholics are the same," he went on.

The other reason that the Rome posting was not popular in the United States Foreign Service was financial. It was not as well paid as other foreign posts. The administration believed that it would open itself to public criticism if the holder of a diplomatic post the existence of which was barely tolerated were to be lavishly compensated. Poor pay was the reason given by Alexander Randal when he wrote to Secretary of State William Seward on September 29, 1862, requesting a transfer from the Vatican post, and his successor resigned for the same reason. Rufus King, a Republican from Milwaukee, took over in 1863, arriving in Rome in the midst of strife on both sides of the Atlantic— the Civil War in his own country and in Rome the forcible dissolution of the Papal States and the birth of the Italian nation. King was to be the last American representative to the Vatican for a long while.

In the prevailing atmosphere of uncertainty, every gesture could backfire, and often did. In 1863 Pope Pius IX wrote to the archbishops of New York and New Orleans urging them both to work for a peaceful solution to the American conflict. It was a typical Vatican approach, balanced and carefully neutral, but the Americans were in no mood for balance and neutrality. The Catholic Church in the United States had taken a similar position of extreme caution toward the issue of abolitionism. Monsignor Martin John Spalding, later archbishop of Baltimore, had sent a report to the Vatican proposing that Rome should not take sides on the issue. In Spalding's view, abolishing slavery would bring economic ruin to the South, and moral ruin to the slaves it was supposed to liberate, because the slaves were not prepared for freedom. Spalding called President Lincoln's emancipation act "an atrocious proclamation." There were several factors behind this rigid approach. One was the hostility of Irish immigrants toward African Americans, especially emancipated African Americans, who would compete with the Irish for the same jobs. There was also the conservatism of the American hierarchy, which was opposed to any change in the established order and fearful that emancipation could be the prelude to a revolution.

Considering the attitude of the American Catholic clergy it was hardly surprising that when it was learned that Jefferson Davis had replied to a letter from the pope, Northerners began to suspect that Pius IX favored the South. It didn't help matters when the pope wrote back, addressing his letter to "The Distinguished and Honorable Jefferson Davis, president of the Confederate States of America." For the North this was an indication that the Vatican had chosen sides, even though Cardinal Giacomo Antonelli, the secretary of state, asserted that Rome remained neutral in the conflict. The bigger problem for the Vatican was that the American Catholic hierarchy's fence-sitting was also seen as support for the South, which was both the reactionary side and the losing side—thus the banner of progress was left to the Protestants. The attitude of the American Catholic Church, which was wrongly thought to be following instructions from Rome, was the final nail in the coffin of Vatican relations with the United States.

In the prevailing atmosphere of hostility toward the Vatican for its alleged sympathies with the South, the last thing the central government of the Church needed was the suspicion that there was a link between the Church and the assassination of Abraham Lincoln. Yet it emerged that John Surratt, one of the coconspirators with John Wilkes Booth in the assassination of Lincoln, had taken refuge in the ranks of the pontifical army, which in those days was quite large. Surratt, a Roman Catholic, escaped the noose by fleeing to Canada (unlike his devoted mother). He was finally tracked down in 1867 and found to be serving in the Vatican's service as a soldier. A photograph in the archives of the Library of Congress shows a heavily bearded Surratt in the uniform of a papal Zouave. It is not clear how a fugitive from justice in the United States could talk his way into a papal regiment. The pontifical army was a kind of foreign legion drawing on volunteers from all over the world. But unlike the French Foreign Legion, which asked no questions about a recruit's past, letting it remain his own affair, the Vatican must have screened its applicants for service, but it was clearly a cursory scrutiny. The Vatican swore total ignorance of Surratt's alleged role in the Lincoln assassination, but in the United States a skeptical public drew its own conclusions. In the North the Vatican was seen as having given refuge and protection to a fugitive involved in the assassination of a leader who was the symbol of freedom, democracy, and the fight against slavery: the very opposite, in fact, of the Papal States themselves.

From Pius IX's viewpoint, the incident threatened to demolish decades of effort to consolidate the Catholic Church's position in America. One complication to setting things right by handing over Surratt was that no extradition treaty existed with the United States, and there was thus no legal arrangement for handing him over for trial. As a conciliatory gesture and to demonstrate its good faith, the papal government detained Surratt before Washington had made any formal request along those lines. The government in Rome determined that he was to be held "until such time as he could be handed over to the

American authorities." The papal Zouave ultimately was tried twice and released. His mother, who ran the boardinghouse where Booth had lodged in Washington, was the first woman executed under the United States justice system.

Rufus King explained to the secretary of state in a letter that Surratt's arrest in Rome was a measure of the Holy See's desire to repair the damage to relations caused by the wanted man's discovery in the pope's army. But the memory of the Vatican's alleged support for the South in the Civil War—or at any rate the Church's failure to take a stronger position against slavery—was harder to explain away. The Vatican had in effect backed the wrong horse, and could expect to suffer the consequences.

PROTESTANTS EXPELLED FROM THE VATICAN

THE FEELING IN Washington was that the Vatican's days as a major political player on the Italian stage were numbered, and that Italy was going through its own north–south struggle. In the north was the kingdom of Savoy, where Camillo Benso, Conte di Cavour, chief architect of Italian unification, supported the idea of "a free church in a free state." The south opposed democracy, and included the Papal States. On March 17, 1861, the kingdom of Italy was proclaimed, and for years after that Washington and Rome drifted further and further apart. The alienation deepened when, in 1867, it was reported that the American Protestant church in Rome had been forcibly moved outside the city walls. In reality the move of a Protestant place of worship away from the center of Rome had more to do with space considerations than complex transatlantic relations. However, rumors proved to have greater longevity than fact, and the one-sided version of the story persisted as an example of papal hostility to Protestantism.

Following the establishment of an American legation, the Vatican authorities had permitted Protestant services to be held at the residence of the United States representative. As word spread, the congregation gradually grew too large for the minister's home, and an apartment was rented by the American legation to be used exclusively as a place of worship by the city's Protestant community. The Vatican tolerated the move and continued to allow regular services there to avoid provoking American reaction. But early in 1867 the rumor began to spread that the Vatican's attitude toward non-Catholic religions had hardened, and that Protestants had been barred from worshipping within the city limits of Rome despite a tacit understanding to the contrary with Washington. Anticipating an anti-papist storm, particularly after this story was reported in the *New York Times,* Rufus King immediately telegraphed Washington on February 19 that "there was no truth" to the stories surrounding the closing of the American chapel in Rome. He reminded Secretary Seward of the importance of keeping open the diplomatic presence in Rome in what he called Europe's period of "profound change." In the circumstances, he said, the Holy See was as valuable as ever as an "intelligence emporium" on the Old Continent. But the rumor about the barring of Protestant worship in Rome, however untrue, was eagerly seized upon by the Vatican's enemies with disastrous results for the shaky structure of bilateral relations.

The Protestant chapel incident was not an isolated criticism of the papacy. Pius IX's suspected sympathy for the South in the Civil War had not been forgotten; and there was also a growing interest in a newly unified Italy, which had established a rival authority in the Italian capital. Henceforth the pope's territorial empire was reduced in size to a small walled enclave. Gone was his temporal power, and with it the arguments for diplomatic relations that had been used to convince an American public that had been skeptical to start with.

AND THE ROME MISSION WAS CLOSED . . .

ON FEBRUARY 28, 1867, the other shoe dropped when the U.S. Congress effectively ended diplomatic relations with the Holy See by the simple expedient of cutting off funds for the Vatican legation. There was no formal breaking off of relations, but any future American representative to the Vatican would have to finance the mission out of his own pocket. An act of Congress now blocked even one cent of taxpayers' money from going to the Vatican legation. The development was a victory for anti-Catholics, but Pope Pius IX had contributed to the debacle by mistakenly equating the growth of the

Catholic Church in the United States (more parishes, more clergy, and more schools) with a wider popularity when, if anything, the reverse was true.

It was, in any case, a unilateral break, and not formally declared as such. There is a diplomatic formula for breaking off relations, for example, following a declaration of war. But Rufus King had no instructions on how to explain his recall to Washington to the Vatican authorities. He left Rome without presenting to the Vatican authorities a formal letter of recall from his government, as the protocol requires, and relations simply went into suspended animation—a state of affairs that would prove helpful later on. The rumored removal of the Protestant place of worship from the city was certainly not publicly cited as the reason for the rupture. Indeed, the Vatican had strongly denied the rumors, and the departing American minister had strongly supported the Vatican's denial. Still, the act of Congress was to have a more lasting impact than the Vatican had anticipated. Rufus King was to be the last United States diplomatic representative to the Holy See until 1940. In his last dispatch to Seward, King reported the pope's bitter disappointment at the latest setback. Pius IX was wounded by America's hasty and ill-considered action, considering it an "ungenerous response to the good will he had always shown towards the American government and people."

Following the break, relations became formal, intermittent, and on occasion far from cordial. The Vatican shifted its attention from Washington to the American Catholic Church hierarchy and the rapidly expanding Catholic community in the United States. In 1830 there were 318,000 faithful in the United States. By 1840 the number of Catholics had more than doubled to 663,000. A decade later it had more than passed the million mark; and by 1878 the total had reached 6 million.

LEO XIII: "THE BISHOPS THERE DON'T WANT ME"

IN 1875 ONE American in eight was a Roman Catholic. In the southern states the picture was somewhat different: the proportion there was only one Catholic for every twenty-five inhabitants. Why? The cheap African-American labor force discouraged European immigrants from settling there. The Irish and the Italians—the mainstays of the American Catholic community—preferred to settle in the urban areas of the East Coast, where they often had family connections and were immediately absorbed into a community that attempted to replicate as much as possible life in the Old Country. The American Catholic hierarchy encouraged this trend. The "Bible Belt" was seen as impenetrable Protestant territory. In 1875 this eastern Catholic concentration received official Vatican recognition of sorts when the archbishop of New York, John McCloskey, was named the first American cardinal. But the American Catholic hierarchy was anything but a united front, with conservatives and liberals feuding over the shaping of the burgeoning American Catholic Church. Liberals supported the creation of a uniquely "American" Catholic identity while simultaneously working to convince new immigrants to shed their burdensome ethnicity. Conservatives opposed this view of a "nationalist" church, which they believed would dilute the authority of Rome. The Vatican was deluged with complaints from American parish priests against certain bishops; and the bishops, displaying the usual opposition to Vatican interference, resisted the appointment of an apostolic delegate from the Congregation for the Propagation of the Faith to investigate and resolve internal differences.

The challenge facing the central government of the Roman Catholic Church was how to restore its authority over a fractious and divided American clergy that was resolutely pushing the boundaries of its autonomy. In 1891 Pope Leo XIII, successor to Pius IX, summoned Archbishop O'Connell to complain to him about the defiant attitude of the American bishops. "Why don't they want the pope there?" he asked. If Christ returned to earth the hierarchy would unite in welcoming him, so why was his vicar not welcome? Things would go better if there was a papal nuncio, the pontiff went on. The American Catholic hierarchy would be free of the Congregation for the Propagation of the Faith, and would come under the aegis of the Secretariat of State. It was an old lament, and a familiar one. When, some years earlier, the Vatican had sent Monsignor Paolo Mori to test the U.S. administration's reaction to resuming diplomatic relations, Bishop John Moore complained to Cardinal James Gibbons of Baltimore that Rome was once again up to its old tricks of trying to encourage the United

States government to interfere in the affairs of the American Catholic Church, which had always been free of such pressure.

Rome now saw in the internal divisions within the American Catholic Church an urgent need to insinuate a papal representative to the episcopate. Liberal bishops recognized the new pope as an ally, even a protector, and supported his efforts.

ARCHBISHOP SATOLLI AND ROME'S "MOSAIC DIPLOMACY"

THE WINDOW OF opportunity opened in Chicago, of all places, and the occasion was the World's Columbian Exposition in that city in 1892. On behalf of the United States government, Secretary of State John W. Foster inquired of his counterpart in the Holy See, Cardinal Mariano Rampolla, whether Rome would consider the loan of certain ancient mosaics and historic sixteenth-century maps from the Vatican Library for exhibition in Chicago. Today, the Vatican is a regular lender of its art treasures for blockbuster exhibitions in museums around the world, but in 1892 its affirmative response was a breakthrough. Along with the mosaics and the valuable maps came Archbishop Francesco Satolli, a senior Curia prelate. The Vatican's loan was widely publicized, but Satolli's inclusion and his mission were known only to the pope's inner circle of advisers, and to a handful of American cardinals and bishops. He was smuggled into the country past the vigilance of the American Catholic Church hierarchy, especially the archbishop of New York, Michael Corrigan, an implacable enemy of the Catholic liberal faction. Satolli arrived in New York on the liner *Majestic* without Corrigan's knowledge, was immediately transferred to a government boat, and then taken to a secret destination.

After Chicago, the Vatican emissary toured the United States from coast to coast. In speeches in Tacoma, San Francisco, Salt Lake City, and Butte, he spoke of the new directions of the papacy under a more enlightened occupant of the throne of Peter, a modern pope for the modern age. He was careful to distance himself from the disastrous mission of Gaetano Bedini of forty years earlier, which was still vividly remembered. Satolli's low-key approach and his caution helped reassure

European refugees that quite possibly things were at last changing in the Vatican. Satolli's cross-country journey brought him into contact with the various currents of ecclesiastical thought across the vast nation. In the process, wrote Cardinal Gibbons, "he learned to know the territory on which he had been called to work," and people were able "to know his way of thinking, his fears and his hopes."

Satolli spoke little English and Gibbons recalled that his preferred way of communicating was to dictate what he had to say in Italian or Latin to his secretary or an interpreter who would in turn write out an English translation. Satolli knew enough English to check the translation for errors, and would then often read it out himself. Despite this convoluted method of communicating, his message appealed to American Catholic opinion, and the visitor avoided rousing the ire of anti-Catholics. He spoke of the papacy, the constitution of the Church, and how the spirit of Catholicism was compatible with the American spirit and American institutions. He showed no fear of American liberty; rather he embraced it and declared that the Roman papacy now shared the same principles. Speaking at a Catholic Congress in Chicago in September 1893, Satolli urged his audience to go forth "in one hand carrying the book of Christian faith, and in the other the Constitution of the United States." He said truth was accepted equally by Protestant, Catholic, and nonbeliever if they were honest in their convictions.

The Vatican prelate's message was meant to reassure Americans that Leo XIII respected the republic's institutions, and that "freedom of expression, and freedom of worship had nothing to fear from the Catholic Church," as Satolli said in an address at the Carroll Institute in Washington in 1895. "America seems destined for great things. It is our wish that the Catholic Church should not only share these aspirations, but should contribute to these great designs." The Church teaches that government by the people is just and proper, he said. "There is no instance of the pope interfering with civil government. History offers enough indications that problems have arisen when government has exceeded the boundaries of its authority and has tried to intervene in religious matters. But the United States was protected from such danger by the spirit of the Constitution, and the loyalty of those who guard it," he went on.

This was Satolli rewriting papal history to fit the changing times:

there were many instances of Holy Mother Church proving anything but the champion of liberty and universal suffrage. But Satolli maintained that the Catholic Church was not opposed to these values, and never had been. "There are those who maintain that only now, under Pope Leo XIII, has the Church become a friend to democratic governments," Satolli declared. "The Catholic Church has always shown great sympathy for such systems of government." To support his argument the prelate cited the tiny republic of San Marino, "which has existed in the heart of Italy for over a thousand years," and Andorra, an autonomous hilltop state sandwiched between Spain and France. "Both are small states, but they have been in existence long enough to show that republicanism is not incompatible with the Catholic religion," he added. He also listed other Italian republics—Venice, Pisa, Florence, Padua, and Bologna. He even recalled that William Tell, who gave his life for freedom in Switzerland, was a devout Catholic.

But what struck home was not Satolli's deliberate distortion of historical fact to reassure his audience of Rome's intentions, but his accurate reference to America's dominant problem at the dawn of the twentieth century: immigration on a massive scale, and his assurance that the Church could help to handle it. In his Washington address, Satolli warned that "all the horrors of a social revolution" were about to be visited upon the United States, and "this country will experience some of the worst unrest that has ever threatened society." The Catholic Church, he suggested, had the solution to the coming crisis created by the human flood of Irish and Italian newcomers who filled the factories—and the labor unions—tipping the balance of the population even further away from its Anglo-Saxon Protestant origins.

AMERICANISM: A PHANTOM HERESY

SOMEWHERE ALONG THE way Satolli's status changed from distinguished visitor to the Chicago exposition to apostolic delegate to the Catholic episcopate of the United States. His appointment was coolly received by the American bishops, who were fearful that the assignment of an Italian would strengthen the image of Catholicism in some quarters as the religion of foreigners. The American bishops were struggling with an identity crisis, or at the very least their loyalties were divided between the pope in Rome and the United States. Cardinal Gibbons was at the head of an effort to get the Church to recognize and take into account the distinctive American ways and ideals: to bring the Catholic religion to Americans in a form that would not offend the American idea of freedom of conscience. This view became known as the "phantom heresy." The mixture of patriotism and faith was viewed with suspicion in Europe, where it was misinterpreted, misunderstood, and labeled "Americanism." The efforts of Gibbons and others drew a carefully worded warning from Pope Leo XIII in the form of a letter to American bishops, the gist of which was that the proper way to go about establishing Catholicism in the United States was to clarify the place of American life in the Catholic faith, and not the other way round.

The fear in Rome was that American attempts to reconcile Catholic and Protestant beliefs would blur the lines of separation. When Gibbons proposed reciting a prayer for American political leaders on Thanksgiving Day, Bishop Benjamin Keiley of Savannah, Georgia, one of his critics, accused him of trying to supplant Christmas with Thanksgiving. The controversy went on for years. Gibbons wrote to the pope that his enemies were using Americanism as "a scarecrow—a line of reasoning that was not just suspect but almost heretical, and a schismatic doctrine." The idea that it was possible to be at the same time a loyal American and a Catholic had not yet been accepted either by the majority of Americans, or—for that matter—by the Vatican hierarchy, and in his dealings with Rome, Gibbons experienced many disappointments.

GHOSTS OF THE
KU KLUX KLAN

HOW THE VATICAN VIEWED AMERICAN
SECRET SOCIETIES

IN 1925, *La Civiltà Cattolica,* the Rome-based fortnightly published by the Italian Jesuits, carried a long report on the Masonic movement and other secret societies in the United States. The article was ostensibly a review of a published survey on such organizations, but it went beyond that scope to focus on the complex challenge the Vatican faced in dealing with American Catholic attitudes toward secret societies. The catalyst for the article was a review of Arthur Preuss's *A Dictionary of Secret and Other Societies* (St. Louis and London: 1924), a work based on information provided by almost all the secret societies and charitable institutions Preuss had been able to identify in the New World in response to his query requesting information on their aims, achievements, and activities. Preuss was identified by *Civiltà Cattolica* as "an American Catholic scholar who has studied the Freemasons and other secret sects for the past thirty years, and collected a great deal of material." The purpose of the dictionary was to make available to "Catholics, and in particular the American clergy, accurate information . . . so that Catholics will know how to deal with the situation." The publication of Preuss's dictionary was well timed: the Holy See felt it needed to provide some firm guidance on the relationship of Catholics to such organizations. The Catholic population in America was growing, and the allure of joining secret societies as a means of becoming integrated and gaining acceptance was causing concern in the Vatican.

"The number of religious sects and secret societies in America is proportionately equal to those in England," stated the *Civiltà Cattolica* article. They had similar rituals, oaths of office, secret signs of recognition, networks of contacts, and a shared love of mystery. But these groups also reflected "Protestant religious practices and a degenerate rationalism," cautioned the Jesuit publication. Anglican Protestantism and Masonic practices, the enemies of Holy Mother Church, had been exported from England to America. Members of clandestine orders, such as the Freemasons and, for example, Yale University's "Skull and Bones," had assumed prominent posts in the United States since the nation's earliest years. Attractive as they doubtless were to immigrants seeking status and the security of belonging to an influential organization, these organizations were nonetheless thought to be a danger to Catholic beliefs, and thus the understandable temptation that they represented was to be avoided at all costs.

Meanwhile, one particular secret society had flatly refused Arthur Preuss's request for information about its inner workings, and that was the Ku Klux Klan. "It's impossible to give you any information precisely because ours is a totally secret organization, and we don't want to see information published about us," Imperial Wizard H. W. Evans said in his reply to Preuss's query. But by then the KKK was notorious in Rome. Already in 1923 the Secretariat of State had information on the activities of a sect which—as *Civiltà Cattolica* described it—"dared to intimidate anyone it considered an enemy of the state, starting with Catholics. Thus today Catholics are assailed by the Masons, the Ku Klux Klan, and by the Protestant church." By then, too, links between the KKK and certain strains of Protestantism were no longer a suspicion but a certainty. Among the episodes cited to support this connection was a visit by Klansmen to a Baptist church in Paterson, New Jersey, "in their white tunics with their faces covered by their pointed headdress. They gave the minister a statement to read to his congregation, lauding him as a patriot and a man of the cloth." In another such instance KKK members entered a Baptist church in Peekskill, New York, during a service on Sunday, November 19, 1923, and presented the pastor with $100 as a tribute to his patriotism.

BETTER THE MASONS THAN THE KU KLUX KLAN

IN THE UNITED STATES the thorny issue of the appropriate relationship between Catholicism and secret societies was a part of a larger civil and religious war. For some years the Secretariat of State and the Propaganda Fide had been receiving requests from the American Catholic episcopate for guidance on how to deal with Catholics who joined Masonic lodges or secret societies—many of which were little more than social clubs. The bishops would, for example, ask what to do when a priest wanted to conduct the funeral service of a Catholic Mason; or whether and when to give dispensation for a "mixed" marriage involving a Catholic member of a secret society. The American Catholic episcopate also questioned the Vatican's reservations regarding the Knights of Columbus on the grounds that, though very Catholic, the organization was also semisecret. Clearly, the rigid Roman approach caused problems in the United States, where the circumstances were different from those in Europe. Nobody in America was prepared to go all the way in condemning membership of secret—which often just meant exclusive or very private—societies across the board.

The article in *La Civiltà Cattolica* cited three published sources in which, it said, good guidance could be found: *The Christian Cynosure*, the Protestant, Chicago-based National Christian Association monthly, founded in 1868 to campaign against "secretism"; *The Cyclopedia of Fraternities*, a compendium of over six hundred secret societies published in New York in 1907; and *An Encyclopedia of Freemasonry and Its Kindred Sciences,* published in Philadelphia in 1906. But this was not enough, and from a European perspective it was hard to arrive at a satisfactory understanding of the issue. There were theological questions, but also economic questions. For example, how could Catholics avoid losing income and social position if they were barred from membership in such organizations? Vatican officials were concerned that Catholicism in America was being put to the test.

The Jesuit publication cited instances in which members of the Knights of Columbus had "believed they could take part in meetings and banquets with Masons. Such involvement leaves a bad impression in Europe, where Freemasonry is openly anti–Catholic and anti–

religious"; but in America it was different. American Masonic groups "are not as rigidly anti-Catholic and against religion as in Europe," *Civiltà Cattolica* went on. Besides, "the great proliferation of religions and sects [in the United States]" rendered it "almost impossible for American Catholics to avoid contact with individuals, societies or groups of different religious persuasions." In a country built on tolerance and good neighborly relations "Catholics would be advised not to isolate themselves in public life, and to participate in gatherings even when they don't conform (to Catholic principles)," the article said. Certainly, such contacts "always carried risk." But the Vatican needed to recognize that the situation called for an approach that was less rigid than the traditional approach in the Old Continent.

The bottom line of the Jesuit message, in the report on the Masonic movement, was that the Catholic Church in America had enemies far more dangerous than the traditional Masonic organizations. Thus *Civiltà Cattolica* called for a benign coexistence with at least some secret societies, and a tactical alliance between Catholics and some Protestant groups against a newer enemy—a secret, but at the same time different, movement that was blatantly antireligion and xenophobic while also violent and hell-bent on inciting racial terrorism. It was necessary to "unite in vigorous opposition against the fanatical rage of the Ku Klux Klan," stated *Civiltà Cattolica*.

In 1925 the bishop of Cleveland, Joseph Schrembs, delivered an address in a new synagogue before an audience of members of the B'nai B'rith organization, described by the Jesuit magazine as "a Jewish semi-secret body for mutual help." The bishop had spoken out against "attacks by fanatics claiming to be acting in the nation's interest, against people of certain races and religions (principally Catholics, Jews, and African Americans), invoking not the Constitution of the United States, not the principles enshrined in the Declaration of Independence, but a non-existent imperial power with terrorist laws." The fact that a bishop had addressed a seemingly covert Jewish organization at a synagogue raised eyebrows among some senior prelates in Rome. But the Jesuit response to the official Vatican objections seemed to be that "to avoid wrongly passing judgment it was important to understand fully the prevailing social conditions in America."

It seemed that Rome regarded the KKK as so dangerous that even a temporary truce with the Masonic movement, the Church's eternal enemy in its European manifestation, was considered acceptable—at least in the American context. The Klan threat was not just cultural and religious, but actually physical. The Vatican files contain a report on a priest, Father Joseph Keller, being violently attacked by Klan members in Dallas. In Alabama the Klan went further and murdered a Catholic priest.

A MURDER JUSTIFIED

IT HAPPENED IN Alabama in the early part of the twentieth century when racial prejudice was a way of life in the Deep South, and the Ku Klux Klan was a force to be feared and reckoned with. This southern saga is of particular interest because one of the protagonists was the controversial Hugo Black, lawyer, judge, later United States senator, and later still associate justice of the Supreme Court. In 1921 a Methodist minister, the Reverend Edwin R. Stephenson, enraged when his daughter changed her religion to Roman Catholicism because she wanted to marry a Puerto Rican, took his shotgun and killed, not his daughter or her husband, but Father James Coyle, who had performed the marriage. At the subsequent trial Hugo Black defended the Methodist minister, a Klansman. Black is reported to have approached prosecution witnesses with the question, "You're a Catholic, aren't you?" in an attempt to discredit them before a Klan-dominated jury, and as a result Stephenson was acquitted. It was later revealed that Black himself had also been a member of the Klan.

The Catholic priest's murder, though an isolated incident, reflected a climate of violence and intolerance that extended beyond Alabama. In the early years of the century the flood of European immigrants, usually poor, and mainly Catholic, had revived old prejudices and justifications. In Birmingham, Alabama, the Klan put pressure on local businesses to fire Catholic employees. But in the 1920s and 1930s Klan terror spread to Tennessee, Texas, as far north as New England, and as far west as California. David Chalmers, in his in-depth study of the Klan, says the organization was rooted in what he calls "hereditary" anti-Catholic sentiment, an atmosphere of witch hunt in the aftermath of the Civil War, Prohibition, and a talent for salesmanship. The Puritan spirit was in rebellion against the changing times, stirring up the centuries-old Protestant hostility to combat the Roman threat.

The charge of pope-ism was enough derail a governor's election, bankrupt a business, or bring ruin to a family. "Patriotic" pamphlets pushed under the door warned of a "papist plot." In Marshfield, Oregon, the editor of a town newspaper who questioned the veracity of stories spread by the Klan was branded a papist, and his paper boycotted. Catholicism was characterized as "the foreign religion" controlled by the Vatican and a threat to American independence; and there was no shortage of immigrants with bitter memories of life in the Old Country ready to confirm and embellish accounts of subversive Vatican activity in America.

THE GUNS OF GEORGETOWN UNIVERSITY

THE NINETEENTH-CENTURY "Nativist" movement was not primarily aimed at promoting Protestantism, or targeting Catholics or Jews on account of their faith. Nativist organizations considered themselves guardians of American culture, acting on the fear that immigrants would undermine the evolution of a distinctive American national identity. So their real target was anyone who failed to assimilate—who was not American enough. Only incidentally did nativism favor the Protestant faith, as the religion of the Founding Fathers, and oppose the Vatican because it placed the American Catholic bishops and priests under the insidious and unwelcome authority of the pope, a foreigner. The members of the Ku Klux Klan were mostly Baptists, Methodists, and the Disciples of Christ, the latter being one of the largest religious movements founded on American soil. They regarded the pope as a more emotional target than other stereotypes such as the Jewish banker and the Negro. One of the Klan's most widely diffused myths was that Presidents Lincoln, McKinley, and Harding, respectively, owed their election to the Knights of Columbus, the fraternal society of male Catholics founded in New Haven in 1882. The Klan distributed tens of thousands of copies of a fake oath supposedly taken by each knight on his induction, which included the vow to "burn, hang, boil, and skin" non-Catholics.

The Klan claimed that 90 percent of the American deserters in the

First World War were papists—a doubly questionable statistic since in both world conflicts the United States never officially admitted that there were deserters from its military. In the Oregon chapter of the KKK it was said that the only good Catholic was a dead Catholic; and it was claimed that whenever a male child was born into a Catholic family, the father donated a new rifle to the local parish arsenal. The pope was said to have acquired property on the strategic heights over-looking West Point and Washington, DC. The Klan also claimed that two eighteenth-century cannons on the campus of Georgetown University, the Jesuit college in Washington, DC, are pointed at the Capitol building. All it took was a rumor, of course totally without foundation, that the pope was arriving by rail in North Manchester, Indiana, for hooded Klansmen to converge on the train station by the hundreds ready to defend America's freedom against the invader. The mood was one of hysteria, a persecution mania that, once it had taken hold, was hard to expel at a time of uncertainty and transition.

William Simmons, another Alabaman who formed the second Ku Klux Klan in 1915, skillfully exploited the public mood of a large majority of American people by convincing them that they were the besieged minority. "What are the dangers that threaten the destruction of our Anglo-Saxon civilization?" he would ask Bible Belt audiences who sought reassurance and were ready to recognize the "foreigners" as the enemy. The danger, he would go on, came from the tremendous influx of immigrants, "devoted to foreign dogmas and religious convictions alien to our own." Immigrants who arrived from all climes "[are] slowly pushing the white, American-born population into the middle of the country, and are preparing to eliminate it," he would say. The reference to white Americans reflected the view among nativists that immigrants from the Mediterranean, eastern Europe, and even Ireland, were members of an inferior race.

THE DUAL WAR AGAINST ROME AND RUM

IN A LOT OF people's minds—or at least a sizeable number of them—the waves of immigrants babbling foreign languages and practicing alien religions were associated with increased crime, corruption, and chaos.

From this situation stock figures emerged that became immovable in the society, breeding alienation and hate. Blacks, Jews, Orientals, Roman Catholics—foreigners, in general—were blamed for drug trafficking, breaking the Prohibition laws by smuggling liquor, political corruption, fraud, prostitution, and scandalous behavior. In California as in Florida the Klan used the pretext of defending public morality to hound papists. On April 22, 1922, the local Klansmen in Inglewood, California, raided the house of Mexican grocer Fidel Elduayen, who was suspected of smuggling liquor across the border. They searched the premises from top to bottom and found only one bottle. Then the law arrived and in the ensuing shootout a Klansman was killed. When his hood was removed he turned out to be a fellow policeman.

The stigma of Rome and rum died hard, but it was not entirely without foundation. Cardinal Satolli's speeches contain repeated appeals for sobriety coupled with warnings against the sale of liquor. Parish priests, not to say bishops, waged a continuous campaign to stop Irish, Polish, and Italian parishioners from engaging in the illegal booze trade.

American bishops were also both perplexed and embarrassed by the discovery of how little many immigrants knew about their own faith. Archbishop Michael Corrigan of New York wrote that he failed to understand how new arrivals from Italy, where there was no shortage of priests, could be so ignorant. Even the enemies of the Church, he remarked, were surprised that Italians who crossed the Atlantic in search of work and a new life had so little awareness of even the most elementary truths about their religion. On June 12, 1922, the *Sacramento Bee* quoted Methodist minister Rev. W. Redburn's complaint that all the brothels and the speakeasies in the area were owned by "Romanists," or at any rate controlled by them. A Catholic could go to Mass in the morning and then be dead drunk all day, whether on Sunday or any other day of the week.

This, then, is how the followers of "that Dago of the Tiber"—as the Klan often referred to the pope—were perceived by white Protestant America, the same group whose members announced "SAN BOG," for "Strangers are near, be on guard" at the approach of foreigners. Patriotic America was vigilant against possible papist plots. The Roman Catholic Al Smith's candidacy for the presidency in 1928 had the misfortune to arouse these suspicions; and the shadowy but powerful anti-Catholic alliance mobilized to stop this Vatican infiltration. And when in the early 1930s it was revealed that Franklin Roosevelt's campaign manager Jim Farley was a Catholic, support for FDR initially declined, albeit with little effect on the final outcome. Farley was accused of recruiting too many Catholics and Jews.

THE RADIO PRIEST

A THIRD AMERICAN phobia was added to Rome and rum, and that was revolution. The Klan added the virus of Communism to its baggage of prejudices, but the same threatening specter also extended to America's growing middle class. Catholics—the hierarchy in particular—were divided on FDR's social programs. In 1924 some cardinals were against a proposed constitutional amendment to block child labor because it smacked of "Soviet lawmaking." But some of Roosevelt's key early legislation reflected a program assembled by the Catholic bishops some time earlier. The American Catholic episcopate as a whole supported union organization; and Roosevelt had the support of the Catholic community generally. The Radio Priest, Father Charles Coughlin of Royal Oak, Michigan, first gained public attention during the presidential election of 1932 as a Roosevelt supporter. His radio talks blamed bankers for the Depression, lavished praise on the labor unions, quoted papal encyclicals, and coined the war cry "Roosevelt or ruin." It was never quite clear whether Coughlin was backed by the American Catholic episcopate, or even by the Vatican, and the ambiguity probably suited the priest.

The adulation of Coughlin turned to vituperation when the priest decided, halfway though Roosevelt's term, that FDR had reneged on his campaign promises. To Coughlin the populist, the politics of the New Deal smacked of Communism; direct state intervention in the nation's economy was the sovietization of America and a threat to the country's freedom. Because of his huge public following it was hard for the American Church hierarchy to restrain the Radio Priest. In 1937 the Roosevelt administration nominated Hugo Black for a vacant seat on the United States Supreme Court. Coughlin attacked the choice as "stupidity." Picked as a liberal Democrat and a strong New Dealer, Black was, of course, a convert from a lurid past in the racist ranks of the Ku Klux Klan, and his past came back to haunt him. When he ran for the Senate the press unearthed his membership in the Klan from 1923 to 1925. Black's defense was that his Klan grand passport was a dubious honor that had been thrust upon him, unwished and unbidden. But for his media opponents the fact that Black had been born in Ashland, Alabama, the same town as Klan leader Hiram Evans, became an indictment in itself, giving credibility to the other anti–Hugo Black stories that filled the papers. The Klan was getting its revenge for his desertion and his subsequent fame as a civil rights lawyer by leaking stories about his supposed activities as a Klansman. The KKK had not forgotten his efforts to improve the working conditions of blacks and his support of the labor unions. As they grew in strength and influence, the unions had become a favorite target of the Klan. Hiram Evans had urged them to dismiss from membership all Catholics, Jews, and blacks. His followers campaigned against the AFL-CIO, accusing it of being "infested with Communists," and "controlled by foreigners."

The Klan was adapting to the changing times, and had become the instrument of reactionary opposition to the labor unions in which Irish and Italian immigrants were often dominant. The Klan's main spokesman in this offensive was James Colescott, a veterinarian from Indiana. Colescott charged the AFL-CIO with "putting whites and blacks on the same level." Popery continued to come under fire in the United States. When, in 1939, Roosevelt decided to resume the tradition of sending a personal representative of the president to the Vatican, he was accused of "selling out to the Roman Catholic Church." But it was not always smooth sailing for the Klan; there was also the occasional setback. In 1936 an insurance company in Atlanta acquired the Imperial Palace of the Klan on Peachtree Street and resold it to the Catholic diocese. The sacred ground of a one-time Protestant stronghold was about to become the rectory of the new cathedral of Christ the King.

The bishop, Gerald O'Hara, invited the Imperial Wizard to the inauguration of the new rectory. Whether Bishop O'Hara's gesture was Irish irony to celebrate the conquest of a corner of racist America or an olive branch extended to the pope's enemies is not known; but Hiram

Evans, no longer the Klan's leading light, called O'Hara's bluff—if that's what it was—accepted the invitation, and attended the ceremony. But the Klan's deep hatred was not lessened by these events. The old religious wars of Europe had been transferred to the United States. But Europe itself was on the verge of a bloodier conflict that would in time draw in the Americans, as an indispensable ally in a struggle first against Nazism, and then Communism—a struggle in which the Vatican would emerge as a key player.

A WARTIME EXPEDIENCY

MYRON TAYLOR'S "HUMANITARIAN MISSION"

THESE DAYS WE would say that the challenge was in choosing the right spin to sell the decision. Back then, in 1939, they probably thought of it as the right catchphrase. But the problem was the same, to allay sectarian suspicions at home that the Vatican was once again putting an American administration in its pocket, and at the same time avoid causing lips to be pursed in disapproval in the protocol-minded central government of the Catholic Church. Some senior Roman prelates were bound to see it as another stalling tactic to avoid resuming bilateral diplomatic relations that had been broken off almost seventy years earlier, but Washington hoped that the more perceptive and pragmatic officials in the Roman Curia would understand the need for continued caution, and accept President Roosevelt's compromise formula for what it was—a cover for the real thing.

The United States felt the need to keep a close watch on Fascist Italy, Hitler's ally in the Mediterranean, and a "humanitarian mission" seemed the best explanation for a presence in the Vatican; the Roosevelt administration would not need to face objections that it was setting up an embassy. Roosevelt was also looking for support from leaders who sought to contain the Fascist threat. His "Containment" speech in Chicago in October 1937 in effect ended American isolationism by calling on the international community to ostracize Germany and Italy. By February 1939, when Pope Pius XI died, relations between the Vatican and the United States were good—three years earlier, Catholics had voted in large numbers for Roosevelt in the presidential elections—and it was in the course of renewed contacts that the question of resuming diplomatic relations resurfaced. The middle man between the Holy See and the Roosevelt administration was Francis Spellman, a young auxiliary bishop in the Boston archdiocese, who, during his days as a junior prelate in Rome, had been a close friend of the Vatican's secretary of state Cardinal Eugenio Pacelli. This was a powerful relationship indeed, because Pacelli was shortly destined to become Pius XII. In the fall of 1936 Pacelli visited the United States and—to the annoyance of several more senior American Catholic bishops—from New York to Philadelphia, Baltimore, and Washington, and on to Cleveland, Chicago, San Francisco, Los Angeles, St. Louis, and Cincinnati, Bishop Spellman never left his side. On October 28, Franklin D. Roosevelt was elected president, and Spellman was able to put into operation his masterstroke—a meeting between the president and Pope Pius XI's secretary of state.

When Archbishop Amleto Cicognani, the apostolic delegate to the American Catholic episcopate, contacted the White House to arrange a meeting, he learned that it had all been taken care of: Pacelli was to meet Roosevelt at his mother's home in New York for greater privacy. Cicognani was furious at being sidestepped. He knew this was Spellman's doing, and it soured forever his relations with the man who would become the most powerful figure in the American Catholic clergy for the next twenty years. Once Pacelli became pope, almost one of his first acts was to pluck his American friend out of relative obscurity and elevate him to the post of Archbishop of New York, over the heads of several more senior candidates. It is said that Spellman's name wasn't even on the terna, the list of three names from which the pope traditionally makes his choice; the names are generally submitted to Rome by the papal representative in that particular country (in this case, it was Cicognani). But in choosing Spellman, Pope Pius XII was not guided solely by friendship. He also saw Spellman as a valuable link to the Roosevelt White House; and Spellman would use his friendship with the president's son, James, to maintain a channel of communication to Roosevelt himself. The American episcopate's support for Roosevelt in the years of the New Deal had helped to rekindle the administration's interest in closer contacts with the Vatican. As usual there were differences in perception: Pope Pius wanted the papal representative to be the dean of the Washington diplomatic corps from the moment of his accreditation. In fact, the pontiff was claiming a diplomatic privilege going back to the peace agreement of the Congress of Vienna of 1815, and still observed to this day in countries around the world where the majority religion is Roman Catholicism; but the Americans would have none of it. For its part, the White House expected the United States ambassador to Italy to wear the extra hat of representative to the Holy See. But the Vatican insists even today that countries with diplomatic relations maintain a separate embassy to the Holy See.

A PRAGMATIC DECISION

THE IDEA OF relations with the Vatican had two well-placed supporters inside the administration. One was Cordell Hull, the U.S. secretary of state, and the other was Sumner Welles, the undersecretary of state whose influence on decision making in American foreign policy extended beyond his rank, and who was later to have a key role in creating what was to become the United Nations. Roosevelt was won over by their argument that an American presence in the Vatican would be another useful observation post from which to monitor developments in Fascist Italy; but as Roosevelt explained to Spellman, the fact that he intended to send his representative to the Vatican did not mean that the United States was ready to accept a papal nuncio in Washington. The U.S. President proposed to create a special United States mission to help deal with the thousands of refugees that were converging on the Vatican from all over Europe, but he also saw the mission as a possible way of jump-starting bilateral relations with the Holy See, which had languished for decades in limbo. The arrangement would bypass the necessity of begging Congress for money to fund the mission, even though Roosevelt must have realized that if things progressed that hurdle would have to be confronted sooner or later.

Pius XII and his secretary of state, Cardinal Luigi Maglione, went along with the idea of a humanitarian mission. "The Holy Father has welcomed with great satisfaction the president's decision to appoint a mission to the Holy See to assist with the refugee problem and to deal with other issues of mutual interest," the Vatican declared. Time was of the essence. For one thing war seemed imminent; for another, Roosevelt wanted to act before the implications of his decision became clear to possible opponents in the Congress. On Christmas Eve 1939, the president announced the appointment of Myron C. Taylor, lately chairman of the U.S. Steel Corporation and already active in international refugee relief on behalf of the United States, as his representative to the Holy See. At the same time Roosevelt took care to send copies of his announcement to Cyrus Adler, an influential Jewish theologian who taught at the Jewish Theological Seminary of America, and to George A. Buttrick, a prominent Presbyterian minister, thereby hoping to forestall criticism. To Pope Pius XII he wrote in his own hand naming Taylor as his personal representative. The letter was delivered to Archbishop Spellman who immediately telegraphed its contents to Rome.

SPELLMAN AND AMBASSADOR JOSEPH KENNEDY

ROOSEVELT'S DUAL-ROLE strategy for Myron Taylor (humanitarian efforts and diplomatic representation) had the desired effect of dampening public opposition, and it would not need congressional approval for its appropriation, because diplomacy came under the humanitarian umbrella. As an added precaution, the president insisted—and the Holy See reluctantly accepted—that Taylor would not have the formal rank of ambassador. It was still a risky business, but Roosevelt was convinced that there were advantages to the United States' establishing a presence in the Vatican's corridors of power. One motive, according to Pope Pius XII's biographer Andrea Tornielli, was "to gain the pontiff's acceptance of American cooperation with the Soviet Union"; or at least to ensure that the pope, who was among those who believed Communism was a greater threat to Christianity than Nazism, did not publicly denounce it. No, it was not all smooth sailing. When the administration announced that it was sending Joseph Kennedy—father of the future president and at the time American ambassador to the Court of St. James—to the installation of Pius XII, there were immediate protests and the government was accused of violating the sacred rule of the separation of church and state.

Spellman owed his own installation as archbishop of New York on May 23, 1939, to his friendship with Pacelli, but also to the fact that he had won the confidence of the president and could help with problem solving. A marginal, but important, factor was the case of Father Charles Coughlin, whose weekly "sermons" on radio were by this time more often harsh political diatribes against Roosevelt and his policies. At the height of Coughlin's popularity, forty million Americans listened to his weekly broadcasts, and the Vatican was in a quandary over whether to do Roosevelt a favor and silence the priest's politically damaging attacks, or to stay out of the fray. Any intervention would have revived charges that the Vatican was authoritarian and opposed to free speech; doing nothing at all implied Rome's approval of Coughlin's weekly attacks on the president—a claim that was made by the Radio Priest's archbishop, Michael Gallagher of Detroit. Gallagher was called to Rome, at least partly to explain this assertion, and in September 1936 the Vatican took a stand when Coughlin himself was rapped on the knuckles in an article in *L'Osservatore Romano,* the Vatican paper.

"YOUR HOLINESS, THESE CATHOLICS ARE ANTI-SEMITIC . . ."

COUGHLIN'S BROADCASTS WERE eventually halted by his superiors in 1940. But when Myron Taylor, a Protestant, presented his credentials to the pope on February 27, 1940, the envoy raised President Roosevelt's concern about the anti-Semitism that the Radio Priest was said to have spread among Catholics in America, a central issue for the White House, along with global disarmament, freedom of speech, and world trade. If the differing views among American Catholics regarding the coming world conflict had one common thread it was that few agreed with their president. There was little enthusiasm among Irish Catholics to rush to the aid of the hated English in their fight with Nazi Germany, particularly when Éamonn de Valera, the prime minister in the Old Country, chose to remain neutral.

The Spanish Civil War that had devastated the Iberian Peninsula between 1936 and 1939 and served as a grim overture to the world conflict that followed had divided American opinion, with the Left sending volunteers to fight with the Republic as the Abraham Lincoln Brigade. But American Catholics, shocked by stories of Republican atrocities perpetrated against priests and nuns and the willful destruction of churches, and aware that the Republic had the backing of the Soviet Comintern, had generally supported the Fascist insurgency led by Francisco Franco. "Fascism seemed a preferable alternative to communism," notes Father Gerald Fogarty in his account of Vatican relations with the American Catholic Church hierarchy. When Germany opened its Russian front in August 1941, the Roosevelt administration's support for the Stalinist regime produced mixed reactions among American Catholics, with even some of the bishops questioning the wisdom of that policy. In turning public opinion round to back a pro-British policy Roosevelt found an ally in Spellman and—at least by extension—in Pope Pius XII himself, although the latter tried to keep his distance from the belligerents. Not surprisingly, Mussolini's government had long since identified Spellman as an enemy of the regime. The August 1940 issue of the party organ *Regime Fascista* had accused the archbishop of being "an agent of the United States Jews." The specific charge was that he sent money to finance anti-Fascists in the Vatican.

So Father Coughlin was a minor issue in the memorandum of instructions that Myron Taylor had received from the White House prior to his departure for Rome. Taylor's immediate mission as Roosevelt's personal representative was to discover Mussolini's intentions in relation to what was already being called the Second World War, and—somewhat improbably—to do what he could to try to prevent the Italian dictator from falling into the arms of Adolf Hitler. But in June 1940 Italy entered the war on the German side, and the only thing left for the new Vatican mission was to be another set of eyes and ears reporting to Washington on developments in Italy in particular, and in Europe generally.

A ROOM IN THE EXCELSIOR HOTEL

TAYLOR WAS NOT the ideal person to dig for information. For one thing he lived in Schifanoia, near Florence, where he had bought a villa, and he visited Rome only occasionally. An Italian writer, Gaetano Salvemini, described the American tycoon as "a plutocrat who had many times expressed his enthusiasm for Mussolini." At first, until Hull relented, Taylor wasn't even authorized to use official State Department stationery. Later still, a consular officer from the United States Embassy in Rome, Harold Tittman, was loaned to the Vatican mission. When Taylor fell ill and had to return home to Philadelphia for treatment, it was agreed after lengthy negotiations that Tittman would temporarily take on his assignment. The Vatican had sensed that the United States was to play a decisive role in the burgeoning conflict and more than ever wanted to maintain diplomatic contact, however ambivalent and middle-level. Tittman established a temporary mission to the Holy See in a room of the Excelsior Hotel, on Rome's Via Veneto, and set about studying the ancient and complex institution that was now his bailiwick.

The image of the Vatican as being solidly behind the Western democracies and anxious for the United States to join in the fight against the evil of Fascism was misleading. It was soon driven home to Washington that influential Vatican prelates were divided on how to approach the conflict, as were the episcopates of Europe, not to mention those in the United States. Tittman had an eye-opening interview with the Superior General of the Jesuits, Wlodimir Ledóchowski, a Pole who hated the Nazis. Ledóchowski told him that there were Fascist and Nazi fifth columns everywhere, and particularly in the United States and in Latin America. Furthermore, some American cardinals did not perceive Hitler as a danger to the Catholic Church, and some German-American bishops were equally soft on the Nazis. Tittman reported to Hull that the Society of Jesus showed a courage and a will to fight that was in sharp contrast to the timid and irresolute stance at the Vatican.

The Roosevelt administration had confirmation of at least some of this in June 1941, when Hitler invaded the Soviet Union. Many American Catholics, already tending toward isolationism (which is where Coughlin comes in) were shocked at being asked to help the Communists, even if it was to fight the Nazis. Pope Pius XI's encyclical *Divini Redemptoris* expressly barred Catholics from collaborating with communists, and as far as anyone knew the papal ban was still in force. For Roosevelt, the support of American Catholics was indispensable if the United States was to fulfill the president's promise to Churchill and enter the conflict. To the Vatican it seemed clear that the future of Europe depended on American intervention. That required some creative thinking to clear the way for Catholic support. The risk for an overcautious Vatican was that it would seem to be publicly taking sides in the conflict, for or against the Axis powers—with possible consequences for Catholic communities in Germany, Italy, and elsewhere in Europe. The message from Rome, when it finally came after much discussion, gave new meaning to the old theological conundrum about angels balancing on the head of a pin. While Fascism and Marxism were both enemies of religion, the Vatican stated, it was important to distinguish between the Soviet regime and the Russian people, just as there was a distinction between Nazism and the German people.

THE SPIES' CAROUSEL

WITH THE ADVENT of the U.S. involvement in the war, the Vatican became a center of strategic importance for the United States. With U.S. diplomatic missions in Rome and Berlin closed, Washington's small outpost inside the Vatican walls in the heart of the Italian capital became a valuable source of information on both regimes. Washington was convinced that the Vatican's diplomatic service was the best in the world. Tittman moved his family into a small apartment in the convent of Saint Martha in Vatican City, where other diplomats from nations at war with Italy were also housed, and began to cultivate a network of reliable ecclesiastical sources. Washington had once looked on spying with distaste, but one of the lessons of Pearl Harbor was the need for better intelligence to avoid being caught unprepared again. Nixon's secretary of state Henry Kissinger liked to quote a late 1920s remark of one of his distinguished predecessors, Henry Stimson, who believed that "a true gentleman" didn't open other people's mail. But this was the 1940s, the nation was at war, and the mail needed to be opened, scrutinized, and deciphered. The offensive was being waged with all available means; and learning the enemy's secrets was a vital—indispensable—operation. Thus the resumption of diplomatic relations with the Vatican turned out to be vital to the national interest.

In 1939 the American embassy in Italy had advised Washington that diplomatic relations with the Vatican would open an extremely important source of political information. The American ambassador in Berlin, Hugh Williamson, said the Holy See had "the best secret service in Europe." And Sumner Welles, echoing the "emporium of intelligence" assessment of an even earlier generation of American diplomats, once remarked that the Holy See's profound and detailed knowledge of certain parts of the world, particularly Europe, was "proverbial." But the Vatican's reputation had—and still has—its skeptics. David Alvarez, professor of politics at St Mary's College of California, maintains in his book on espionage and the Vatican "from Napoleon to the Holocaust" that the Holy See's reputation for being all-knowing is a myth based on the papacy's image of secretiveness and mystery. In 1939 the Holy See had diplomatic relations with thirty-seven countries, with apostolic delegates in twenty-two others, among them the United States. Alvarez observes that the main source of information for Rome was its diplomatic service, the same one of which the legendary Monsignor Domenico Tardini once observed dryly, "They say that the diplomatic service of the Holy See is the best in the world. If ours is the best in the world I'd like to see the second best!"

With Myron Taylor not able to return to Rome once the United States had declared itself, Tittman remained as Washington's sole contact in the Vatican. The ex–World War I pilot, who had lost a leg in combat and disabled a hand, had limited Vatican sources. However, his few connections were high placed, starting with the substitute secretary of state, Giovanni Battista Montini, the future Pope Paul VI, who—it was said—also gave Latin lessons to Tittman's son. In fact, Vatican officials were more interested in expressing concern that the Allies might bomb Rome than in breaking their neutrality, at least most of the time.

Tittman's sole means of sending his reports to Washington was through the Vatican's diplomatic bag to Switzerland, a neutral country. From there they were forwarded to the United States. It wasn't a completely secure route: secret agents were everywhere. Moreover, because he was neither an ambassador nor a full consul Tittman was not entitled to use the State Department code book to compose his reports, and the department was not about to make an exception for the "Personal Representative of the President to His Holiness Pius XII." So he banged out his dispatches on his typewriter and sent them uncoded. Knowing the risk of his information falling in the wrong hands, Tittman used circumspect language. Toward the end of the conflict things improved. But by then the enemy was not Nazism but Communism, and on that score the Catholic Church and Washington were of one mind. Even so, anti-Catholic prejudice made the going far from easy.

THE ANTICOMMUNIST TRIANGLE

COSSACKS IN SAINT PETER'S SQUARE

IN 1944, when it became clear that the United States–Soviet alliance would not outlast the war but would be transformed into an ideological, military, and economic rivalry, the American way of mobilizing a war-weary public to the dangers that lay ahead was to put the emphasis on religion: a victory for the Soviet Union would mean the end of freedom of worship. A striking image had to be found that would implant in people's minds the nightmare of Communism ascendant in the West—one that would make Americans understand once and for all that the tactical alliance with Moscow had run its course, and that it would be replaced by a conflict destined to last for years, decades.

The Vatican was a suitable symbol of this strategic reversal. It could be portrayed as the incarnation of a defenseless Europe, a moral survivor of the world conflict, and now threatened by Stalin's Cossacks, a new Barbarian horde watering their horses at the fountains in Saint Peter's Square. This was the theme of a lengthy article in *Life* magazine of September 4, 1944: "The World from Rome: The Eternal City fears the clash between Christianity and Communism." The author was William Bullitt, an American diplomat who had served in Paris as well as in Communist Moscow. But what made the article worthy of special note was not the author's bona fides, but in the first place the claim that his work was based on interviews with senior, well-informed Vatican sources, including Pope Pius XII himself. The article reflected the very real fear among the pope's inner circle that Pius XII might have to escape from Rome as Soviet forces took over the city. Second, the article was noteworthy because at the time of publication American and Soviet troops were gearing up to deliver the death blow to Nazi Germany. But *Life* was looking beyond certain victory to the inevitable breakup of an alliance of convenience against the common enemy.

"What is the picture of the situation as seen from Rome?" Bullitt asks.

> It is an old picture, familiar to Romans since the time of the Caesars when Europe and Western Civilization were threatened by invading hordes. The task of the Caesars was to hold them back, and to preserve within the limits of the Roman Empire the civilization that had its origins in Athens and its strength in Rome. In the end, the Caesars failed; Rome was reduced to rubble. Successive waves of barbaric hordes swept over Western Europe, and through the dark ages Western Civilization was preserved only by the church.

This was the message of the Holy See, transmitted through the pages of *Life* magazine. But it was also the message that the United States wanted to convey. Bullitt's anonymous Roman sources spoke of the decline of British influence in Europe and the resulting crucial role of the United States. They perceived Italy as the frontier between East and West and the new battleground in the struggle between the "good" Americans and the "bad" Russians. The talk of Rome was "Will the result of this war be the subjugation of Europe by Moscow instead of by Berlin?"

The answer was that it could happen. The sources cited the strength of the Italian Communist Party in the Italian resistance during the war, particularly in the northern industrial triangle of Turin, Milan, and Genoa. They warned Bullitt that Moscow-trained party leader Palmiro Togliatti was an able political strategist committed to the Marxist revolution, and that an alliance between the Communists and the Socialists could have emerged as a majority had the Allies not stepped in to avert food shortages and to reduce galloping inflation. And the threat from the Left was still real as long as the situation in Europe remained unstable and confused.

But, Bullitt added, the Communists would have to deal with a factor in Italian life that they would find hard to overcome. That factor was not the royal house of Savoy, Italy's monarchy, because King Vittorio Emmanuel III had been discredited by his collaboration with Mussolini's Fascist regime; and his son, Prince Umberto, was not popular and would probably never rule as king. It was the Vatican—and it was to be a cornerstone of American strategy for the years to come. "The authority of the pope over the hearts and minds of Italian men and women has never been greater," Bullitt wrote. Pius XII was credited with saving Rome from destruction by Allied bombing or by the retreating Germans. Moreover, in a world turned upside down, people turned to God for guidance and comfort.

Bullitt's article identified the battle lines: Catholic Italy versus Communist Italy. "The Italians know that should the Communists rule Italy the hand of Moscow would be laid on the Holy Father. The Vicar of Christ would have to escape from Rome," Bullitt continued. The point was that the loss of Italy to Soviet control would also mean the loss of the Vatican, the spiritual core of Roman Catholicism, whether the pope managed to escape or not, and the psychological impact on the West would be disastrous. Whatever might have been said later about Pope Pius XII's wartime behavior, with rumors and controversial speculation about his attitude toward Hitler's treatment of the Jews, the Washington view at the time was that the Vatican had emerged from the war with its moral standing untarnished. Washington's respect for Alcide De Gasperi, the architect of Italy's postwar reconstruction, was not so much based on his achievement in forming a Catholic political party (the Christian Democrats) and launching it on its long span of election successes that lasted until the late 1980s, but on his close ties with the Vatican, which acted as his guarantor. In other words, the United States initially trusted De Gasperi because the Vatican did.

THE STRUGGLE TO CONTROL EUROPE

THE FLEDGLING AMERICAN intelligence service, newly named the Central Intelligence Agency, was impressed with the closely knit central administration of the Vatican and the complete discretion of the minuscule state, which had one of the smallest armies in the world, consisting principally of a company of the Swiss Guard created in 1503 under Pope Julius II, and armed only with "faith, hope, and charity," as Bullitt put it. The CIA saw potential in the Church's network of priest-informers in Italy and across the continent. What would eventually emerge as a formidable anticommunist triangle made up of the United States, the Italian Christian Democrat Party, and the Catholic Church had its origins in a dialogue between President Harry S. Truman and Pope Pius XII, with the pope's friend Cardinal Francis Spellman acting as intermediary and cheerleader.

A key factor for the Vatican was the belief that Britain could no longer alone guarantee Europe's geopolitical equilibrium. Britain had emerged from the war "a tired victor," with a heavy debt to repay to the United States and an empire in need of attention and restructuring. London therefore needed its traditional special relationship with the United States more than ever. At the same time the United States had lavished aid on Stalin without extracting any commitment from him that he would not invade central and eastern Europe. "When Myron Taylor saw Pius XII again for the first time in June of 1944, following the liberation of Rome, the pontiff was worried about Russia's attitude towards the Catholic Church," writes the historian Ennio Di Nolfo. Taylor reported to Roosevelt that Pius XII "expressed concern at the lack of confidence in Stalin's word, and in particular the growth of the Communist Party in Italy."

Already in 1944 the Vatican was casting off its Eurocentric approach and was seeing international politics in global terms. Pope Pius XII seemed to have a clear vision of what was taking place and was well disposed to an alliance with the real winner of the Second World War. "Pius XII understood the United States: He was the first pope to fully appreciate its power," says Andrea Riccardi, president of the Community of Saint Egidio, a movement founded by Monsignor Vincenzo Paglia, and close enough to the Vatican to be considered by some as a parallel ministry of foreign affairs. The Vatican was aware that while Poland was ostensibly governed by the Polish Committee of National Liberation, the country was in fact already in the Kremlin's grip. The Vatican received reports of Polish dissidents being taken to Siberia— about 1,700,000 since 1939—and knew that was merely a prelude to what was to come as the Soviet net closed in around eastern Europe.

The Vatican had written off as lost to the enemy Lithuania, Latvia, Estonia, Finland, Poland, Romania, Bulgaria, Hungary, and Czechoslovakia, although ultimately Finland was saved. Austria teetered on the East-West brink, and a division of Germany, with East Prussia coming under Soviet rule, was beginning to seem inevitable. Rome had information that Churchill and Stalin would agree that Hungary would remain in the Soviet area while Greece would come under the British sphere of influence.

The unknown quantity for the Holy See was Yugoslavia, Italy's neighbor on the Adriatic. The Vatican secretary of state disagreed with the Anglo-American policy of supporting Marshal Tito: Rome perceived him as Moscow's ally and was not taken in by his professed independence. The Vatican also wanted to be kept in the loop about the Allies' plans for resolving Austria's future. At one point Moscow proposed the restoration of Hapsburg rule in the person of Archduke Otto von Hapsburg, but the Vatican saw this as a move to gain popularity. To the Church, the Soviet regime represented a threat that Pius XII on various occasions during his life had described as more serious than the threat of Nazism. If the predictions in *Life* magazine seemed alarmist at the time they were to prove extremely accurate within a few months. America understood the full impact of the Soviet menace when Winston Churchill gave his famous Iron Curtain Speech in Fulton, Missouri, in 1946. The papacy had identified the new postwar balance of power two years earlier, when it made its decision to align the Church with the United States.

Cardinal Spellman was one of the leading figures of Catholic anticommunism both in the United States and in Europe. He was a member of the National Committee for a Free Europe, an ostensibly private citizens organization started by Allen Dulles, then director of the Central Intelligence Agency. The committee set the pattern for CIA-sponsored and -financed propaganda "cutouts." Henry Ford II and the historian Arthur Schlesinger were also among its prominent members.

It is hard to determine whether Spellman was the Vatican's man in Washington, or Washington's man in the Vatican. But it is even harder to underestimate the part he played in shaping Washington's Italian strategy in those early years of the cold war, and to a lesser extent its European strategy. He was a strong advocate of the Vatican's potentially strong role in the cold war. He also urged the Truman administration to give its full backing to the Italian Christian Democrats, and he pressed

Washington to keep both the Vatican and the Italian government informed of American intentions in the area. He was probably behind the decision to send Roosevelt's special adviser Harry Hopkins to Rome prior to the 1945 Yalta Conference. Myron Taylor took Hopkins to see the pope on January 31, after which Hopkins joined Roosevelt in the Crimea for the summit at which he reported the Vatican's views.

A DISPENSABLE MISSION

WASHINGTON'S STRONG COMMITMENT to Italy was soon obvious. Early in 1947 De Gasperi was brought to Washington where he addressed a joint meeting of the United States Congress. Italy received $227 million in aid between 1947 and 1948, and then became a beneficiary of the Marshall Plan, America's landmark postwar reconstruction program for Europe. De Gasperi's Christian Democrats, with their labyrinthine internal alliances and rivalries, were to enjoy continuous American support at great expense for almost four decades.

But Vatican hopes of strengthening diplomatic ties with the United States as a consequence of their joint anticommunist offensive came to nothing.

Yes, Myron Taylor was back in Rome since 1939 as the president's personal representative, but for how long? The Philadelphia executive did not hide the fact that he expected to be recalled and the American mission to the Vatican to be closed, to avoid renewed attacks on the administration for failing to keep church separate from state. Taylor's impending recall was even reported in *Newsweek* magazine in January 1946; and in the Vatican it was believed that Taylor's removal was probably a concession to American voters. When a distressed Spellman sought confirmation from Truman that Taylor would not be withdrawn, the reply was not reassuring. The cardinal attacked critics of U.S. diplomatic relations with the Vatican as "bigots." He tried to persuade Harry Truman to replace Taylor with the real thing—full diplomatic ties. He assured the pope that Truman was determined to keep the mission open "in spite of continuing and growing pressure." But the pope saw the American presence being cut back and knew it would soon disappear altogether. Pope Pius XII protested about these intentions to the White House; Spellman continued to pressure Truman, and the dismantling was halted, but only temporarily.

The Vatican-Washington collaboration still had its supporters inside and outside the administration. In 1946 Myron Taylor wrote to Truman that the pope and the Catholic Church were "the great bulwarks" of democracy in Europe. The Communist threat to Christianity and democracy transcended "minor differences" among Christian religions. Andrea Riccardi defends Pope Pius XII's foresight and courage in supporting the Europe of De Gasperi, Robert Schuman, and Konrad Adenauer, aiming for a European union that included the major Protestant countries, and not backing the narrower dream of some others of a Latin Union with membership limited to Italy, France, Spain, and Portugal. But Pope Pius XII's American alliance also had many detractors, particularly in Germany, where even in West Germany loyalties were divided between Washington and Moscow. When Taylor visited the archbishop of Berlin, Cardinal Konrad von Preysing, Spellman's friend, he was shown an article in the paper *Berlin am Mittag,* which had ties with the Russians. It said that the Jesuits had joined forces with American Protestants and capitalists, with the backing of the Holy See, to combat Moscow.

The intention was to destabilize Vatican-American cooperation, already unsettled by the diplomatic issue, and further complicated by the forthcoming Italian elections scheduled for 1948. There were also growing differences between Taylor and Spellman. The White House's man in Rome (for the moment) found the cardinal's attempts to influence the elections by working through the Italian-American community particularly heavy-handed and tried to distance himself from them.

Taylor had his own problems arising from the ambivalence of his position and the uncertainty about the future of the United States mission. Between 1949 and 1951 the Holy See pressed Truman further to firm up the arrangement. The substitute secretary of state, Archbishop Domenico Tardini, a prelate known for his blunt manner and acid tongue, asked Spellman to explain to the White House that the pope could not accept as special envoy from the president someone who was also a representative to other religious leaders in Rome in addition to the Holy See. It seemed as though the pontiff was being placed on the same level as other figures whose importance in Italy was not comparable with his own. Tardini's complaint was based on Washington's attempt at thinly disguising Taylor's appointment by saying that he was the president's representative to all religious leaders in Rome. Reminding Tardini of his position, Myron Taylor trotted out the official explanation that in sending him to Rome the United States had had to sidestep a constitutional issue on the separation of church and state.

Tardini was the wrong man with whom to take this line. In the war years Pope Pius XII had acted as his own secretary of state, assisted by two extremely able *sostituti*, or deputies, who played a Vatican version of "good cop/bad cop." Archbishop Giovanni Battista Montini was the good cop; Tardini was the bad cop. Characteristically, Tardini snapped back at Taylor that Brazil, Chile, and France, where the same doctrine of separation of church and state was in force, had diplomatic relations with the Vatican, as did Britain, where Anglicans were in the majority and Catholics a minority, and Egypt, which was not a Christian country at all.

MONSIGNOR MONTINI VENTS HIS ANGER ON SPELLMAN

IT WAS THE usual dialogue of the deaf. Recognition of the need to cooperate in the fight against Communism had not diminished anti-Catholic prejudice in America. If the Vatican was, as Bullitt wrote, "a permanent factor" in Italian life, so was the shibboleth of anti-popery in the United States. In May 1951 Spellman sent the pope a list of fourteen eminent Americans who supported the continuation of a presidential representative at the Vatican, and among the names were Sumner Welles, Harold Tittman, Bullitt, and Myron Taylor himself. Five months later, on October 20, 1951, Truman went beyond that formula and announced the nomination of General Mark Clark as the first ambassador of the United States to the Holy See. The matter seemed settled, but that proved to be one more illusion. Clark's nomination ran into a storm of Protestant protest. Cynics suspected that Truman was simply too savvy a politician not to have known that Congress would block the appointment; but he was probably hoping that if he was seen to be well intentioned, he could placate Vatican anger and ensure its collaboration.

Congress duly—and predictably—rejected the nomination and Clark withdrew in early January 1952. Truman announced that he would name another ambassador, but he never did. It was a deeply disappointing setback for Cardinal Spellman, who while visiting Rome in 1953 said gloomily that he had begun to doubt that there would ever be diplomatic relations between the United States and the Vatican because a recent survey of the Senate had shown that only five of the ninety-five senators were prepared to approve the nomination of an ambassador. In reply, Spellman received a furious letter from Archbishop Montini, who for once forgot his "good cop" reputation and let the United States have it. He denounced what he called the "unreasonable and unreasoned" attitude of American non-Catholics, calling their repeated attacks on the Vatican "harsh, vulgar, and totally unjustified." Their actions were "hardly compatible with the American perception of themselves as champions and guardians of liberty." And finally, the zinger: "I cannot conceal from your eminence the impression that the reaction of Catholics in the United States to these attacks has not been adequate." Spellman was stung by Montini's letter and quickly replied, quoting the strong reaction of Catholics in his community to the failed diplomatic effort. The harsh tone of Spellman's letter reflected his frustration at seeing a diplomatic initiative that had seemed on the verge of success finally and irreparably going up in smoke. He reminded Montini of the support given to Italy by American Catholics to prevent the Communists from gaining power. "The hierarchy, parishes, and faithful of the United States are militant, motivated, and as capable of achieving good results as any other nation on the globe," Spellman wrote. "We are second to no one, I repeat, no one in our devotion to the Vicar of Christ." He reminded Montini of the $200 million in aid distributed in the past decade by the Catholic War Relief Services, but "more valuable" was the work of "the American religious, both men and women, who leave their country to preach the word of Christ in the pagan world." But for all the sharp rhetoric both Spellman and Montini knew the matter was now closed.

"AMERICA IS OUR NEW PROTECTOR"

DESPITE THE SETBACK, both parties recognized the urgent necessity of continued collaboration, and the anticommunist triangle remained intact. The Holy See appreciated that the strategic core of the democratic fight against Communism was Washington. It was the new imperial power destined to protect a war-battered and melancholic Europe from the threat of new dictatorships. In 1959 Cardinal Alfredo Ottaviani, the prefect of what was then called the Holy Office and a champion of Catholic orthodoxy, visited the United States and in a speech paid America the compliment of comparing its "support and protection" of the Vatican with that of the Holy Roman Empire in the Middle Ages, and in later centuries France, but without being a threat to the Church's power. "Never was help given with less self-interest," the cardinal said.

It was an odd analogy, reflecting the Vatican's tendency to put the present in the context of history, but to Ottaviani it made sense. America, he said, always seemed to be "the New World." Early in the twentieth century the United States was still missionary land. They were not "missions among non-believers, but among non-Catholics, yet still missions," he declared. "Today, yours is the most developed Catholicism known anywhere, and you offer your arm to support the Apostolic See in the world." Coming from one of the most senior Vatican prelates, it was a kind of legitimization of the new alliance, and yet the residual memory of the struggles of that "mission among non-Catholics" lingered. It made American Catholics reticent about their religion, gun-shy. So that when in 1959 John F. Kennedy, the Democratic candidate for the presidency and a Catholic, promised in advance that as president he would not establish diplomatic relations with the Vatican, Rome was stunned, realizing that a Catholic in the White House would not advance the cause, but the prejudice. The project advanced by Kennedy's father, and of late by Spellman, was still out of reach.

KENNEDY'S "NEXT TIME"

"I AM NOT THE CATHOLIC CANDIDATE"

THERE WAS NO way around it. He could talk as much as he liked about the Soviet threat, or Fidel Castro, or poverty in West Virginia, or the embarrassment of not having put a man into space. But in the end the number one issue of the presidential campaign was that he was a Catholic, and nobody was more aware of the problem than John F. Kennedy himself. The fact that he was the Democratic Party's presidential candidate mattered less than that he was a member of a religious faith that had weighed heavily on the shoulders of successive American politicians for a century and a half. Kennedy faced head-on the challenge of proving that the interests of his country mattered more to him than the interests of that other country, the seat of his religion—that as president he would not "take his orders from the pope."

He would later say that "the so-called religious issue" had been blown out of proportion by his political opponents to undermine his campaign. But if he genuinely believed that is was not a real issue with American voters, he certainly gave a convincing imitation of a candidate anxious to lay it to rest. As, for instance, the time—it was September 12, 1960, two months before the election—when he flew to Houston to address the Greater Houston Ministerial Association, a gathering of Protestant, mainly Baptist clergymen. On that occasion he disarmed the audience, the majority of whom had regarded him almost as an agent of a foreign power, by declaring bluntly, "I'm not the Catholic candidate, I'm the candidate of the Democratic Party, and I happen to be a Catholic. I don't speak for the church on public issues, and the church doesn't speak for me." Because "I am a Catholic, and no Catholic has ever been elected president, the issues of this campaign have been set aside, perhaps deliberately, perhaps not." So it seemed necessary, he went on, to spell out the kind of America he believed in. What followed was an indirect refutation of all the charges brought against him. "I believe in an America where the separation of church and state is absolute," he said, "where no Catholic prelate would tell the president (should he be Catholic) how to act, and no Protestant minister would tell his parishioners for whom to vote—where no church or church school is granted any public funds or political preference, and where no man is denied public office merely because his religion differs from the President who might appoint him or the people who elect him."

Kennedy recalled the story of a Catholic soldier who had fought on the Pacific front in World War II, while his brother died fighting in Europe. "Nobody mentioned divided loyalties then, or that the brothers belonged to a community that was a threat to the liberty for which our forefathers gave their lives," he said. It was the same critical litany with which he had been bombarded by his political adversaries, as his candidacy had revived the anti-Catholic prejudice that was never very far beneath the surface. He told his audience that he had earlier visited the Alamo, where along with a Bowie and a Crockett, a McCafferty, a Bailey, and a Carey had also died, and nobody knew whether or not they were Catholics. At the Alamo no one was asked to state their religion.

In attempting to reassure the American electorate, Kennedy was also disappointing some of the members of the American Catholic episcopate, Cardinal Spellman first and foremost among them, to say nothing of the Vatican itself. It didn't seem believable that a newly elected Catholic president should, on entering the White House, declare himself opposed to diplomatic relations with the Holy See, and against federal aid to parochial schools. A president who, moreover, stated that his religious views were his own "private affair," who would not subvert the First Amendment, and would not take orders, or even advice, from the pope. He had also said that he was as critical of a nation that denied the presidency to a Protestant as to one that blocked a Catholic. In Houston he had pointed out that Chancellor Konrad Adenauer in Germany and President Charles de Gaulle of France were Catholic leaders of great independence.

Once in the White House Kennedy would do his utmost to dispel any hint of susceptibility to the Vatican's wishes. His "private affair" was safeguarded with almost obsessive determination. He simply couldn't afford to allow his religion to become an issue. Any contact with Rome was strictly unofficial and always informal, undertaken by trusted intermediaries with no direct role in the White House. It was his way of keeping the lines of communication open (ajar would probably be a better characterization) without breaking the "Houston commandments." In public, of course, the distance maintained was almost total. The Vatican did not appreciate the new arm's-length policy, and neither did Spellman, who in his life had expended considerable personal effort to bring the Vatican and the White House closer together. And, ironically, Spellman had once received influential help from Joseph Kennedy, the president's father. In fact, the American Catholic Church had watched helplessly as Kennedy undid some of the concessions they had fought hard to win from the federal government. In a 1959 interview with *Look* magazine, the future president had already indicated that he would oppose full diplomatic relations with the Vatican because American public opinion did not favor them. That was of less importance to the American bishops than the prospect of losing financial support for Catholic schools. As for Spellman, he was no longer a link with Rome. When the cardinal asked Frank Folsom, a mutual friend, what the devil Kennedy was planning to do, the answer was: exactly what he says.

TOP SECRET CONGRATULATIONS

POPE JOHN XXIII, who had succeeded Pope Pius XII in 1958, was trying to establish a rapprochement with the Soviet Union to help the Church in Eastern Europe, and hoped that the presence of a Catholic in the White House would facilitate the improved relations he sought with the United States to counterbalance his contacts with Moscow. Receiving Archbishop John Wright of Pittsburgh, he made light of

American suspicions of papal influence if Kennedy won the election. He asked Wright how Americans rated Kennedy's chances of winning the election. Kennedy's chances were considered very good, the bishop replied. "Well, don't expect me to run a country with a language as difficult as yours," Pope John XXIII commented.

In Washington, the CIA attempted to assess the impact of the progressive Chilean Catholic hierarchy on the government of Salvadore Allende, and foresaw the emergence of militant social churchmen in the same mold as the Brazilian bishop Helder Camara, who championed the cause of the slum dwellers in his diocese. In the east, the agency attempted to evaluate the Vatican's opening toward the Soviet Union. The CIA station chief in Rome was Thomas Hercules Kalamasinas, the son of immigrant parents who was born in Staten Island and raised in the Greek Orthodox faith but converted to Catholicism after his marriage to a Roman Catholic. A man of strong anticommunist convictions, he found Pope John XXIII's embryonic *Ostpolitik* worrisome, and in fact the Rome station's reporting did little to reverse the impression in Washington that there was a dangerous leftward drift in the Vatican's leanings. Kalamasinas was ordered to raise the priority of the station's spying on the Vatican. Ironically, at the same time, Kennedy was going to great lengths to keep the Vatican at arm's length from the White House.

Years later, Giulio Andreotti, a former Italian prime minister several times over, would recall that when Jack Kennedy visited Rome in 1963, a senior member of the presidential staff told him the story that at the Democratic Convention prior to his election, former president Truman had joked that it wasn't the influence of the *Holy* Father that was worrisome, but the influence of the father, in other words, Joseph Kennedy. It was a funny line, but it cut no ice with the candidate. In the triangle of Bible states with Indiana at the apex and Oklahoma and Mississippi at the base, the key factor was not the racial factor, but the religious factor. The pope's closest advisers told John XXIII that the first Catholic president of the United States was going to lean over backward to avoid any whiff of Vatican influence on his policy decisions, and they were proved right. Of all the messages of congratulations from foreign heads of state received by Kennedy after his election, only the one from Pope John XXIII was kept secret by the White

House, and the Vatican was asked to do the same with Kennedy's own equally harmless reply.

At the root of this concern was an awareness that the cultural core of the country was Protestant, and American Catholics knew it. Daily life in the United States was conditioned by the faith of the Founding Fathers and the influence in the New World of certain fundamental values that were not Catholic. "We American Catholics are psychologically influenced by Protestantism," Cardinal Francis George of Chicago once confessed to Andrea Riccardi, founder with Monsignor Vincenzo Paglia of the community of Saint Egidio. Many hoped that Kennedy would finally exorcise that influence, and that his presidency would represent "the final fusion of the melting pot," as Theodore White put it in his account of a presidential election a decade later. It was as though the ultimate barrier to overcome to unite the country was religion rather than race or ethnicity.

Artificial and politically motivated as the fear of Vatican influence might have been, Kennedy was faithful to his commitment that the pope would not rule by proxy in the United States. Theodore Sorensen, one of Kennedy's closest advisers, was to explain it this way:

> The hardcore religious opposition . . . would remain and flourish, to be cited by future conventions against the practicability of nominating a Catholic, if he (Kennedy) lowered the bars between church and state, yielded to the pressures of the hierarchy, or otherwise confirmed the religious opposition's suspicions. But if his conduct of the office was in keeping with his campaign pledge and constitutional oath, while unreasonable bigotry would always be raised, the unwritten law against a Catholic president would not only be temporarily broken but permanently repealed.

A discreet contact was maintained, however. In Washington, senior State Department officers would, as the occasion arose, meet privately with the apostolic delegate to the American hierarchy, Archbishop Egidio Vagnozzi. A couple of times a year, too, Vagnozzi and McGeorge Bundy, Kennedy's special assistant for national security affairs, arranged to meet purposely by accident at a reception or dinner at the residence of the Italian ambassador. They would slip away unobtrusively to the ambassador's study, conduct their business, and return to the party. In Rome the setting was less grand, but there were more frequent but equally informal contacts between William Sherman, a political officer at the American Embassy, and Igino Cardinale, the Vatican's chief of protocol. These meetings usually took place in Cardinale's cluttered office on the third floor of the Vatican palace. Sherman had the dual function of covering both the ruling and strongly Catholic Christian Democrat Party and the Vatican.

But in these contacts there was no talk of exchanging ambassadors, or even personal representatives. Influential advisers such as the historian Arthur Schlesinger Jr. encouraged the president to think seriously about resuming diplomatic relations with the Vatican, but Kennedy was adamant. When Dean Rusk, the secretary of state, brought up the subject at the close of a cabinet meeting, while the cabinet room was emptying, Kennedy listened to Rusk's arguments. Then he shook his head firmly. No, he said, that was going to have to wait. It was an issue for another president—or at any rate, for a second term.

The policy of distance was again confirmed in September 1962 when the Vatican invited some eighty countries, including the United States, to send an official delegation to the opening ceremony of the Second Vatican Council. Washington's official refusal, transmitted through the Rome embassy, explained that the principle of the separation of church and state precluded representation at a religious conference. Igino Cardinale immediately sought a meeting with Sherman. "If the Holy See as much as dropped a hint that Russian official attendance would be welcomed, (Soviet leader Nikita) Khrushchev himself would be on the next plane," Cardinale told the American diplomat, appealing to Washington's sense of competition with Moscow. Sherman realized that the United States was about to make a diplomatic error and advised Washington of the Vatican's intense irritation. Back came the prompt reply that the White House, not the State Department, had decided "at the highest level" that the answer was still no.

But the Vatican was not prepared to take no for an answer. The pope sent Vagnozzi to the State Department with a personal message for President Kennedy. The pope was sorry to hear that the United States would not be represented at the opening of the Second Vatican Council, and he hoped that the American ambassador would be able to

attend. In other words, the pope was whittling down the Vatican's invitation from "a delegation," which in diplomatic parlance normally
meant a high-level person or group, to a token representation. He was
suggesting a double compromise because the Holy See normally refused to do business with diplomats accredited to the Italian government. The American ambassador in Rome, Frederick Reinhardt,
meanwhile, had also advised the White House to revise its original decision, which, he said, would be a political error. Kennedy relented.
Reinhardt was told to attend the ceremony at Saint Peter's, taking
William Sherman with him. His instructions were specific and came
from the Oval Office: If queried he was to say that his attendance was
absolutely natural, and to underline the routine nature of his being
there he was instructed that instead of the white tie and tails normally
worn by diplomats at papal functions he should wear a business suit.

The more Pope John XXIII was drawn into the political sphere, the
more Kennedy's Washington kept its distance. The pontiff felt it was his
duty to try to ease cold war tensions. The effect on him of the Cuban
missile crisis had been profound; and he made it clear to both Washington and Moscow that his services as mediator were available. In the
Kremlin, Nikita Khrushchev reacted with curiosity and perhaps more
than a small dose of opportunism. The Kennedy White House hesi-
tated, wary. The CIA argued that the pope and his advisers were taking the signals from the Soviet regime too much at face value. But as
the Vatican's contacts with the Communist world grew more ambitious
and more complex—this in a country where the Italian Communist
Party regularly emerged as the biggest single winner in elections, and
where the name of the political game was to keep forming alliances to
keep them out of government—the policy planners in Washington began to think that perhaps it was best to keep the little walled state in the
heart of Rome under close scrutiny. When Pope John XXIII published
his landmark encyclical *Pacem in Terris,* its conciliatory tone toward
Communists as people, if not to the Marxist ideology, made the West
nervous. The director of the CIA, John McCone, asked for an audience with the pope.

McCone began by telling the pope that he was speaking on behalf
of the president of the United States. He said it was dangerous for the
Church to deal with the Communists because they could not be

trusted. Pope Pius XII had excommunicated Catholic members of the Communist Party, yet now Pope John . . . The pope replied gently that his perception of world affairs was not necessarily the same as that of the United States government. Following the audience McCone continued the attack in his talks with the pope's advisers. While Moscow was cooperating in Eastern Europe, the CIA had reliable information that the Communists were persecuting Catholic priests in other parts of the world, for example, in Latin America. In the United States many were getting the impression that the pope "ha[d] communist sympathies," McCone said.

"Does the United States government have communist sympathies?" asked one of Pope John XXIII's associates. "Of course not," McCone replied sharply. "Yet the United States maintains relations with the Soviet Union," the prelate observed. "But that's different," the CIA chief argued. "There are many practical reasons for regular contact—trade, for example." The prelate smiled. "But the pope has to consider his trade too," he said. "The trade of the soul, the good of mankind."

A PROVIDENTIAL DELAY

THE KENNEDY ADMINISTRATION watched as Pope John and his inner circle of collaborators, notably his private secretary Loris Capovilla, and Agostino Casaroli, rising star in the Secretariat of State, carried out their own "parallel diplomacy" in Soviet-controlled Eastern Europe. In June 1963 Pope John XXIII passed away at the age of eighty-five, and the five American cardinals went to Rome for the conclave that would elect his successor. Topping the CIA's list of possible papal choices on the progressive side was Cardinal Giovanni Battista Montini, the archbishop of Milan, with his counterpart in Genoa, Cardinal Giuseppe Siri, favored by the conservative wing of the Church. Montini was elected on June 20 as Pope Paul VI. The news reached Kennedy in Ireland, where he was in the course of a European trip; he had been scheduled to visit Pope John XXIII in Rome on July 2.

Within a couple of hours the CIA had supplied the president with a detailed profile of the new pontiff, his family background, his political ties with Christian Democrat Party leaders Aldo Moro and Giulio

Andreotti, both of whom he had known from their time as members of the student Catholic Action movement, FUCI. The agency included Pope Paul VI's contacts with the Italian Socialist Party, once allied to the Communist Party, but no longer, and his likely interest in continuing his predecessor's *Ostpolitik*. The new pope was equally interested in learning more about the president he would meet on July 2. The evening following his election he summoned the archbishop of Boston, Cardinal Richard Cushing, and asked him what topics the prelate thought Cushing's fellow Bostonian would want to discuss with the pope.

Cushing's advice was to avoid any issue that could be used as political propaganda in the United States against the "Catholic White House," such as Catholic schools and the race issue; in fact, it would be best to avoid American domestic issues altogether, and talk about world peace instead. Then the new pope had a really bad idea: since Kennedy's schedule had him arriving in Rome on June 30, Pope Paul VI sent Igino Cardinale to the American Embassy to invite the president to his solemn installation, which was fixed for the afternoon of that day. The pope's invitation threw the White House into a panic. For a president who had studiously avoided paying any public tribute to the Catholic Church there was only one answer, even when the Vatican pressed for acceptance, seemingly unaware of the domestic impact of Kennedy's presence at such a high-level, high-visibility Vatican ceremony. On the other hand, being in Rome and not attending the ceremony was equally out of the question. A less offensive answer had to be found.

The solution found was for Kennedy to delay his arrival in Rome by twenty-four hours, until July 1. While Pope Paul VI was being crowned in Saint Peter's Square, Kennedy was spending the night in a luxury hotel on Lake Como, a prudent three hundred miles or so north of the Italian capital; and the official United States delegation to the pope's installation was headed by Earl Warren, Chief Justice of the Supreme Court. The official reason for the president's unscheduled stopover was that he needed a rest.

On July 2 Kennedy sped through the streets of Rome in the presidential Lincoln heading for the Vatican. He wore a white tie and tails, and on his knee was the CIA backgrounder that even included advice on correct dress and suitable conversation topics for his meeting with the new pope. His advisers suggested that he propose to the pope bringing back President Roosevelt's compromise formula of appointing a personal representative to the pontiff with limited diplomatic powers. There had also been a CIA suggestion that the president should try to induce Pope Paul VI to bring the influence of the Vietnamese Catholic hierarchy to bear on the Buddhist monks to soften their antiwar stance. A succession of acts of public self-immolation by the monks, televised throughout the world, had not helped the American case.

I CAN'T GENUFLECT TO THE POPE: I HAVE A BAD BACK

DURING THE RIDE Kennedy was more interested in the Italian political situation. At an official reception in his honor the previous evening he had met Palmiro Togliatti, leader of the Italian Communist Party. The encounter had piqued his interest, and he bombarded Rusk with questions. It was clear that he regretted not having had the opportunity for a longer conversation with the head of the largest Communist Party in the West. At the same time he told Rusk that he was not interested in raising the issue of diplomatic relations in his meeting with the pope. That chapter was closed. If Harry Truman, a Baptist, had thought it prudent to steer clear of the problem, he was certainly not going to step in.

As the presidential motorcade drove into the Cortile San Damaso, a company of Swiss Guards presented arms with their halberds and a squadron of prelates of the papal household waited to receive him, Kennedy made one final adjustment to the visit. He mentioned to Monsignor Cardinale with studied nonchalance that he did not intend to follow the practice of Catholic heads of state and genuflect before the pope, nor was he going to kiss the papal ring. No need, Cardinale replied, a cordial handshake would suffice. Kennedy seemed satisfied, and went on to explain that he would not bow as he shook hands because for years he had suffered with a bad back and might not be able to straighten up again.

The meeting lasted half an hour, and Kennedy emerged visibly relieved. But he did not reveal what had been said, at least not immediately. He seemed satisfied to have steered clear of the diplomatic issue and any discussion of domestic American problems. The separation of church and state was safe. But the Vatican managed one last try, using the good services of Andreotti, a close friend of Pope Paul VI and Cardinal Spellman. Then Italian minister of defense, Andreotti met Kennedy at the American ambassador's residence in Rome, Villa Taverna. "I asked the president if he did not consider it an anomaly that both Washington and Moscow did not have ambassadors at the Vatican," Andreotti would recall years later. "He replied that following his election he had had to go to great lengths to prevent the so-called 'Catholic issue' from exploding."

Kennedy was even criticized for receiving Cardinal Cushing, a friend of the family, more frequently than senior Protestant clerics and rabbis. Andreotti reversed Kennedy's own argument and asked him whether he thought there was any hope that a Protestant president would take the diplomatic step when a Catholic president would not. After a long pause, Kennedy replied that he might consider it in his second term. But Kennedy was assassinated on November 22 of that year, and the Vatican had to wait another twenty years—for a determined Polish pope and a former Hollywood actor—Pope John Paul II and Ronald Reagan.

AN ALMOST HOLY ALLIANCE

FROM HOLLYWOOD TO THE POTOMAC

JANUARY 1981: The line of distinguished guests shuffled slowly through the White House, foreign ambassadors in the lead followed by an elegant flurry of Ronald and Nancy Reagan's jubilant friends, a blend of Hollywood aristocracy and skillfully preserved bicoastal socialites. Screen names from the past, in their heyday more famous and more successful than Reagan had been in his: Frank Sinatra; the tall, craggy presence of a no-longer-young Gregory Peck; the luminous, ageless beauty of Lauren Bacall and Katharine Hepburn. In the United States, after the grim, humiliating reality of the Americans' being held hostage in the embassy in Tehran, the 1980s had been ushered in by a newly elected Republican president who would make optimism his guiding star. Between the parading diplomats and the assembled stars was a kind of no-man's-land inhabited by a balding man in his sixties, his athletic figure encased in a well-cut, conservative black topcoat. Visible under it was a clergyman's collar; the man was Pio Laghi, the apostolic delegate to the Roman Catholic bishops of the United States. He was on good terms with Reagan, and he would later truthfully claim to be a friend of Reagan's successor George H. W. Bush, and of the Bush clan.

Laghi was a Vatican diplomat, but not its representative in Washington because, of course, there wasn't one. He had been invited to the White House in his secondary capacity of permanent representative to the Organization of American States, which has its headquarters in the American capital, and in protocol terms this posting was a kind of postscript to the Washington diplomatic corps. A seasoned Vatican diplomat despite the ambivalence of his current, actually new, appointment,

Laghi, born in Faenza, Italy, knew the United States well, having previously lived there from 1954 to 1961. Returning twenty years later, he sensed that Washington had begun to regard the Vatican in a new light. In 1978, the Polish Cardinal Karol Wojtyla had been elected pope. A leading figure in the so-called Church of Silence behind the Iron Curtain, Pope John Paul II was an implacable enemy of Communism, as was the whole Polish Catholic Church hierarchy. In Washington Wojtyla's election was seen as a geopolitical miracle, an act of providence, and an opportunity.

Laghi had received the news of his Washington assignment in late 1980. He was then nuncio in Buenos Aires, where he had gained some notoriety for playing tennis with the generals of the highly unpopular Argentine military junta. Shortly after his appointment to the OAS, while still in Argentina, he received—to his great surprise—a telegram from the United States. It said: I BELIEVE WE BOTH HAVE NEW JOBS IN WASHINGTON. WELCOME. It was signed Ronald Reagan. To his knowledge, Laghi had never met the president-elect. He believed Reagan's message was more than a mere courtesy. He saw in it at least the promise of less distant relations between the Vatican and the White House. And he was right.

3339 MASSACHUSETTS AVENUE

ARCHBISHOP PIO LAGHI had the good fortune to be in Washington when the impact of Pope John Paul II's fame, popularity, and sense of purpose were at their highest. The Vatican was equally fortunate to have in the American capital an experienced diplomat (who had served in Jerusalem, Cyprus, Nicaragua, and, most recently, Argentina) to be its voice in the strategic dialogue that took shape out of Ronald Reagan's admiration for, and curiosity about, the pope. Laghi was to remain in his highly sensitive post for nine years, as the conviction grew inside the Reagan administration that the new papal team in Rome were natural allies with the United States in what was to be the final push against the Soviet Union.

With this changing perception came a reevaluation of the Vatican's storehouse of global information. Henry Kissinger had once said famously that the Holy See collected a great deal of intelligence through its ecclesiastical network all over the world but didn't know how to use it. One way to use it was to pass on valuable information to a friendly government in Washington prepared to be less distant and to suspend traditional American suspicion of papal interference. In Central and South America, for example, then battlegrounds of conflicting ideologies involving Sandinistas, liberation theology, left-wing "bandolero priests," and right-wing paramilitary death squads—some of them said to have close ties with American intelligence—the Reagan administration saw the Roman Church as an instrument of stability and mediation.

To the Reagan administration, then, the Polish pope was the hammer with which to destroy the Iron Curtain, corroded by the rust of economic disaster and a failed system but still resilient. On his historic homecoming to Poland in 1979, Pope John Paul II had issued a call for the freedom of all peoples. His speeches had been a thinly veiled public endorsement of the new independent labor union, Solidarnosc. The visit was a stone cast in the pool of cold war, East-West politics, and its ripples were felt in Washington—and Laghi was there to follow up, to explain, and to build on the impact of what the pope had said.

The ninth apostolic delegate since Francesco Satolli lived in a neo-Renaissance stone house directly across Massachusetts Avenue from the Naval Observatory, once the residence of the chief of Naval Operations and now the official home of the vice president of the United States. The Vatican prelate made the most of this proximity. "The Elder Bush and I could wave to each other from the window," Laghi likes to say. In reality, they did more than wave from a distance. They met privately and with increasing frequency, Bush being both a neighbor and more accessible than Reagan. Their conversations ranged over current developments. Reagan's holy war and the pope's may have had different motivations, but there was a common objective—the total defeat of Communism.

REAGAN'S CATHOLIC NETWORK

LAGHI'S INTERLOCUTORS WERE for the most part members of Reagan's influential network of Roman Catholics positioned inside the

White House and at other strategic points in the administration. They served as his best conduit to the president himself, relaying communications from the Vatican Secretariat of State headed by Casaroli, and on occasion from the pontiff himself. There was a Catholic, William Casey, at the head of the Central Intelligence Agency. Alexander Haig, the secretary of defense, was another. The wife of Secretary of State George Shultz was also a Catholic with her own contacts in Rome. She was a friend of Giulio Andreotti, the former Christian Democrat prime minister. The Catholics inside the White House itself included Reagan's own chief of staff, William Clark, and Richard Allen, who headed the National Security Council. Reagan had appointed William Wilson to fill the post of his personal representative to the Holy See. Wilson was to become the first United States ambassador to the Vatican. His Catholic wife, Elizabeth, was a close friend of Nancy Reagan, the president's wife.

The last Catholic link, but by no means the least, was Reagan's ambassador-at-large, Vernon Walters, an accomplished linguist who was able to converse with Pope John Paul II in fluent Polish. Walters was a frequent visitor to Rome, where his usual ports of call were the Vatican Secretariat of State, the United States embassy, and Giulio Andreotti. Sometimes he came armed with the latest satellite photos of Soviet troop movements and missile sites around Poland or other Warsaw Pact countries.

In short, Laghi had valuable contacts with key administration officials in a dialogue that was authorized but not official, conducted on the Vatican side by an interlocutor whose credentials were as ephemeral as early-morning mist on the Potomac. When he visited the White House, usually to meet with Clark, but on occasion with Reagan himself, Laghi arrived in a car with normal, not diplomatic, plates and certainly no Vatican flag flying from the hood. The anonymity suited the White House. Laghi increasingly felt robbed of his true identity.

Meanwhile, the Vatican prelate's contacts with Bush developed into a cordial relationship, almost a friendship. Every year Bush came to the apostolic delegate's reception marking the accession of Pope John Paul II, where he would stay and chat with many of the other guests, mostly foreign diplomats. In protocol terms Bush's presence was highly unusual, not to say unorthodox, and over the years became a silent reminder that, despite their unprecedented cooperation in the fight against Communism, the Vatican and Washington still had no diplomatic relations. This did not stop Reagan from seeing the pope as a strong, strategic ally. At first, Laghi was to recall many years later, "the president was interested in Cuba, in Nicaragua, and in liberation theology. He asked me what was meant by liberation theology. What were its implications? The Sandinista movement he regarded as anti-American. His understanding of theology was limited, but his instinct told him that the liberation theology movement was subversive."

The pope had left no doubt where the Church stood on liberation theology: The movement had no legitimacy and deserved no support. In an address to the Mexican bishops (but in reality directed at the whole Central American episcopate) he made it clear that the notion of two churches—a "popular church" that supported the Sandinista regime in Nicaragua and an "institutional church" whose bishops were loyal to Rome and therefore were out of touch with the needs of the people—did not sit well with him. The papal line was that a "liberation" that went hand in hand with Marxism was blasphemous and a dangerous illusion, and the Church could not ally itself with a Socialist regime. This was clearly music to the ears of the Reagan administration.

Reagan himself gave every indication of enjoying his conversations with Laghi, even the more intricate ones, such as Laghi's expostulation that "the Church must know how to conjugate three verbs: to proclaim (the word of God), to condemn, and to practice charity. If the process begins with the second, the risk is that the approach is emotional and not intellectual, and the process runs into trouble." At first sight they were an unusual pair: the skilled Vatican diplomat, a product of the rarified atmosphere of the Pontifical Academy in Piazza della Minerva, behind the Pantheon in Rome, and an agile navigator in the world of Vatican Curia intrigue; and the famous Hollywood star and onetime actors' union leader who had somehow evolved into an icon of the American Right, a champion of the military-industrial complex and the oil lobby, governor of California, and president of the United States. But Reagan was a good listener who was amused by Laghi's use of whimsical metaphors to illustrate serious points: "Theology is like spaghetti, Mr. President. Served with too much sauce and too much salt, they are bad for the digestion. Liberation theology, as served up by the Sandinistas and the priests who support them, is ruined by too much seasoning."

THE KGB AND THE HOLY ALLIANCE

THE POPE AND Reagan were "profoundly aware that Poland, the most populous of the Soviet satellites, was also the most vulnerable politically," recalled former ambassador James Nicholson. "If they could work together to bring about the collapse of the communist regime in Poland, the rest of Eastern Europe would follow." There is an unmistakable note of satisfaction that the pope had enlisted in "the American party," without a passing thought given to the reverse, or at least complementary, possibility that it was the pope who was taking advantage of American policies for his own ends. But at the time the convergence of objectives was so obvious that the dominant reading of the situation was the former.

The other convergence was between Washington and Moscow. "When the archbishop of Krakow was elected pope, the head of the KGB and later Soviet leader Yuri Andropov believed that the United States had wanted the Polish prelate at the head of the Roman Church," wrote Paolo Mastrolilli in the geopolitical magazine *Limes*. In *Witness to Hope* the theologian George Weigel, considered the best of Pope John Paul II's American biographers, spells it out:

Andropov called the chief KGB agent, the *rezident*, in Warsaw and demanded, "How can you possibly allow the election of a citizen of a socialist country as pope?" The *rezident* is said to have suggested that the Comrade Chairman make his inquiries in Rome, not in Warsaw. Andropov then ordered an analysis of the election from Section 1 (Reports) of the First Chief Directorate of the KGB. The report, which reflected the KGB spymaster's view that history worked through plots, concluded that Wojtyla had been elected as part of a German-American conspiracy in which key roles were played by the Polish-American archbishop of Philadelphia, Cardinal John Krol, and Zbigniew Brzezinski, national security adviser to President Jimmy

Carter. The goal of the plot was, presumably, the destabilization of Poland as a first step toward the disintegration of the Warsaw Pact. The analysis was almost comical, but the threat analysis was acute.

There were those who couldn't resist the temptation to complete the circle; and the term "the Holy Alliance" to describe the relationship between the former movie actor and the pope who came in from the cold was first used by Carl Bernstein, half of the famous Watergate reporting team at the *Washington Post,* in an article in *Time* magazine, precursor to a book coauthored with Marco Politi, the Vatican correspondent of the Rome newspaper *La Repubblica.*

Mostly citing American sources, Bernstein describes in considerable detail an iron pact. He quotes Richard Allen: "It was one of the greatest secret alliances of all times." Holy it was not, but it was extraordinarily timely. Some saw it as farsighted; others as merely far-fetched, contrived. "One cannot speak of a formal agreement or alliance," Pope John Paul II himself told the writer Luigi Geninazzi in February 1992. The pope called Bernstein's holy alliance thesis an attempt to fill in the blanks in history. Causes are invented to explain subsequent developments, he said. Writing in *Avvenire* about Reagan's death on June 5, 2004, Geninazzi, an expert on Poland and Solidarnosc, concedes that there was "an extraordinary meeting of the minds, but not an alliance."

When the regime declared martial law in Poland in 1991, Reagan decided to impose economic sanctions. "The pope was against sanctions, arguing that they imposed hardships on the people but did not harm the regime," Geninazzi wrote.

> The truth is that both [Reagan and the pope] were determined to defeat the totalitarian system, but their strategies were different. For Reagan, Poland was one battlefront in a broad political offensive to weaken the Soviet regime. The pope, on the other hand, focused on the grassroots level, invoking the Polish national conscience. Still, there existed a great feeling between them. Both had been actors, and athletes, and both had become great communicators. True, Reagan was moved to tears by the television images of the pope in Poland in 1979, but the idea of a secret alliance is absurd.

William Clark, Reagan's national security adviser, recalled that Reagan and the pope shared a common view of the Soviet empire, and that in the end justice and law triumphed. Lech Walesa's labor union Solidarnosc—Solidarity—emerged from the shipyards of Gdansk to challenge the regime in Warsaw. Whatever its organizers' initial intentions, Solidarnosc quickly became a fifth column for the Reagan administration and the Church to be supported, enlarged, and developed into an opposing force destined to break the power of the Communist regime.

In the summer of 1982 Ronald Reagan had his first private audience with Pope John Paul II. The outcome, according to Carl Bernstein, was Reagan's secret decision to give Solidarnosc Washington's full support. Lech Walesa and the other Solidarnosc leaders began to receive strategic advice, often from American or European priests and union officials operating undercover. The CIA, the AFL-CIO, and the Catholic Church worked together to support Walesa's organization; and the U.S.-Polish-Vatican collaboration became a thorn in the side of the government and remained so until the collapse of Communism. Until 1990 the "evil empire" clung to an ailing system like survivors of a shipwreck clinging to flotsam in the water. But to the Reagan administration, the potential collapse of the Soviet Union had looked promising from the early 1980s.

America's military might couldn't undermine the balance of power between East and West established at the Yalta Conference, but Pope John Paul II's unarmed "divisions" could, and they were destined to do more damage to Moscow and Warsaw than any ballistic missile. Throughout four decades of Communist control Polish fidelity toward the country's bishops had never faltered. Now Poland's Catholic episcopate emerged as a vital force in the final showdown.

JANUARY 10, 1984: THE FIRST AMBASSADOR

IT WAS MONUMENTALLY risky work, exposing priests and union activists to intimidation, prison, and even death. But Pope John Paul II pushed the cause with the determination of a Pole who had lived through the darkest days of the system. Even after moving to the Vatican it took time before he shook off the fear of being spied upon by the secret police, and began to talk freely on the telephone. So, with the world watching in fascination, the Vatican took the lead in the final battle. At the same time, Vatican diplomacy in the expert hands of the secretary of state, Agostino Casaroli, the architect of the Church's *Ostpolitik* with the Soviet Union, was closing in on an objective in "Westpolitik" that had eluded Rome for more than two centuries: the establishment of diplomatic relations with Washington.

Typically, the Vatican chose an unrelated occasion on which to make its decisive move. In 1896 the contribution of precious ancient mosaics to the Chicago exposition opened the way for successful negotiations to send an apostolic delegate on the Catholic episcopate of the United States; this time the event was the centenary of the founding of the Knights of Columbus, the influential Catholic welfare organization formed as a rival to similar Protestant groups from which Catholic immigrants were once barred membership.

The celebrations were in Connecticut, and Casaroli himself was to represent the pope. Casaroli contacted William Wilson, Reagan's personal representative to the Holy See, and suggested that Reagan might want to be present. The invitation was relayed to the White House and was duly accepted. In the course of the afternoon the president and Casaroli had a private meeting lasting more than an hour, and the outcome was an agreement in principle to appoint an American ambassador to the Vatican, and an apostolic (papal) nuncio to Washington.

In June 1983 the U.S. Senate voted to repeal "a provision of Federal Law prohibiting appropriations for the support of U.S. diplomatic relations with the Vatican," and the House took similar action. Congressman Clement Zablocki (D-WI), a Catholic, introduced the amendment in the House, and Senator Richard Lugar (R-IN), a Methodist, did the same in the Senate. There was no mention of actually establishing an embassy, thus reducing the likelihood of objections. That decision was left to the president.

The American change of direction was one more indication that the Reagan administration recognized the pope's determination to play an active role in promoting peace and the Vatican's engagement in international relations. The determining factor in the decision was the president himself. On January 10, 1984, the Vatican announced the establishment of diplomatic relations with the United States; the White House announcement followed a few hours later.

To his great satisfaction, William Wilson was confirmed as the first United States ambassador to the Holy See. The ambivalence of his previous position had irked him. "When you realize that you are the representative of the president of the world's greatest nation, politically, economically, and militarily, to the leader of the most important spiritual and moral state you begin to understand that you occupy a truly important position," he told James Nicholson, one of his later successors, in the summer of 2002. "You hold the appointment, but you're not an ambassador. You have to ask yourself why that is." Not that the Vatican had ever given any hint that he was considered anything other than America's full-fledged diplomatic representative. "It was as though the Vatican was anxious for the United States to have an embassy," Wilson recalled.

Laghi was appointed the first papal nuncio to the United States but retained his former duties as apostolic delegate. Years later he would recall that "eighty percent of the time I functioned as a consultant. Every year, about twenty new bishops had to be appointed. It was my task to gather information about possible candidates and to give advice [about them]."

Yet even otherwise well-informed and sophisticated officials had difficulty understanding fully what the Vatican was all about, and what the precise role of its diplomat-priests was. Somewhere in the recesses of the mind there remained the residual suspicion that their mission was to infiltrate the government of the United States in order to bring it under the Vatican's domination.

REAGAN ON TRIAL

YET TWO CENTURIES of separation of church—any church—and state in the name of the First Amendment of the Constitution could not be unceremoniously pushed aside without striking a nerve, especially when the church in question was the Church of Rome. The Vatican–United States agreement brought long-standing antagonisms rushing to the surface. That it was Ronald Reagan who had made this pact with the Vatican devil came as a shock to his conservative constituency and strained its loyalty. But in the end opposition was confined to the religious Far Right. Jerry Falwell, the well-known fundamentalist Baptist minister, protested that establishing diplomatic relations with the Vatican set "a bad precedent. I wonder what will happen when Mecca wants an ambassador. I told the White House that if they give one to the pope, I could ask for one myself."

In November 1984 Reagan's decision, taken in the interest of Realpolitik to strengthen his ties with a key ally against Communism, was challenged in a United States District Court located in Philadelphia, Pennsylvania, by a coalition of churches and religious groups consisting of the American Jewish Congress, the Baptist Joint Committee on Public Affairs, the Seventh-day Adventists, the National Council of Churches, the National Association of Evangelicals, and the Americans United for Separation of Church and State. They charged among other things that diplomatic ties with the Vatican were an infringement of their rights as taxpayers, and as Americans, and discriminated against their own respective religious communities.

The Philadelphia court found in favor of the White House, quoting legal precedent going back to the nineteenth century, congressional records, Vatican diplomatic documents, and the *Encyclopaedia Britannica*. The lower court's ruling was upheld on appeal and reaffirmed in 1986 by the Supreme Court. The fact that the president himself had taken the decision on his own initiative was a determining factor. That, said the Supreme Court, made it a political issue, and not a legal one.

Summing up two hundred years of history in a few lines, the district court ruling said:

> The Vatican City State is an area of 109 acres within the city of Rome. The pope of the Roman Catholic Church is the spiritual sovereign of this city-state (see 22 Encyclopedia Britannica 905 [1971]) . . . The Holy See "occupies a position that is recognized in international law (Ponce vs Roman Catholic Church, 210, US296, 318 [1908]) and

consequently had diplomatic relations and sends representatives to various international organizations, including the United Nations."

The Supreme Court added that

the United States established consular relations with the Holy See for the first time in 1797. Relations between the two governments were formalized in 1848, and from 1848 to 1867 (the United States) sent four official delegates, all approved by the Senate, to represent it . . . Diplomatic relations were interrupted in 1867, and the two governments did not exchange representatives until 1939, when President Roosevelt and Pope Pius XII reestablished informal relations . . . in 1984 . . . President Reagan exchanged official diplomatic notes with the Holy See and named William A. Wilson United States ambassador to that government.

In upholding the decision by the court of appeals the Supreme Court justices first ruled that the appellants "do not make any concrete allegations that they personally have been treated unequally" and "failed to allege any personal injury suffered . . . as a consequence of the alleged constitutional error." In addition, the recognition by the United States of a foreign state like the Vatican was assigned "exclusively to the executive power." In making his decision, "the president clearly viewed the Holy See as a government, and not as an exclusively religious authority, and that determination conclusively limits the courts." The fact that the Vatican had declared that the United States had established diplomatic relations with the Catholic Church in Rome was irrelevant to the court. For the justices, "the relevant question does not relate to the Holy See's view but to the president's view concerning the diplomatic relations that he has established."

Public opinion was more favorable than in the past, although the numbers were far from overwhelming. A Gallup poll taken at the time showed that 57 percent of Americans supported Reagan's action. However, 79 percent of *Catholics* were in favor of establishing diplomatic relations with the Vatican, but only 48 percent of Protestants. The American Catholic bishops had questions about how this new arrangement would affect their freedom of action. Many Catholics perceived the agreement as clearly a political step that at best would have little impact on their relationship with the Vatican.

The Vatican could not resist a note of suppressed triumph in announcing its diplomatic reinstatement in Washington. The Vatican newspaper *L'Osservatore Romano*'s front-page headline said tersely, "Diplomatic Relations between the Holy See and the United States." A commentary alongside by Paolo Befani, the paper's highly respected foreign editor, carried the equally laconic heading: "After 117 Years," but the undertone of self-satisfaction was unmistakable. The reference to 117 years recalled the length of time that had elapsed since the 1867 cutoff, which the Vatican still resented. This was clear from Befani's article, which certainly had the Secretariat of State's stamp of approval. Reagan's decision, Befani wrote, "corrected a historic anomaly." The article pointed out that the Vatican at that time already had "diplomatic relations with more than a hundred countries from every continent, culture, race, and every form of government," and "in at least half of those diplomatic partners the population was predominantly Catholic."

The article pointed out that it had been a unilateral American decision to interrupt relations in 1867. The early missions in America were mentioned, and the first contacts in Europe between emissaries from Washington and the popes, but Cardinal Gaetano Bedini's traumatic trip in 1853 was passed over without a word. Befani jumps to the suspension by Congress of the appropriation for the maintenance of an American legation in Rome "from and after June 30, 1867," and says that the move was unexpected considering that relations "between the two capitals were more than cordial, to the point that two years earlier President Lincoln had urged the pope through diplomatic channels to consider creating American cardinals, and Pius IX had immediately responded by elevating to the purple the bishop of New York, Monsignor John McCloskey. So why break diplomatic relations?"

The Vatican journalist answered the question with a historical explanation that was subtly critical of the American government of the time. "There were apparently two reasons," wrote Befani.

On the one hand there was the belief that the Papal States' days were numbered and that, therefore, it was prudent to anticipate that development, thereby gaining the sympathy of the new Italian state. On the other hand, there was the sharp dissension between the administration and the Congress on the problems of Post-bellum reconstruction . . . Throughout the conflict Pope Mastai had maintained a policy of non-interference in the internal affairs of the United States, except for expressing his support for the abolition of slavery. After the war the pope had spoken in support of reconciliation, and the United States representative in Rome, Rufus King, had publicly voiced the same views. The closing of the Rome embassy was a form of reprisal by Congress against both the pope and the American diplomat.

That was not all. The Vatican newspaper said that Washington's "unilateral decision" of 1867 had been unreasonable, and it had been a long road to January 10, 1984, and normalization. Some of the milestones along that road had included the first visit by a pope to the White House "as the president's guest"—Pope John Paul II in 1979—to "significant progress in Vatican Council II" toward "the ecumenical dialogue among Christian churches."

The article paid tribute to Vatican patience and its perseverance for decades in remaining open to dialogue with Washington in the face of repeated slights. The inference was that not only had the papal state survived the defeat at Porta Pia and the royal house of Savoy; it had also forced the United States to come to terms with its diplomatic importance.

L'Osservatore also carried the reaction of the American episcopate: Bishop James Malone of Youngstown, president of the United States Conference of Catholic Bishops; Cardinal John Krol, archbishop of Philadelphia; Bishop William Hickey of Washington. Krol's comments were the most pertinent: "The president and the Congress have had the courage to banish to history the remnants of the pride of origin and religious prejudice that have had such a negative influence on our national politics." Clearly, Krol went on, "it was the government and not the [American] Catholic church that would benefit most from full diplomatic relations with what is today one of the most respected centers for world peace."

The establishment of full diplomatic relations was obviously a welcome relief, but the Vatican could not resist removing the stones that had accumulated in its shoes for decades. And beyond the Atlantic, in the United States the most frustrated were the believers in the total separation of church and state. For them what had transpired confirmed their view that the Vatican was plotting to gain control of Washington. For the enemies of popery there was nothing left to do, no more battles to fight, at least politically and legally. But the public had to be informed that the Vatican now controlled American politics. In fact, it always had covertly: now it would do so openly. After 1984 a literary genre reemerged with stories about secret operations by world governments, incidents verging on the diabolical, and always in the background the Vatican.

At the same time there was a real Vatican scandal that outdid any fiction and involved a powerful American monsignor who headed the Istituto per le Opere di Religione, in other words, the papal bank, from 1971 to 1989. This was Paul Marcinkus, a prelate of Lithuanian origin from Cicero, Illinois, and a genial giant who had run crowd interference for Pope Paul VI, and then Pope John Paul II, on their foreign travels. It was a sordid story, with, clinging to it, the odor of the Mafia—which is hardly surprising since one of the key figures was Michele Sindona, a Sicilian international banker who is alleged to have laundered money for the Mafia; another was Roberto Calvi, head of the Banco Ambrosiano. On June 18, 1982, Calvi's body was found hanging from the neck under Blackfriars Bridge in London. The supporting cast included members of Italy's ruling Christian Democrat Party with ties to the Vatican.

The scandal cast an aura of intrigue, mystery, and unchecked power. Marcinkus, who according to the Vatican expert Giancarlo Zizola had "performed important tasks for Wojtyla in Krakow, raising money from Polish Americans for a church in Nowa Huta and other projects in the archdiocese," was quietly removed from his sensitive post. He first took refuge in the Vatican (where he was out of reach of the Italian police), and then was sent as administrator to a parish in Arizona, with a Vatican diplomatic passport for protection. Marcinkus died there on February 20, 2006. Soon, however, another scandal—the clergy sex abuse crisis—was to emerge in the United States, which would prove more damaging and more costly to the Vatican, the American hierarchy, and American Catholics than a score of financial scandals.

THE WOMAN FROM THE FBI
AND THE PEDOPHILES

THE CATHOLIC HIERARCHY FACES A SCANDAL

ONE OF THE noticeable domestic aspects of the second Iraq war and its immediate aftermath was the muted tone of American Catholic reaction. Faced with a policy that was becoming increasingly critical, the United States Conference of Catholic Bishops seemed in its comments to be timid, even defensive. The American Catholic hierarchy issued some statements, carefully retooling the Vatican's much more assertive position for local consumption, its bishops being fully aware that any outspoken criticism of the war would have been deemed unpatriotic. But even within these parameters the Church seemed to many to be holding back and not speaking with the authority with which it had spoken in past situations. Although the hierarchy represented a large and influential community of 67 or so million members, with 195 dioceses, 45,000 priests, and 19,000 parishes, at that moment, it seemed to have lost its moral authority. The problem was not the old prejudices against immigrants, and neither was it pressure from a Protestant lobby. Rather, it was that American Catholicism was facing the most critical moment of its existence. In a sense, the Church was also at war, but against itself, and against a nation that had put the institution on trial, pointing an accusing finger at the scandal of its pedophile priests, which according to some Vatican officials may have been somewhat overblown, but was real and devastating nonetheless.

It exploded in Boston, the archdiocese of Cardinal Bernard Law, and between the end of 2002 and 2003 it had spread throughout most of the United States. The cardinals and bishops faced a collective trial that prevented them from taking a strong public stance on any major issue, and against any group, including the Pentagon's neoconservative planners of the unilateral war. The moral authority of the U.S. Conference of Catholic Bishops was challenged by hundreds of relatives of individuals who had allegedly been sexually abused in parishes and schools. The pope had to issue draconian directives to block the wave of disrepute that threatened to overwhelm an American institution that had taken two hundred patient, determined years to establish in the face of a thousand obstacles and prejudices. Burdened with this shame, it is not surprising that even the Holy See failed to make its voice heard in a Protestant White House determined to launch a holy war against the villainous Iraqi leader.

In November 2002, after months of shocking revelations in the *Boston Globe,* the bishops had their backs to the wall. They had to show strength of will in ridding themselves of, and dealing with, the pedophile priests in their midst—and in paying out millions of dollars in damages. In a desperate and atypical move, they turned to an agent of the Federal Bureau of Investigation to probe the scandal and prepare a report. The bishops engaged Kathleen McChesney, a Catholic and a highly respected FBI veteran.

THE McCHESNEY REPORT

"IN NOVEMBER 2002, in response to the problem of sexual abuse of minors by Catholic priests, I was asked by the American Conference of Bishops to leave the FBI and set up an office for the protection of minors and young people. I was asked to prepare an annual report on progress in each diocese," McChesney stated a year after her appointment, having finished her investigation. Her main job, between confessor and policewoman, was to verify that parishes, religious communities, and seminaries were obeying the minors' bill of rights drawn up following the scandal. Her brief included discreetly interviewing all those who were allegedly responsible for allowing sexual abuse to occur. But the bishops also insisted that no names should be mentioned in the final report, possibly for legal reasons. To scour all the parishes within the prescribed six-month deadline fifty-four investigators were hired, mostly former FBI officers.

Investigators were given special training on how to work in the closed, rarified world of the clergy that included parish priests, professors, theologians, seminarians—all persons of the highest level of respectability, responsible for the development of young men and women and children. McChesney engaged William Gavin, president of a Boston private investigators firm, the Gavin Group. Gavin himself was a twenty-four-year veteran of the FBI and was serving as deputy director of the bureau's New York office when he retired. He had been in charge of the investigation into the World Trade Center bombing in 1993. In 2004 McChesney told the Italian newspaper *Avvenire* that the investigation had been conducted by laypeople. Of the 195 dioceses, 4 had not been included in her report because of various problems in carrying out the probe, but 171 had developed support programs for the abuse victims and their families.

THE GEOGHAN CASE

COMPLAINTS AGAINST Catholic priests for sexual abuse had been made for years; and for years the hierarchy had either minimized such cases or settled them quietly, usually by moving the alleged pedophile from one parish to another, from one state to another. But the situation was never seriously addressed. Early in 2004 the recurring scandal resurfaced with a virulence that made it difficult to sweep under the carpet. While the United States was engaged militarily in Afghanistan, and the first Taliban detainees were arriving at the U.S. Marine base in Guantánamo, the city of Boston was consumed by revelations in the *Boston Globe* that Father John Geoghan had been a serial molester and had been transferred from one parish to another in the archdiocese despite numerous complaints against him for child sexual abuse.

Geoghan stands out as one of the worst offenders in the recent history of the Catholic Church in America. Published reports said he had been an active pedophile for at least twenty years, and one of the complaints against him referred to an episode in 1979. When the Boston Police met with one of the auxiliary bishops of Boston to follow up some of the more specific allegations, they were told Geoghan was "undergoing treatment." This was the hierarchy's frequent solution to the problem, in place of a full-scale confrontation of the sexual abuse crisis and the larger fundamental problem of the selection of priests.

The psychiatric center where Geoghan was being treated diagnosed an extreme case of pedophilia, but added inexplicably that the priest was "psychologically suited" to teach children. Yet some 150 people had come forward claiming they had been abused by him. The 2004 "Report on the Crisis in the Catholic Church in the United States" described him as "insecure, immature, and psychologically disturbed." It quoted the rector of the seminary where Geoghan had studied as saying he was extremely immature. Yet he was admitted to the seminary in 1953, and ordained a priest in 1962, remaining a priest for over thirty years: he was defrocked in 1998. There had been no shortage of alarm bells over the years. In 1984 Bishop John D'Arcy, one of Boston archbishop Cardinal Bernard Law's auxiliaries, wrote a letter warning that "Father Geoghan had a long past history of homosexual relationships with boys." But the warning was ignored, and by the time Geoghan had been sentenced to ten years in jail, the scandal had spun virtually out of control. (Geoghan was murdered in jail.)

Father Geoghan was not the only pedophile priest in Boston. Father Paul Shanley was arrested about the same time. In 1978 the Vatican had written to the then archbishop, Cardinal Humberto S. Medeiros, expressing concern that some of Shanley's public comments "seemed to indicate homosexual behavior involving minors." In all 120 priests were forced to resign nationwide, and the archdiocese of Boston paid $30 million in damages solely to Geoghan's victims.

By December 2003, Boston had paid a further $80 million on 541 other claims for damages, and had been forced to sell the archbishop's imposing residence in the city and close or amalgamate some parishes. But in September 2004 the *Boston Globe* reported that a further 140 complaints had been advanced, some of them going back five decades, and the treasury of the archdiocese had been bled dry. The scandal also had a political impact, depriving the episcopate of its moral force to speak out against the Bush administration's preventive war.

THE DALLAS SEVENTEEN COMMANDMENTS

IN APRIL 2002 the pedophile priests scandal was causing such concern in Rome that Pope John Paul II summoned the American bishops to the Vatican to give him a detailed, firsthand report on the sexual abuse cases and their origins. The meeting took place against a background of differences between the Vatican and the Bush administration over the latter's unilateralism after 9/11. In his assessment of the sex scandal the pope made his stance crystal clear: "There is no room in the priesthood and in religious life for anyone who could do harm to young people," he warned.

Two months after the Rome summit, the American bishops, meeting in Dallas, Texas, began their long, traumatic catharsis as a start to restoring their credibility. The Dallas conference approved rules for the protection of children and young people calling for the permanent exclusion of any priest who was found guilty of sexual abuse of a minor. It seemed unnecessary to establish such a rule: after the crisis it was unthinkable that any priest would be allowed to continue to serve the Church after any such transgression. But in the surreal and confused atmosphere of the time the ground rules needed to be stated categorically. In all, seventeen new rules were promulgated ranging from the obligation of each diocese to work with abuse victims to the importance of priestly celibacy. The resulting document was called "a milestone in the history of the Church in America."

But the scandal remained a millstone around the necks of the bishops, and it would take more than seventeen rules to clear the whiff of squalor and suspicion that had come scudding down on American Catholicism. It was also necessary to face the problem squarely no matter where it led, study it in depth, discover its roots, and in the process repair the lack of confidence it had created among the faithful, as well as the damage done to the hierarchy's credibility. The bishops engaged the John Jay Institute for Criminal Justice Ethics in New York to carry out an unprecedented long-term study of priestly abuse from 1950 to 2002, and the results were more shocking than the immediate cases had indicated.

According to the report, 4,392 priests had been credibly accused of sexual abuse of minors, amounting to 4 percent of the 109,694 clergy active in the ministry during those years. The study put the number of minors who were known to have been abused by members of the clergy at 10,667, and said that the Church had disbursed more than $500 million on the problem. Most of the money went to pay damages to abused minors; the rest went for legal fees and payments to consultants and experts. Most diocesan bishops cooperated in the inquiry, but a few did not, claiming a right to privacy. Religious communities were less forthcoming, refusing to make their archives and their memories available to investigators, reflecting a secretive mentality and—by inference—a right to immunity. The combination of public indignation and at the same time the desire for closure inevitably led to casualties, and the first head to roll belonged to Boston's top cleric, and one of the most influential prelates in the United States, Cardinal Bernard Law.

THE CARDINAL AND FIDEL CASTRO

LAW HAD TRIED for months to marginalize the scandal, and then he hoped to shut it off by publicly apologizing. But that was not enough. The omissions of the past, the secretiveness that had led bishops to cover up past cases of pedophilia, had finally caught up with the American Catholic hierarchy. The cartoons showed the cardinal, with mud on his cassock, saying, "I'm here to clean up this scandal."

In reality his days were numbered. In early December 2002, fifty-eight priests from the archdiocese signed a statement calling on Law to quit as Boston's archbishop. Abraham McLaughlin, in the *Christian Science Monitor,* called the development "a turning point in the sex abuse scandal and in the history of the Roman Catholic Church." And he was right. A few days later, on December 13, while the Bush administration was mobilizing for the Iraq War, the cardinal went to Rome and offered his resignation to Pope John Paul II, and it was accepted. He had lorded over the third largest Catholic diocese in the United States for eighteen years.

He had been appointed archbishop in 1984 and named a cardinal a year later. Law was considered the pope's man through and through, and his profile went well beyond his position as Boston's archbishop. He was active in the fight against anti-Semitism in the United States and a key figure in interfaith dialogue. As a "Wojtylian," he was also a tough opponent of gay marriage and abortion. In the 1984 presidential election campaign he called on Catholics not to vote for the Democratic presidential team of Walter Mondale and Geraldine Ferraro because, for him, vice presidential candidate Ferraro's pro-choice position on abortion was unacceptable. Law was also a close friend of former president George H. W. Bush. By the end of 2002 the cardinal's moral authority seemed irremediably damaged, and the army colonel's son retreated to the Vatican with the media hammering at him without pity.

In the first four months of 2002 the *Boston Globe* published 250 stories related to the pedophile priests scandal. But the media was not the only critic of the cardinal and of the way the Catholic Church in America had dealt with the scandal. A number of grassroots lay organizations were formed in the wake of the scandal. Probably the best known is Voice of the Faithful. It is not popular with the Catholic hierarchy, and some bishops have barred the group from meeting on church property. James Post, its president, warned that Law's successor should once and for all break the hierarchy's "instinct for secrecy." The French newspaper *Le Monde* quoted a Boston priest as saying: "Law wanted to protect the Church's reputation, as though we were still in the time when Irish immigrant Catholics could solve problems among themselves." But that was Law's real mistake. Thomas O'Connor, author of a book on Catholicism in Boston, said he asked several people to sum up Cardinal Law in two words and received no complete answers. "It's difficult to pigeonhole this man: his character is subtle, enigmatic, and he has a brash personality."

In trying to explain the intensity of media attacks on Law, mystified Vatican prelates believed that one factor was the cardinal's contacts with Fidel Castro. Law had visited Cuba in December 1998 to follow up on Pope John Paul II's own controversial visit that had so irritated the Clinton administration. Law was in Havana for four days as a guest of his friend Archbishop Jaime Ortega to assess the impact of the papal visit on religious freedom, an issue Law said he had discussed with Fidel Castro himself.

A MORAL AND FINANCIAL BANKRUPTCY

ACCORDING TO Andrew Cawthorne, the Reuters correspondent in Havana, the cardinal visited Cuba "regularly" in the late 1990s and was opposed to the economic sanctions imposed by the United States against the Communist-run Caribbean island. Law himself said of his meeting with Castro in December 1998, "Our dinner took place in a friendly and respectful atmosphere." Law's main mission in the wake of the pope's trip was to improve the freedom of worship for Cuban Catholics, secure the regime's permission to import priests, and persuade Castro to reinstate the celebration of Christmas, which had been banned since the Castro revolution in 1959. His visit was seen as a friendly overture but it drew fire from Cuban exile groups, particularly from "Little Cuba," Miami's Dade County, and from the United States government whose official objective was—and remains—the defeat of the Castro regime.

The *Miami Herald* voiced the Cuban exile view that religious freedom in Cuba would make Castro look good and work to his advantage. Typical was the article by Juan M. Clark, a sociologist at Miami-Dade Community College who lambasted the cardinal for legitimizing the Communist dictator. Clark said that Castro had expelled 131 priests in 1961, and the Cuban government had since that time kept the number of clergy unchanged even though the population had doubled. "Let's not kid ourselves: Castro is the man who repressed Christians," Clark wrote. Cardinal Law maintained that things had changed, he added. In reality, Castro had opened the doors a little to Catholics, pressured by the economic crisis, the Vatican, and the desire to exploit the pope's visit, as a way of gaining more international support for overturning the sanctions. "Can the church in Cuba achieve what the Polish church was able to do?" he continued.

Following the sexual abuse scandal, some Vatican prelates theorized that Cardinal Law was paying the political price for his dealings with Castro. Another view put forward in Rome was that the attacks on Law were at least partly orchestrated by Washington's Jewish lobby in retaliation for the cardinal's support for the Palestinians. Both theories seemed like attempts to divert attention from his main fault, and the main problem. A former senior Clinton presidential staffer explained, "The truth is that people were furious with the Vatican when Law was recalled to Rome. The way the pope protects him is unacceptable." Pope John Paul II had tucked Law out of harm's way, appointing him archpriest of the basilica of Saint Mary Major in Rome.

Back in the United States the harm was spreading. Faced with claims for $53 million in damages from 133 victims of sexual abuse in his archdiocese, Archbishop John Vlazny of Portland, Oregon, declared bankruptcy early in 2004. Later that same year, the Catholic diocese of Tucson, Arizona, with damages amounting to $16 million, followed suit. The scandal cost the Boston archdiocese more than $87 million as Law's successor, Cardinal Sean O'Malley, tackled the problem head-on and settled 95 percent of the sexual abuse complaints against priests in the city. To raise the money O'Malley sold off church property, including the residence that would have been his home. The archbishop's mansion was bought by the Jesuits of Boston College. But O'Malley also closed more than sixty parishes in a restructuring designed to shore up the finances of the archdiocese.

In December 2004 the California diocese of Orange County paid $100 million to eighty-four abuse victims, which was considerably more than previous settlements of multiple priest sexual abuse claims and set a new standard affecting future claims, and the chain of shameful cases seemed never ending. The other inevitable result of the scandal was to resurrect in Boston's Protestant elite old prejudices against papists. Such sentiments had been laid to rest by the rise to political and social prominence of the Kennedy clan in the city, but they had been revived by the squalor attaching itself to a humiliated diocese.

BOSTON'S PURITAN GHOSTS

ACCORDING TO MICHAEL NOVAK, the neoconservative Catholic theologian, the ghost of anti-Catholicism still haunts old American cities with long histories. Novak maintained that the pedophilia scandal was deliberately overblown by powerful WASP circles to discredit Cardinal Law, Boston's high-profile top Catholic. This is the same city where in 1834 anti-papist arsonists set fire to the convent of the Ursuline Sisters in Charlestown. In a 2002 article on the scandal in the *National Review,* Novak relates a conversation with a young woman who told him, "Everyone votes Republican in Boston." She seemed not to be aware that the Kennedys dominated Boston politics, Novak comments. Then he realized that she meant "everyone who counts." The city—he concludes—is a region of islands, an archipelago of rivalry and difference.

A gulf still separated the first arrivals, the Irish, and successive waves of later Catholic immigrants. Novak says one of his favorite teachers, David Reisman, warned him more than once of the fierce anti-Catholicism that comes up from the roots of the trees in Harvard Yard and Boston Common: They were the ghosts of Puritan Boston. The anti-Catholicism was pervasive, fueled by ethnic rivalries going back generations, and fueled by differences in class and education. The latest arrivals from Italy and Ireland were looked down upon by the first arrivals. "Cardinal Law's tragic fall has brought these memories to the surface," Novak wrote. As a Catholic conservative—he supported President Bush and the war in Iraq—Novak regards Cardinal Law as the victim of a long, downward slide in standards that started long before Law's appointment as Boston's archbishop. He blames institutions such as Boston College and the Weston School of Theology (also Jesuit run) for their excessively liberal teaching over the past decade, holding them responsible for creating moral confusion on sexual matters and division within Catholic culture.

NOVAK AND THE "ANTI-CATHOLIC CATHOLICS"

TO HEAR NOVAK explain it, dissent from Pope John Paul II's teaching, and Pope Paul VI's before that, has had "the inevitable effect of weakening the sense of good and bad, of what is right and wrong" for those who face sexual temptations. This "internal uncertainty" was the root cause of what was happening at the dawn of the twentieth century. But the list of those responsible goes on to include the "Boston elite and the media," the latter virtually controlled by WASPs—liberals who still look down on the Church with contempt. With them he includes a large number of "Catholic anti-Catholics" who end up as bigger culprits than the Protestants.

The worst sin from Novak's point of view was that the scandal offered Protestants a wealth of opportunity to revive anti-Catholic sentiment, and to perpetuate the idea that Catholics are morally corrupt. Law and the pedophile priests were a lethal weapon in the hands of Catholicism's Puritan enemies. But one would have to go back to the McCarthy era to find similar abuses of due process in which salacious sexual details were revealed without restraint to titillate the public. According to Novak the rights of the accused priests were grossly violated, and the Boston elite intentionally allowed this to happen to damage the Catholic Church. That same elite, he maintains, would never have allowed such a thing had their own interests been threatened. His bottom line, however, is that the scandal was a self-inflicted wound by the Catholic community, and one cannot blame anyone else.

The aftershocks are likely to be felt for a long time to come. In July 2007 lawyers for 508 victims of sexual abuse said they had settled lawsuits against the archdiocese of Los Angeles for $660 million. And in autumn 2007 the Vatican hired Jeffrey Stanley Lena, a well-known California lawyer, to deal from Rome with all the cases of sexual crimes perpetrated by Catholic priests throughout the world. Besides the hemorrhage of millions of dollars to pay damages, and the removal of Cardinal Law, and in addition to the monumental report prepared with the help of the FBI, this lurid affair again raises a very American doubt as to whether, for a citizen of the United States, being a Roman Catholic constitutes a potential conflict of identity. In May 2004 the Catholic bishops approved a statement titled "Catholics in Political Life" in which politicians who supported abortion rights were branded as "cooperating with evil," and the door was left open for bishops to deny communion to such lawmakers. This action was in response to Democratic presidential candidate John Kerry's right-to-choose position. The sex abuse scandal also cast its shadow on the debate, but in the end "Catholicism weathered the storm," declared Gordon Melton, a Methodist pastor who heads the Institute for the Study of American Religion at the University of California in Santa Barbara, because the majority of American Catholic bishops are good leaders.

Some analysts believed that being rapped on the knuckles by leaders of the Church actually worked to Kerry's advantage as it showed him to be independent of Rome's influence. The Kerry controversy delved into the heart of the matter. "In one sense," reported the *New York Times,* "the argument is really about how to define being faithful—to religious authority, to the Constitution, or to both."

THE EMPIRE OF RIGHT

GEORGE BUSH'S GOD

THE SPEAKER'S TONE was grave, occasionally slipping into the rapid cadences of a Baptist preacher. The audience of some sixteen hundred religious leaders and social workers from all over the United States responded in kind, shouting "Amen" in all the appropriate places. It could have been a large congregation in the Bible Belt, but it was the ballroom of the Hilton Hotel in Washington that echoed with the audience's incantations, and the speaker was not a minister but the president of the United States, George W. Bush. To a non-American, the scene on June 1, 2004, seemed surreal. Yet the occasion reflected one of the most powerful and at the same time mysterious aspects of this sometimes hard-to-read country. Behind Bush a large banner proclaimed COMPASSION IN ACTION. The president told the story of a convict whose soul was saved by evangelist ministers. Reading the Bible can be the start of a great change in someone's life, said the preacher/president. The convict felt lost but had found the way. Bush added that he was addressing "all faithful" whether they were Jewish, Christian, Muslim, or Hindu, but his real audience was Protestant, in Texas and elsewhere in conservative America. Protestants are his core support. Bush, campaigning for his second term, used the occasion to confirm his intention of channeling funds for social services through religious institutions.

The timing of Bush's initiative was certainly not accidental, and it was calculated to appeal to conservative Christian voters, but the larger significance was that church and state had become less separate in the face of a perceived growing need for religion in public life. It was no accident that the faith-based aid program had been launched by George W. Bush, either. In fact, in recounting the story of the convict who had began reading the Bible in prison Bush was to some extent indirectly speaking about himself. He was perhaps recalling his own mental imprisonment as an alcoholic until that blessed day in 1986 when, urged by his wife, Laura, he stopped drinking and began to study the Bible. This led to his rebirth as a Christian, more specifically to his becoming a practicing Methodist. From then on his public life and his religious beliefs were merged. When in the 2000 presidential election a somewhat questionable handful of votes separated him from his Democratic opponent, Al Gore, Bush told his collaborators not to worry because he would emerge the winner. His victory did not depend on the efforts of his brother Jeb, governor of Florida, in the recount. It depended on the fact that he, George W. Bush, had been talking to God. He had done so at frequent intervals between 1985 and 1986, as he had attended a course in which the main reading was the entire New Testament.

ALCOHOLISM DEFEATED BY FAITH

THE SOLE REASON that he was in the Oval Office and not in a bar in Texas, Bush said in an interview in 2002, was that he had rediscovered his faith; he had found God. "I am here thanks to the power of prayer," he said. It was a sentiment he had expressed on other occasions, including in a conversation with Cardinal Pio Laghi, the former nuncio to the United States. Laghi was in Washington bearing messages from Pope John Paul II on the eve of the second Iraq offensive. As the pope had been openly critical of any American attack on Saddam Hussein, it is not hard to imagine the nature of the pope's message. But people who met Bush in those months were amazed at the way he peppered his conversation with biblical quotations. He seemed to see the war against Iraq as a religious mission as well as a military one. Bush personified and sublimated the American trauma of the September 11, 2001, terrorist attacks on New York and Washington. The tragedy—never fully understood in Europe—gave fresh force to a latent sense of doom in American thinking that has for decades influenced the country's politics. Some fundamentalists saw 9/11 as Divine judgment. Days after the attack, two leading churchmen from the conservative Right, Jerry Falwell and Pat Robertson, appearing in a television discussion, were of one mind that if an angered God continued to allow America's enemies to punish it as it deserved to be punished for the evils of "pagans, abortionists, feminists, gays and lesbians" and others who wished to secularize the country, then America hadn't seen anything yet.

Bush sees himself as the interpreter of this world; he is a restorer of morality after the "immoral" Clinton years. The Bible is Bush's compass. As Bill Keller, then managing editor of the *New York Times,* put it to an Italian writer, Bush's faith is based on a direct relationship between himself and God. It does not recognize priests as necessary intermediaries, or require any books besides the Bible. Born-again Christians consider the Bible all that is needed. Richard Cizick, vice president of government affairs of the the National Association of Evangelicals, says George Bush asks the same question that Abraham Lincoln asked during the Civil War: not whether God is on our side, but whether we are on God's. This moral and moralistic mind-set, eternally waiting for the end of the world and obsessively in search of signs from God, became an element in the decision-making process at the highest level of the most powerful nation on earth in the wake of 9/11. The use of apocalyptic theories gave the policies of the United States a religious dimension that would legitimize any and every decision to intervene.

WESTERN FUNDAMENTALISTS

IN THE WEST, fundamentalism has become synonymous with Islamic extremism. It evokes al Qaeda, Osama bin Laden, suicide bombers in Israel and more recently in Iraq, the madrassas or religious schools of Pakistan and Saudi Arabia. But as the Italian Protestant historian Paolo Naso recently recalled, the term now so closely linked to Islam had an earlier life in Christian theological circles in the United States. He traces its religious origins to twelve pamphlets published by a group of Evangelical theologians between 1912 and 1915. Called *The Fundamentals 1912–1915, Testimony of Faith*, the series spelled out the fundamentals of Protestantism: the need for personal salvation through

Christ, the infallibility of Scripture, atonement, resurrection. The term "fundamentalist" is widely believed to have been used for the first time in 1920 in reference to the writers of the pamphlets as a vocal group attacking the liberal teachings of other members of the fragmented and volatile Protestant church. Though *The Fundamentals* was a conservative reaction to what was perceived as a threat from liberals to traditional beliefs, it also raised questions about when religion needed to be included in the laws of the country. The discussion resurfaced during the Reagan era, and again in the presidency of George W. Bush. In the wake of 9/11 the Presidential Prayer Team was formed, an independent group "designed to encourage a national outpouring of daily prayer for the president," according to its Web site.

Besides, Richard Land, the Princeton- and Oxford-educated president of the ethics and religious liberty commission of the Southern Baptist Convention—the largest Protestant church in America—has said that there have been more born-again Christians working in the Bush White House than at any other time in history. The leading ones have been Secretary of State Condoleezza Rice and John Ashcroft, the attorney general during Bush's first term. Ashcroft even quoted God in denying the existence of a holy war between Christianity and Islam. The war on terrorism was not a religious conflict, he declared in 2002. "It's a war between good and evil." He recalled President Bush's belief that God was not neutral. Bin Laden thinks he knows better. His struggle, the terrorist has said, is "against the new Christian-Jewish crusade led by the great crusader Bush under the flag of the Cross."

The strong involvement of Evangelicals in foreign policy has created a broad new consensus in favor of foreign intervention. Kansas Republican Senator Sam Brownback, a darling of the fundamentalists, but a convert to Catholicism, told the *Wall Street Journal* that as the world's most powerful nation the United States must act responsibly, even with humility, not just in our economic and strategic interests but also for what is morally just. This view was reflected by a 2004 Gallup poll that showed that among Americans who went to church at least once a week 56 percent felt that the situation in Iraq justified the American-led war. Evangelicals supported the export of American values: they felt it was necessary to "Christianize" Islamic Iraq and Afghanistan. Their precondition for helping North Korea should there be an agreement on Pyongyang's nuclear weapons would be that the North Koreans would show progress on human rights.

Christian activism may have originated with the Protestant establishment in the early 1900s, but the idealism of Woodrow Wilson and Franklin D. Roosevelt was elitist. Today's Evangelical movement is a grassroots movement, observes Martin Marty, professor of Christianity at the University of Chicago. Evangelicals are more willing than in the past to act on their convictions. They say that if God calls them to be the virtuous nation, they need to act on it. Michael Horowitz, a director at the Hudson Insititute, a conservative think tank in Washington, recalls that some years ago Arthur H. Sulzberger, then publisher of the *New York Times,* took a group of leaders of the Jewish community to the White House to persuade Roosevelt not to appoint a Jew to the Supreme Court. They were afraid that such an appointment would increase anti-Semitism. But Horowitz said that the Christian community would not make the same mistake as the Jewish group. (This was certainly true in 2004, when there were no fewer than five Catholic associate justices on the bench.)

AMERICA AS THE NEW ISRAEL

THE ALLIANCE OF neoconservatives and Evangelicals was rooted in the latters' belief that the Bush administration doctrine of spreading democracy and religious freedom is not only a moral issue, but a national security issue as well. Some Protestants believe that Christianity should launch a major proselytizing effort among Muslims, even though for Muslims conversion is a crime punishable by death. The conversion theory is based on growth numbers that are worrying for Christians but encouraging for Muslims. According to *World Christian Encyclopedia* (2005) the number of Christians in the world had increased from 550 million in 1900 to almost 2 billion (1,999 million) at the start of the second millennium. Of these, 1,057 million are Roman Catholics, up from 266 million. But what troubles some Christian fundamentalists in the West is that the number of Muslims had grown from 200 million in 1900 to 1,188 million, and is still increasing at a steady rate. Martin Marty says some alarmed Evangelicals have even come to regard militant Islam as the Antichrist. More broadly, this view of Islam as a demographic challenge to Christianity has brought American Evangelicals closer to Jewish pressure groups in the United States. It also accounts for the Bush administration's inertia in seeking a solution to what many regard as the key issue in the Middle East, the Arab-Israeli conflict.

In 1997 a Baptist review named Michael Horowitz "one of the ten most influential Christians." The only problem with that description is that Horowitz is Jewish. But he was being recognized for his efforts to prevent the West from showing the same indifference toward the persecution of Christians in today's world as it had done toward Jews during the Holocaust in Nazi Germany. At the same time, the image of America as the new Israel has acquired some currency among Christian conservatives. "American nationalism is profoundly secular, yet full of religious references," observed Tiziano Bonazzi, professor of American history at the University of Bologna. In fact, he added, "a series of biblical contexts define the United States . . . for example, Exodus transforms the great wave of immigration from Europe, from a wrenching experience into a triumph of hope."

On this perception is based "the notion of America as an antithesis to Europe, set against it as Canaan is to Egypt . . . The United States as the new Israel, a rising nation that has made a pact with God and has a Divine mission to create a brave new world provides an identity for a divided people," says Bonazzi. The Evangelicals apply biblical prophecies to current developments to get the results they want. With the West— or more specifically the United States and Britain—at war in Iraq, American fundamentalists have found legitimacy in the Bible, argues the Italian Protestant scholar Paolo Naso. They have quoted Jeremiah to justify attacking Saddam Hussein. In Jeremiah, a "terrible war" is waged against Babylon because the Babylonians had "attacked the sons of Israel." Naso says the Left Behind series of novels and the film based on them reflect a certain Christian fundamentalist view of geopolitics. He recalls that, with Israel under attack, the character Buck quotes from chapters 38 and 39 of the book of Ezekiel that "a great enemy from the north invaded Israel with the help of Persia, Libya, and Ethiopia."

Furthermore, observes Naso, the Antichrist in the fictional series, Nicolae Carpathia, rises to become despotic leader of world government and ultimately self-declared god with his own global religion from the position of Secretary General of the United Nations. In other words, the Left Behind series, or its authors, identifies the United Nations with the Antichrist. The hostility of the radical right wing of the Republican Party to the United Nations and other international institutions is well known: these organizations are seen as obstacles choking the vitality of the United States. Furthermore, in the Left Behind series, New Babylon is located in Italy, the geographical and spiritual center of the Roman Catholic faith—as though the United Nations and the Vatican are caught up in a grand conspiracy, a diabolical plot. The two institutions are either unable or unwilling to recognize the gravity of the situation, and it is left to the Bible and American Protestants to uncover the truth.

Protestant America considers the government in Jerusalem an ally for symbolic as well as political reasons. Thus an Evangelical figure such as Gary Bauer can found (with Rabbi Daniel Lapin) the American Alliance of Jews and Christians, which has the dual role of supporting Israel and at the same time protecting traditional American values. Christian Zionist groups collect millions of dollars to support the Jewish settlements in the West Bank. John Hagee, the Texas fundamentalist preacher and a strong supporter of Israel, has been critical of the Bush administration's timid approach to the Israeli-Palestinian question. His well-publicized view is that God's law transcends United States law, and the strategies of the State Department.

This pro-Israeli approach puts Christian fundamentalists on a collision course with at least part of Islam. The Muslim religion is portrayed as intolerant. On September 12, 2002, Ashcroft was quoted as saying to the *Washington Post,* "Islam is a religion in which God expects you to send your son to die for him," but in the Christian faith, "God sends his own son to die for you."

THE UNIVERSAL NATION

SUCH POSITIONS MAY seem extreme, but there are leading Republicans who find them acceptable. "Many Americans still believe, like the Founding Fathers, that they are almost God's chosen people," Italian journalist Emilio Gentile wrote in 2004. He pointed out that, according to a *U.S. News & World Report* survey, the number of churches, synagogues, mosques, and temples in the United States is the highest in the world: There is one place of worship for every 865 Americans. As pollster Gallup Jr. puts it, Americans "hunger for God." It is one sign of what has been called American "exceptionalism." The eminent historian Daniel Boorstin has said that individual faiths were not important in American life, but religion is enormously so. And the political philosopher Jean Bethke Elshtain observes that "[t]he separation of church and state is one thing, the separation of religion and politics quite another." In every era, religion and politics have intersected continuously in American society.

It was Seymour Lipsett who in 1963 first defined American "exceptionalism." It reflects the belief—says Tiziano Bonazzi—that "Divine Providence has chosen the United States to advance the freedom of man: a redeeming nation." This view establishes the distinctive nature of the New World. Every act of force, every concept, has to be viewed in that context. "The American people are not just a nation, but a universal nation," wrote Bonazzi, paraphrasing the historian Anders Stephenson. Bonazzi himself says Americans view their nation as perfect, enviable, and a natural model for the rest of the world. "This perception creates a constant battle against imperfection, as right strives to fulfill itself and is challenged by wrong."

In bad times, opposition to Europe as the source of most evils comes easily to Americans. The class struggle, Communism, Nazism— all had their origins in the Old Continent. The same can be said of the most disastrous conflicts of the twentieth century. Colonization of the New World resulted from religious wars in the old one. "Exceptionalism extracted from history a holy place: America," Bonazzi maintains, "rendering it in a certain sense immune from history, unchangeable, self-contained." He quotes from an American propaganda pamphlet of the 1940s designed to counter the Marxist threat. Produced in several languages, it was intended for world distribution. It says that Communism did not invent and develop the great social movements of the past decades. The "permanent revolution" was taking place in America, in an atmosphere of freedom, peace, and harmony. "The international effort of the United States [in World War Two] also brought American freedom to all people," the pamphlet says.

SIX EXPANSIONIST WARS

AMERICANS CONSIDER THEIR nation intrinsically good, almost divinely inspired, and therefore neither imperialistic nor expansionist, neither aggressive nor bent on conquest. Giulio Andreotti recalls having a conversation along these lines with none other than Cardinal Spellman. They were discussing the ongoing war in Vietnam, the former Italian prime minister said. Spellman "told me that if America had to haul down its flag in that conflict, the trauma would have been profound and long-lasting because—the cardinal told me—'We Americans are used to thinking of ourselves as the arm of God.'" Eventually, of course, the United States did haul down its flag in Vietnam; and Spellman's prediction about the trauma being long lasting proved correct. Even so, when Bush says that Americans are willing to pay a price to bring freedom to other nations he is merely dressing a long-standing American policy of expansionism in new clothes.

In Robert Kagan's brilliant distinction, Europe is Venus, feminine and capricious, and America is Mars, the omnipotent god of war, armed but benign. This brilliant neoconservative analyst regards Washington's interventionist policy, its unilateralism, as both just and unavoidable. Why? The alternative is not international consensus but a compromise with terrorism. What he calls America's sixth expansion is a reaction to the terrorist attacks of September 11, 2001. The first expansion, he says, was the war against Britain in the late eighteenth century. The second happened at the expense of Mexico when the United States acquired California and Texas. The third was the Spanish-American War through which the United States gained control over the Caribbean. Then came the Second World War and, after almost half a century, the collapse of the Soviet Empire. Kagan then lists the first Gulf war in 1991 as the sixth expansion, resumed with additional force following 9/11.

Having nominated America the god of just wars, Kagan reverts to the old theme of the struggle between Good and Evil, of an empire that resists the title even though it is, by definition, the Empire of Right. James Nicholson, the former United States ambassador to the Holy See, is mouthing the Bush administration's ideology when he says that the United States does not like to take over other countries, and will only remain in Iraq long enough to bring democracy to that country. September 11 strengthened America's idea of itself. Not only was the terrorist attack the most devastating on United States territory; on another level Americans also saw it as the latest encounter in the long struggle between democracy and tyranny, between morality, order, and democracy on one hand, and blind violence, chaos, and vile criminality on the other. The Empire of Right had no choice but to react, armed with the most sophisticated weapons, and above all sustained by its moral superiority. The fight against international terrorism is seen by many as the ultimate confrontation, Bonazzi states: "If the Soviet Union was the empire of evil, terrorism is the empire of chaos: a menace more subtle and pervasive, and therefore more dangerous. Only one power can confront it, and that is the power that creates order."

THE IMPERIAL THEOLOGY

THE UNDISPUTED FACT is that the 9/11 terrorist attack has shaped the American empire's current course of action and provided its moral justification. It was from that time forward, too, wrote the liberal historian Chalmers Johnson, that some American leaders began to think of the United States as the equivalent of an empire: a new Rome, no longer tied by international law, the concerns of its allies, or any constraints on the use of military force. This transformation, he added, could turn out to be irreversible. Among Bush's closest advisers, the comparison with the ancient Roman Empire is cultivated with relish.

Men like Paul Wolfowitz, William Kristol, Charles Krauthammer, Richard Perle, and Kagan subscribed to the idea of a Roman Washington, with Bush as emperor in the sense of architect of world peace, based on American power akin to the peace the ancient Romans managed to impose on the nations under their control. They saw no contradiction in this vision of the imperial destiny of the United States: it was America's moral obligation. As a benevolent, civilizing power America was almost forced to be a world leader, and to make war.

All of which explains why, in the era of George W. Bush, imperialism is not a dirty word to either Protestants or Catholics. When large, uncomfortable holes began to appear in the White House logic on the

Iraq war, one of Bush's few defenders was Novak, comparing the United States to Sparta. In response to a critical article in the Italian Jesuit periodical *Civiltà Cattolica,* Novak attacked those who—he said—still wrote that oil, not the al Qaeda terrorists, was the real motive behind America's intervention in Afghanistan. He said that the worst blindness of America's critics was not when they focused on financial issues, but when they concentrated on the spiritual. When Americans go to war, their first priority is a quick victory, but their second is to establish an equally rapid exit strategy. Americans don't stay; they are not empire builders. They want to go home. It was a fair defense against growing anti-Americanism. It was also a Catholic intellectual's affirmation of America's exceptionalism, which unites Americans culturally regardless of religion.

Bush is the champion of both the Protestant Right and conservative Catholics. In 2004 he addressed the annual convention of the Knights of Columbus in Dallas. Twenty-five hundred conservative Catholics representing a national membership of 1.5 million gave him a standing ovation. Included in the convention program was a pro-life documentary in which a pregnant woman chooses to die to save her unborn child. The Reverend Jim Wallis, editor of the left-leaning Protestant magazine *Sojourners,* and the man who termed Bush's religion the "theology of empire," says Bush suggests that God is on the side of the United States. The president believes "the success of American military and foreign policy is connected to a religiously inspired mission, and even that his presidency may be a divine appointment for a time such as this." Such declarations as "They are devils, we have right on our side" and "If you are not totally with us you are playing the devil's game" lead, Wallis states, to bad foreign policy, to say nothing of dangerous theology.

Bush's collaborators point out that his public pronouncements don't include the apocalyptic theories of some Protestant groups, and that he has always addressed his remarks to all religious denominations. Tim Goeglein, head of White House outreach to religious groups, says Bush is an Evangelical Christian in the tradition of C. S. Lewis, someone who is not too caught up in the denominational differences but focuses on the common teachings of the universal church. In other words, he supports an ecumenism that is both Neochristian and very American. Bush sees himself as the leader of all Christians. One Italian commentator draws the conclusion that "the United States is not only an empire; it is also a papacy, which expects the world to adopt its principles and values." As such, the United States intersects with the other Christian empire, the papacy in Rome, and the results are not always harmonious.

PACIFISM AND PEACE

THE CHURCH'S 9/11

O N THE AFTERNOON of September 11, 2001, a few hours after the twin terrorist attacks on New York and Washington, and
after the fourth hijacked flight was forced down in Pennsylvania, Pope
John Paul II sent President Bush a telegram saying his prayers were
with him and with the United States "in this hour of suffering and
trial." The pope's spokesman, Joaquin Navarro-Valls, stressed to reporters that John Paul's intention in sending the message was to show
his closeness to the United States. Even in those early moments of horror, uncertainty, and indignation what stood out was the enormity of
what had happened. Anyone who knew America was aware that the
attack had changed the world. It was the first time that the United
States had been hit on its own territory with such devastating effect.
Not even the very heart of the imperial superpower, it seemed, was
immune from the terrorist menace. The real message, according to Va-
leria Piacentini, a top Italian expert on Islam at the Catholic University
of Milan, was to the Arab world: no Islamic regime could rely on the
United States for its protection.

In the avalanche of theories about the causes and effects of 9/11 Piacentini's view is as good as any. But for the Vatican the main concern
was not the geopolitical impact but the georeligious one. The Vatican's
immediate worry was how the West (read: America) would respond to
Osama bin Laden's atrocity, and his perception of himself as an Islamic
fighter against a Judeo-Christian crusade. In other words, the Church
feared the outbreak of a religious war. The then archbishop of Milan,
Cardinal Carlo Maria Martini, warned that the best response "to mind-

less violence was the force of reason." Pope John Paul II, speaking at his general audience on September 12 while the world was still reeling from the impact of the attack, addressed the "beloved people of the United States," imploring them not to launch "a spiral of hate and violence," and urging them to put their faith in "wisdom and peace." The aim was to pull the leaders in Washington into a reassuring embrace, and to demonstrate the West's solid support against the new terrorist threat. But there was also the presentiment that an American military retaliation was predictable, and no one would be inclined to oppose it.

The Vatican realized the need to support the American action, to give it legitimacy as an international response, and at the same time to prevent it from escalating out of control and taking on a religious significance. Rome considered it a priority not to allow American action to destabilize the relationship between the two worlds—Christian and Islamic. The Vatican also saw 9/11 as an opportunity. The unforgettable images of New York's Twin Towers in flames and of the devastation at Ground Zero were a chance to shift opinion away from the anti-Americanism that had flourished in Europe since the antiwar protests against the Vietnam conflict, which had been rekindled by the first Gulf war, in 1991. The day after 9/11 the French newspaper *Le Monde* ran the headline "We are all Americans now." Coming from *Le Monde,* which was, and remains, not exactly pro-American, it was a powerful message. The Vatican had always had reservations about the pacifist movement mainly because of its links with Communism. Pope John Paul II and the cardinals and prelates who shared his views, though men of peace, continued to regard pacifism as too easily exploitable for political ends. Steps were then taken to convince Catholic pacifist groups that anti-Americanism had had its day, and that terrorism could not be justified under any circumstances.

The Vatican's first salvo in this cultural offensive was fired at the post-9/11 meeting of the Italian bishops conference by its president, Cardinal Camillo Ruini. His speech on that occasion was an outline of the Vatican's approach to the United States and to the fight against terrorism. He did not hide the Church's anxiety, not so much about the fact that the Bush administration was gathering an international coalition of support, but about what the Americans intended to do with it. Ruini's main concern was the risk of a "clash of civilizations," thus transforming the historian Samuel Huntington's best-selling theory into a reality. A few days earlier the pope had warned, "Religion should never be used as the motive for conflict." In echoing the pontiff's words, Ruini took what was to become a familiar European, and to a certain extent Arab, route: He identified the Arab-Israeli conflict as the root cause of "Binladism." Although this emphasis ignored bin Laden's and al Qaeda's broader agenda of Islamic dominance, the United States' failure to address the Middle East conflict remained a central criticism of Washington's policy, and in particular its decision to attack Iraq.

"The main knot to untie remains the one in the Holy Land, where the Arab-Israeli conflict has dragged on for more than fifty years," Ruini declared. But the real novelty of his address was his statement that the Catholic Church recognized the right and the duty of the United States to strike at international terrorism, its protectors and defenders. This message supplied the ethical green light to the American attack on Afghanistan and the Taliban fundamentalists, the enemies of moderate Islam and of the pope. "It's been widely noted that what happened on September 11 profoundly changes the world situation," the cardinal said. "What remains unclear, however, is the nature and direction of that change. The more immediate question is how the United States will respond to the attack—and there is no doubt that it has the right, indeed the duty and necessity to combat and neutralize international terrorism, including those who, at any level, sponsor or defend it." But then came the caveat. "It's equally important and indispensable that this right and duty not be limited to armed force, which should in any case be contained and not indiscriminate. It should concentrate its greater efforts on removing the motivations and breeding grounds of terrorism."

Ruini also cautioned against what he called "simplifications and generalizations that could have serious consequences at the global level." For a senior Vatican prelate this was uncharacteristically plain speaking, devoid of the traditional Roman opaqueness. Subsequent developments would also show it to have been prophetic. But the cardinal was working up to his central message to the Italian bishops: On the one hand terrorism was not solely the product of the Islamic world, and he pointedly mentioned Catholic terrorism in Northern Ireland. On the other, he went on, "We need to unmask and overcome the pseudomoralism also present in our country, and even among Christians, that tends to identify the United States as the cause and the catalog of the world's ills, and to see it as a civilization that is intrinsically and irremediably mendacious and wicked." He was attempting to change the thinking of pacifist and anti-American left-wing Catholics who believed that 9/11 had been an American-Zionist plot to justify going to war. The same belief had taken hold in the Arab streets, and was beginning to make headway among some European intellectuals, particularly in France.

THE POPE PRAYS WITH AMBASSADOR NICHOLSON

TWO DAYS AFTER 9/11 James Nicholson, then United States ambassador to the Holy See, had a twenty-minute audience with the pope at Castel Gandolfo, the papal summer palace in the Alban Hills north of Rome. As Nicholson would later write, not surprisingly, "the events of September 11 dominated the conversation." Nicholson and the pope prayed together and the American envoy "had the time to explain to the pope the necessity of my country to respond to the terrorists for our own defense and for the defense of our allies." Pope John Paul II replied that he believed the events of 9/11 were attacks not solely on the United States, but on "all humankind," and furthermore that the United States was "justified in undertaking defensive action." For Nicholson, the meeting "laid the basis for the Holy See's support of our campaign against terrorism." He thought it extraordinary that the pope and the Church should be so supportive. The Vatican had not supported the first Gulf war and was opposed to economic sanctions against Iraq and Cuba. But "to have the moral support of the Holy See" in the coming offensive "was very precious to President Bush" as leader of the coalition of nations united against international terrorism.

For Nicholson, 9/11 had its own personal significance. A Vietnam vet and the third son of seven children in a farming family in Iowa, he had risen in the Republican Party ranks to become chairman of the Republican National Committee, and the post at the Vatican had been his reward. He had presented his credentials as the seventh American ambassador to the Holy See on August 10, 2001, and a month later found himself in the maelstrom of diplomatic activity following the terrorist attack.

For the Bush administration, Pope John Paul II's support counted. If the pope himself accepted the inevitability of American action it meant that Bush had right and morality on his side. But Rome's *nihil obstat,* or no objection, specifically covered the action against Afghanistan's fundamentalist regime. That way the Vatican left open the possibility of acting as a brake on further interventions in other countries that could spark a wider reaction from the Islamic world.

For months, in that first phase of the antiterrorist war, Washington and the Vatican followed a common line that the United States had the right and the duty to capture the terrorists and those who had sent them, and to "excommunicate" politically and morally anyone who used violence against the civil society to gain their objectives, including those who used the Islamic faith as a pretext for terrorism. "The pope is not a pacifist because terrible injustices can be committed in the name of peace," explained Navarro-Valls at the time. "Either the criminals who have perpetrated a horrible crime are not in a position to repeat it, or the principle of self-defense comes into force, with all its consequences."

THE DEVIL IS A UNILATERALIST

BUT THE CATHOLIC world was divided on the issue. Battle lines were drawn, with one side trying to prevail over the other. One side would point out the horrors of terrorism; the other would allege human rights violations by the Americans in Afghanistan. There were protests from organizations such as Pax Christi against the American aerial bombing that caused Afghan civilian casualties, and also against the Italian government's support of the American-led military operation. In November 2001 about thirty bishops, mainly from Latin America, also condemned the American bombings. They called them "another form of terrorism, this time practiced by governments that claimed to be democratic, civil, and Christian."

But the first significant crack in the international coalition's global solidarity followed the deportation of six hundred prisoners to a specially prepared camp at the United States military base in Guantánamo, an American enclave on the island of Cuba. The first wave arrived on January 11, 2002. Three hundred Taliban suspects made the twenty-hour flight, and the first images showing them handcuffed and in their orange suits became an instant symbol of an America that seemed ready to sacrifice its reputation as the cradle of democracy and human rights in the name of its war on terror.

What rang alarm bells in the Vatican, however, was the publication of an administration document in September 2002 called the National Security Strategy defining new, extended parameters of preemptive and preventive uses of force against so-called rogue states. Released on the first anniversary of 9/11, the document spelled out the Bush administration's new stance on occasions when force might be used even without evidence of an imminent attack to ensure that any serious threat to the United States did not "gather" or grow in time. The document showed clearly that the United States had not recovered from the trauma of the terrorist attack. On the contrary, 9/11 seems to have conditioned the Bush administration's strategic thinking. The new strategy also reflected Washington's frustration with its failure to capture Osama bin Laden, and its impatience with what the Bush administration perceived to be the less than passionate support it had received from its European allies and the United Nations. The United States was slipping into a unilateralism that the United Nations and the Vatican considered a devastating development in international relations, foreshadowing a deterioration of relations between the West and the Islamic world. In the circumstances it was hard not to read into the new Bush antiterrorism doctrine an excuse for launching an attack on Iraq without the approval of the Security Council of the United Nations.

The Europeans had come to perceive the United States as "a rogue colossus," in many ways more dangerous to Europe's peaceful ideals than either Iraq or Iran, the American neoconservative Robert Kagan admitted at the September 15, 2002, conference on security organized by the International Institute of Strategic Studies in London. As preparations continued for an armed action against Saddam Hussein, there were reports that Iraq possessed stockpiles of weapons of mass destruction, in particular chemical and bacteriological weapons capable of killing hundreds of thousands of people. But inspectors from the International Atomic Energy Agency, the United Nations nuclear watch-dog, failed to uncover these weapons, and the conflict seemed daily more inevitable. The Vatican watched with apprehension as the situation rapidly worsened, but it was powerless to reverse the precipitous rush toward a calamitous war. Furthermore, striking a balance between the opposition of the Catholic Left and the need not to abandon the United States to its own devices was becoming increasingly difficult. In those months there wasn't a bishop in Italy who did not point out in sermons and statements to his faithful the danger from fundamentalist terrorism while at the same time defending the American right and duty to retaliate against the authors of 9/11. But the prospect that Bush's preventive war doctrine would soon be put into practice against Iraq reinforced the most virulent anti-Americanism.

SYMMETRIC DIPLOMACY

THE VATICAN MAINTAINED a posture of equidistance between what were now viewed as "the belligerents." When Washington officials complained bitterly that the Vatican was not showing enough support for the just cause of the West, Rome replied sharply that the Vatican was the West, and if anyone was deviating from the right path it was the United States. "When the pope speaks, he does so for everyone: Americans and Iraqis," the Catholic newspaper *Avvenire* commented tartly. For the Holy See, the two countries were on the same plane. The Vatican was determined not to show any favoritism toward the United States. When Washington sent a request to some sixty countries that it considered allies asking them to expel all Iraqi diplomats, the Italians complied, but the Vatican said no, on the grounds that even the most tenuous line of communication should be kept open. Then, in February 2003, Tariq Aziz, Iraq's deputy prime minister and Saddam's conduit to the outside world, arrived in Rome. Tariq Aziz is a Chaldean Christian. The Iraqi's visit was arranged by French-born Father Benjamin, a color-ful former pop singer turned priest with long-standing Baghdad connections and an equally long history of anti-Americanism.

Tariq Aziz's visit, which had been approved by the Vatican's minister of foreign affairs, Archbishop Jean-Louis Tauran, also French, was

Saddam's last attempt to save himself and his regime by trying to engage the pope on his side. Pope John Paul II was willing to be used provided there was even a slim, eleventh-hour chance of avoiding the conflict. The Bush administration was also pressing the Vatican—but to gain papal approval for what Washington had taken to calling "a just war." Ambassador Nicholson brought Michael Novak to Rome to lobby Vatican officials. Novak quoted Saint Augustine, who had defined a just war in his monumental work *De Civitate Dei*. But quoting Saint Augustine was not enough to convince the Vatican to overcome the widespread concern that the United States seemed willing to attack Iraq without United Nations cover. *L'Osservatore Romano,* the Vatican newspaper; Radio Vatican; *La Civiltà Cattolica;* and *Famiglia Cristiana* formed a media quartet of opposition, hammering on the importance of saving the peace. At the same time, Vatican diplomacy, in the hands of Tauran and Archbishop Angelo Sodano, the Vatican secretary of state, continued to send signals to both sides with the evenhandedness of Solomon.

Cardinal Roger Etchegaray was sent to Baghdad to try to convince Saddam Hussein to give the Americans the answers they said they wanted regarding the weapons of mass destruction. Etchegaray had to wait for several days for his meeting with the Iraqi leader, and eventually returned to Rome with a tenuous agreement to cooperate. Shortly afterward Cardinal Pio Laghi, the former nuncio to the United States, went to Washington on the same voyage of hope. Meanwhile Pope John Paul II had inevitably been co-opted by the protesting Left as its symbolic head. Those who met with him at the time, however, found his views to be different from those of the anti-American pacifist position that was being attributed to him. Gian Guido Vecchi reported in *Corriere della Sera* that the Catholic picture was far from homogenous: "If the Catholic Action (movement) shouts 'No to war, yes to peace,' Communion and Liberation says 'No to war, yes to America.'"

PEACEMAKERS NOT PACIFISTS

THE VATICAN TRIED to avoid seeming to be in confrontation with the White House. "Making out John Paul II to be the pacifist pope is misleading and belittling," warned Lorenzo Ornaghi, rector of Milan's Catholic University. "One has to first understand what is happening inside these Catholic movements both here and elsewhere . . . Peace is not an acquired commodity that needs to be defended, it's something more dynamic that has to be constructed without taking anything for granted." On February 18, Sodano told the paper *Avvenire,*

> The Holy See is not pacifist at any cost, because it admits the right of states to legitimate defense. But it must be said that the Holy See is always a peacemaker working intensively to prevent the outbreak of war. Three days ago, Cardinal (Roger) Mahony, the archbishop of Los Angeles, wrote that the war would not solve the problems of the Middle East. He said war would be the worst solution.

For Sodano, pacifism was, if not a dirty word, at least highly suspect.

His view was widely shared in the Vatican, and in the Italian hierarchy. When the rainbow protest banners carried in mass antiwar rallies in the squares of Europe began to appear in the churches, the Italian bishops conference did not remain silent. Bishop Giuseppe Betori, the conference secretary, warned against what he called "ideological theories" at the peace demonstrations, which he said, were always "an ever-present menace." As for the rainbow banner, "in a church it would seem to be overdoing things, even pointless: the crucifix has been for 2,000 years a symbol of peace, and doesn't need additional symbols."

The Vatican strategy differed from that of either the United States or Iraq, or America's European opponents. Yet the differences with Washington widened as Archbishop Tauran insisted that the sole way to give legitimacy to armed intervention was through United Nations resolutions. Things got worse when he declared that unilateral American action would amount to "a war of aggression and therefore a crime against humanity." Other Vatican officials felt that in calling the war a crime, the cardinal went too far, but they insisted that the Holy See was not being pacifist. Pope John Paul II did not support the antiwar positions of France and Germany. The Polish-born pontiff was in any case surprised and angry when President Jacques Chirac criticized the Poles for supporting the war. "It's an oversimplification to say that the operation represents Christianity and the West," declared Bishop

Vincenzo Paglia of Terni, founder of the Saint Egidio community, which often reflects Vatican thinking on foreign affairs. "That would make the war a conflict between Christian fundamentalism and an Islamic one."

CONDOLEEZZA RICE:
"I DON'T UNDERSTAND THE VATICAN"

THE VATICAN POSITION was too subtle for the American palate. Washington did not understand and was very irritated. The pope's apparent opposition to the war seemed an incomprehensible choice, almost a betrayal. After 9/11 the United States had come to regard Pope John Paul II as an ally; he was considered to be firmly on the U.S. side. Now he was seen to be distancing himself from the American position and standing with the United Nations, an organization widely distrusted by the Bush administration and its conservative allies. "I don't understand the Vatican position," said Condoleezza Rice, then national security adviser to the president and the high priestess of unilateralism, in an interview with the Italian newsmagazine *Panorama*.

> I don't understand how it can be considered immoral to try to prevent the deaths of tens of thousands of people, perhaps hundreds of thousands, perhaps millions, by intervening against a brutal regime that has already killed 100,000, that has used chemical weapons against its own people and its neighbors, that tortures, mutilates, and violates. I don't understand how it can be immoral to use force against a regime of this type. And we have seen how, sometimes, inaction can lead to even more immoral actions.

At the beginning of March the pope started a fast in the hope that a war might be averted. On March 4 Ambassador Nicholson told Italian television that he intended to fast as well, but he also defended Rice's criticism of the Vatican's opposition. "I believe that Miss Rice was referring to the crimes committed by Iraq, and she doesn't understand why the pope has not addressed them as well," Nicholson said. "Unfortunately, the Holy See doesn't mention the crimes against humanity committed by Saddam Hussein. We didn't hear them mentioned even after Cardinal Roger Etchegaray's mission to Iraq." Nicholson's blunt comment reflected the level of American disappointment. The White House seemed to think it, and not the Vatican, had the moral high ground. *Corriere della Sera* carried a cartoon of President Bush and the pontiff. Bush was wearing a papal crown and was called the "anti-pope" in the caption. Pope John Paul II was the "anti-Bush." The strongly pro-American academic Massimo Teodori felt that the pope's position was not just a moral one; it was also the result of a desire to let the world know where, as a world leader, he stood on the major developments of the day. In other words, in opposing the Iraq war the pope was making a political judgment. Cardinal Laghi's trip to Washington had to be seen in this context.

The ex-nuncio, who knew the way Washington worked, had already sensed from Novak's visit to Rome "a hardening of the American position," according to *Corriere della Sera,* which broke the story of the cardinal's American mission. "Cardinal Etchegaray's visit to Iraq had caused some doubt, even disappointment, in the United States," because it seemed as though an ingenuous Vatican had been fooled into aiding Saddam Hussein in his delaying tactics. Laghi had in his favor his personal friendship with the Bush family, but it promised to be a challenging undertaking all the same. The cardinal was to urge Bush not to take any "irreversible decisions," and to give the United Nations time to evaluate Saddam's latest offer. But on his first day in Washington, Laghi already knew that his meetings in the White House would be a dialogue with the deaf. Condoleezza Rice had already sent a message to that effect through the four American cardinals who had met with her on the eve of Laghi's arrival.

CONDOLEEZZA AND THE CARDINAL

THE LAGHI VISIT

"WHAT IS Cardinal Laghi coming for?" Condoleezza Rice asked the four American cardinals. Her irritated tone was unmistakable, and the question required no answer. Bush's national security adviser could well imagine Pio Laghi's special mission as the pope's personal envoy. But the future secretary of state's manner left little doubt that the cardinal was neither welcome nor likely to be successful. From the Bush administration's point of view Laghi's visit was inopportune, futile, and destined to complicate things, without altering the inevitable prospect of war. Rice's challenging question set the tone for the meeting, which was documented in a confidential report sent by one of the four cardinals to the papal nuncio in Washington and by him to Rome in case it could be of use to Cardinal Laghi.

It was March 2, and Cardinals Anthony Bevilacqua of Philadelphia, William Keeler of Baltimore, Edward Egan of New York, and Theodore McCarrick of Washington met with Rice in the White House. What was striking was the somber tone of the discussion even as Pope John Paul II was making his final effort to yank President Bush back from the brink. The two-page report shows that the Bush administration was unappreciative of what Washington saw as the Vatican's interference in a situation that had already been decided both politically and militarily. Rice's first question to the cardinals had been an inquiry into "the scope of Cardinal Laghi's visit." The cardinals replied that Laghi, a seasoned diplomat, had a message to deliver to the president explaining the pope's position on the war. The pope also wanted to assure Bush that their "difference of opinion" over Iraq in no way diminished the pontiff's esteem for the United States, and he would pray for peace and for America.

The cardinals told Rice that they had two concerns. First, not enough information had been made available to the public in support of the administration's case for attacking Saddam Hussein. Second, there were the potentially devastating unintended consequences of the war. Their main fear was that the attack would detonate an explosion in the Middle East, or worse a massive protest throughout the Islamic world, with a serious impact on the Holy Land, and possibly reprisals against Christians. The cardinals told Rice they were getting messages of concern from bishops throughout the country. Wherever they went they heard the same view: Bush's foreign policy was making the international·community uneasy, and people were very concerned about the forthcoming conflict. Moreover, it seemed to them that the information about Iraq's weapons of mass destruction was flimsy.

Rice listened with obvious impatience as the cardinals assured her that they supported Bush and hoped that his preparations for war were intended to scare Saddam Hussein into quitting Iraq. They apparently failed—or refused—to understand that the decision to attack Iraq was locked into place. Rice replied that Bush did not want war, but 9/11 had cast the Middle East situation in a clearer light, and it was no longer possible to accept Saddam's negative influence in the region. A Russian specialist, Rice could not resist dropping in a reference to her area of expertise. The strategy of containment that had proved so effective with the Soviet Union in the cold war would not work with Iraq, she told the cardinals. Moscow was not prepared to take too many risks, and had in any case achieved some of its objectives. Saddam had not.

HITLER, SADDAM, AND THE NUCLEAR FEAR

RICE SAID THAT the Iraqi leader had managed to hoodwink the United Nations for twelve years, exploiting the divisions between the five permanent members of the Security Council. She reminded the cardinals of the $3 billion a year Saddam had managed to siphon off illegally from the United Nations Oil for Food program, money that was designated to provide food and medicine to the Iraqi people and relieve the deprivations caused by international sanctions. She claimed that Saddam had used the money to construct eighteen mobile chemical weapons laboratories, which the United Nations inspectors had been unable to locate. Saddam had also started building a nuclear bomb, and would shortly be able to use it unless he was stopped in time. There was no longer any margin in which to maneuver with Saddam, Rice argued: Containment was simply not an option. It was dangerous to pretend that Saddam could be forced to quit the country: the United States had certain information to the contrary.

At that moment the telephone that linked her to the Oval Office rang, and the caller was President Bush. She told the president that she was meeting with the four cardinals, and relayed his greetings to them. At the end of the call she resumed her exposition of why the White House had reached the end of the road with Saddam, even though the administration was fully aware of the collateral danger in going to war. But not confronting the Iraqi dictator would lead to worse consequences, she argued. He had to be stopped.

The cardinal's report quoted her as saying that by stopping Saddam Hussein the United States would be opening the way for a new era in the Middle East, and the United States would use all the economic and political muscle at its disposal to consolidate and advance the future stability of the Middle East. "We need to act," stressed Rice. If not, Americans would be perfectly justified in no longer believing in their leaders. Her review of the Bush administration's thinking left little room for argument. Cardinal Egan pointed out that if Saddam were cornered he would be more likely to use his arsenal of weapons of mass destruction because he would have nothing to lose. Rice shook her head. Then she pointed out that the population of Iraq had been living for years "in a torture chamber." The war couldn't make their condition any worse than it already was.

She further told the cardinals that the United States truly wished to resolve the Arab-Israeli problem. The Bush administration was ready to put pressure on Prime Minister Ariel Sharon, and there had been an improvement in the situation in the Holy Land. But Rice quickly came back to the attack on Iraq, saying the war was necessary to prevent Saddam Hussein from using his weapons in the already unstable Middle East. And so the conversation went, with the gap between the two sides widening. The cardinals had the impression that Bush and his associates had a war plan ready, and had calculated the consequences. On the latter point the Vatican and the administration differed significantly over what the consequences would be.

Cardinal Bevilacqua tried to chip away at Rice's rocklike resolve by asking why Europe did not seem convinced that "we Americans were right," and Cardinal McCarrick added that the U.S. position would have been better if other nations supported it. But Rice countered that the United States had the support of many nations—probably twenty—including some eastern European countries recently freed from Soviet control. This was seen as a reference to Poland, the pope's own birthplace. Saddam believed that he had the support of the international community, and that impression needed to be corrected. "To delay in taking action after 9/11 would be like delaying in 1938 and 1939 in taking action against Hitler," she was quoted as saying. She seemed to be making the point that Europe had been slow in reacting to Nazi aggression in 1938—an unpardonable error.

Rice's conclusion to the American cardinals was that the United States wished more than anyone to have the support of the United Nations. But it was too late to talk of anything but armed intervention against the Iraqi regime. The ninety-minute meeting was ending in a stalemate. McCarrick told Rice that the American Catholic Church still hoped that war could be avoided, but in the event of a conflict the bishops would support their country while at the same time working to limit the confrontation. Rice's response was that the United States had the same objective. Finally, according to the cardinal's report, Rice asked what they thought she should tell Laghi. "The same things that you told us," was the response. "Fine, I'll probably see him Tuesday or Wednesday," she said.

NOT A DIALOGUE BETWEEN FRIENDS

FOR PIO LAGHI, arriving at the White House on the morning of March 5, 2003, was like going back in time. As nuncio to Washington he had been a regular visitor. This time, however, he had neither illusions nor expectations: this was mission impossible. He tried to introduce a friendly note to ease the stiffly formal atmosphere, perhaps thinking that because she was the daughter of a Presbyterian minister Condoleezza Rice would warm to another churchman. "I hope that we can understand each other: Condoleezza is after all an Italian name . . ." was the cardinal's opening gambit. But it soon became clear that there was no margin for understanding. Rice seemed to regard the cardinal's visit as almost frivolous at a time when the president was occupied with momentous decisions. The conversation quickly degenerated into a cold exchange. "Saddam Hussein and his government are a cancer, and we must stop it from spreading," said the president's national security adviser. The same words were repeated by President Bush when Laghi was ushered into the Oval Office.

As a friend of the Bush clan, the cardinal knew the president. Every Christmas he received a card from George senior, always a portrait of the former president and his wife Barbara and their dog, Sadie, in the center, encircled by photos of the Bush sons, their wives and children. But before leaving Rome Laghi had spoken to *Corriere della Sera* about his forthcoming American mission. "We'll look each other straight in the eye and speak courteously, but it won't be a meeting of friends," he predicted. And he was right. The encounter with George W. Bush was polite but formal—the president of the United States receiving a veteran Vatican diplomat. Laghi had instructions from the pope to speak plainly to ensure that the United States fully understood Pope John Paul II's aversion, and that of the Catholic world, to this unilateral decision to attack Iraq. He also handed Bush a letter from Pope John Paul II, which the president placed on his desk, without opening it.

Bush was not as sharp-tongued as Condoleezza, but there was certainly nothing approaching a meeting of the minds. When the president replayed the cancer remark the cardinal answered: "Mr. President, the cancer has already spread, it has spread into a conflict between the Arabs and Israelis." This was the main point on which the Vatican wanted to focus attention. Bush pointed out that he was the first U.S. president to call officially for the establishment of a Palestinian state. Laghi countered that it would have been better to have done so much earlier because Palestinian Islamism had different characteristics from Islamism in Pakistan or Indonesia. Not to have acted quickly to remedy the crisis that had beset the Holy Land for decades, and now instead to pour weapons into Iraq, would result in spreading tension throughout the Muslim world. The cardinal's point was that by letting the Palestinian-Israeli situation fester it had grown from a local situation into a regional one, and it could not be solved by going to war in Iraq. Laghi made a second point, that because the United States and its ally Britain were seen as Christian countries, an attack on Iraq would destroy the bridges with Islam. "We'll rebuild them stronger than before," answered Bush. Laghi explained that any military action would be interpreted in the Arab world as a neocolonial operation or, worse, a new crusade, not with an aim to liberating the Holy Sepulcher but with geopolitical and economic objectives.

This was one of the key points of disagreement between Rome and Washington. For the Holy See, the idea of resolving the Palestinian-Israeli situation by beating up on Saddam Hussein as one of the financial backers of anti-Israeli terrorism represented a dangerous shortcut. It was an illusion destined to provoke more terrorist attacks, not fewer, and to increase the number of terrorists. For the Bush administration, destroying Saddam Hussein was meant to deliver a warning to other regimes in the region. But how effective would this objective be? Al Qaeda had been undermined at its very base in Afghanistan and its finances assailed, yet it continued to flourish.

A wall of incomprehension separated the Holy See and Washington on Israel. The Bush administration regarded the issue as unassailable, and the meeting skirted round the issue. The Catholic Church viewed the way that Bush and Ariel Sharon were handling the Palestinians as clumsy. They were neither engaging the ailing Yasser Arafat, nor, at the time, the prime minister of the Palestinian Authority. Deep down, the Vatican had the impression that the United States and Israel were wearing themselves out and even destroying themselves with their Middle East policy. Without wanting to or realizing it, they risked dragging the entire Western world into a conflict with Islam. But the Arab-Israeli issue, which the Vatican regarded as the core problem in the region, floated unresolved over the conversation.

The other question, embarrassing to the Vatican, was the scandal of pedophile Catholic priests. It was not mentioned, but both sides were certainly conscious of its implications. Laghi felt that Bush and Condoleezza Rice and the staff members in attendance were silently reproaching him that the pope would have done better to deal with the problem within his own church before questioning the morality of the Iraq war. Bush claimed the right to judge the justice or otherwise of the war. As he repeated more than once to Laghi: "I'm the one who decides whether or not to initiate the conflict." He told the cardinal that Jesus had "saved me from alcoholism," and now Jesus was guiding him in making a more difficult decision. The meeting made no progress, but it placed on record the Vatican's opposition, and its efforts right up to the end to dissuade the Bush administration from embarking on a shameful action.

"THEY HAD ALREADY DECIDED ON WAR"

"I HAD THE impression that they had already decided," Laghi recalled months later at a seminar organized by the Catholic monthly *Il Regno*, published by the Dehonian Fathers in Bologna. When the cardinal entered the Oval Office the president had launched into a lengthy explanation of the reasons for the war. Laghi cut in saying, "I'm not here just to listen, but also to ask you to listen to me." The president did listen, and occasionally interrupted. He interrupted when Laghi explained the Vatican's moral objections to the use of force and to a preventive war; and again when the cardinal spoke of the possible collateral damage that the Iraq war could cause in other countries. On the other hand, Laghi broke in when Bush claimed that Saddam had allowed al Qaeda to set up terrorist training camps in Iraq. "Are you sure? Do you have proof showing this?" the cardinal wanted to know. Laghi also questioned Bush's claim that the administration knew Saddam Hussein had weapons of mass destruction and was preparing to use them.

But Bush had no doubts: he knew reason was on his side. So was God, as he told Laghi. He quoted verses from the Bible. "He spoke and behaved as if he was divinely inspired and seemed genuinely to believe that it was a war of right against wrong," Laghi told the seminar. "We spoke at length of the consequences of the war. I asked him: Do you realize the consequences of occupying Iraq? The confusion; the fighting between Shiites, Sunnis, and Kurds." But at that moment, Bush saw only the triumph of democracy. And at the end of a half-hour meeting, Bush pointed out that he and the pope saw eye to eye on such issues as the defense of human life and opposition to stem cell research. "But I am here to talk about Iraq, not about these problems," the Vatican diplomat told the president as he departed the White House. It had all been useless: useless to inform the president that the pope was "very, very concerned"; useless to point out that the pope was praying that "the Lord would guide (Bush) in his search for peace." The strategy had been set and nobody could halt it—or indeed challenge it. Not, at any rate, in the White House.

Laghi had to call a press conference at Washington's National Press Club, "because they told us we couldn't hold it at the White House," as he recalled later. To the Washington media Laghi spoke plainly, making no attempt to hide the differences between the Vatican and the Bush administration. "To the American people I want to say, think carefully about the possible consequences [of war]! The Church is above it all. We don't want to create any rifts." The cardinal was no longer addressing the White House: through the media, he was sending a message to the American Catholic episcopate, and all those who defined themselves as Christians in America. But his words were also directed beyond the Atlantic to the Mediterranean and the Islamic world. At the same time the secretary general of the American Council of Christian Churches was said to have asked the pope to come to Washington to make a last-minute appeal against the war at a joint meeting of the U.S. Congress. As for the American Catholic bishops, it was common knowledge that their moral voice had been weakened by the sex abuse scandals. Donald Wuerl, then bishop of Pittsburgh, declared at the time that, "in spite of the scandal, the American bishops had continued to speak out with their moral authority. But it's euphemistic to say that their authority had not been blemished by the scandal."

Laghi's mission had failed, and war was imminent. Less than three weeks later the United States and Britain would attack Iraq without a United Nations mandate, and with a large section of the international community in an uproar. The United States and the Vatican, the West's two parallel empires, were poles apart. Before leaving for Rome the cardinal called on Colin Powell, the U.S. secretary of state. He had learned that the former general had many private doubts about the conflict. It had also become apparent that senior generals were warning that the invaders would face many imponderables, whereas Donald Rumsfeld, the secretary of defense, and the Pentagon civilians, classic Second World War images vivid in their memories, saw only a certain American victory and the troops welcomed in triumph as liberators with cheering and flowers. Laghi recounted to Powell the details of his meeting with Bush, hoping perhaps for some sign that the secretary of state dissociated himself from the White House, or was prepared to use his authority to halt the preparations for war.

Although Laghi could sense Powell's unease, the general remained impassive. But when the cardinal commented that going to war could have potentially disastrous consequences, Powell replied laconically, "You're telling me, a military man? I know what war is." No one could reverse the course of events. As Condoleezza Rice had put it bluntly, it was the end of the road, and Laghi had understood this both from his conversation with the presidential adviser and even more so from President Bush. No one had actually said that war had been declared. The Vatican envoy could have clung to this very slim hope. But even that was dashed before his departure when U.S. Marine General Peter Pace, then vice chairman of the Joint Chiefs of Staff, and incidentally an Italo-American, accompanied him out of the White House after the meeting with Bush. The general gave him a friendly tap on the shoulder and said, "Don't worry, your Eminence, we'll do it quickly and well."

For months after the first shots were fired relations between Rome and Washington seemed to be in limbo. The Vatican obstinately left its nuncio, Archbishop Fernando Filoni, in Baghdad, even during the worst of the fighting. Rome also continued to insist on the need for United Nations involvement. The United States pressed on with its offensive, convinced that God and the American armed forces would prove that the United States had right on its side. But buried in the folds of the Rome-Washington dispute was a mutual reluctance to break off contact. For one thing, about a third of the 150,000 American troops in Iraq were Roman Catholics, and the Holy See wanted to avoid making them feel that they had been abandoned by their religious leaders. On May 1, 2003, President Bush staged his famous "Mission Accomplished" appearance on the carrier USS *Lincoln*. When it became apparent that the claim was premature, and the postwar situation in Iraq would continue to be difficult, bloody, and chaotic, the administration began to realize that the Vatican could play a useful role in talking to the imams, and calming the anti-American sentiment that was dominant in the European Union.

NASIRIYAH AND ITALIAN CATHOLICISM

"WHEN THE IRAQ situation worsened for the Americans the Vatican refrained from making any comment so as to avoid the charge of stabbing Washington in the back," commented *Corriere della Sera*. "But behind the silence was still the conviction that the war was illegal. With the cessation of the actual fighting, the Vatican issued a declaration expressing the hope that the Iraqis would receive prompt humanitarian aid." The Church was hoping that the United Nations would now step in, that other countries would become involved in Iraq's reconstruction, and that as soon as possible political power would be transferred to an Iraqi government. But the Holy See perceived the rise of terrorism in Iraq as confirmation of its belief that the war had been wrong, and an armed opposition was now in place to impede the pacification and normalization of that country.

Even so, Cardinal Achille Silvestrini, a former senior member of the Secretariat of State, warned against isolating the United States and allowing it to close in upon itself. America's historic merits were well remembered and acknowledged, but it also had to be remembered that the Iraq conflict was not based on "a faultless presumption of legitimacy." Above all, Silvestrini challenged what he called the "infantile" policies of Pentagon neoconservatives such as Richard Perle. There was a slight thaw in Vatican-Washington relations when Powell visited the pope—the first high-level American meeting with John Paul II since the outbreak of the war. But a more effective rapprochement followed the death of nineteen Italian soldiers in a suicide car bomb attack in the town of Nasiriyah, in southeastern Iraq on November 12, 2003. Differences between the Vatican, the Italian opposition, and the conservative government of Prime Minister Silvio Berlusconi, a staunch ally of the Bush administration, were laid aside as the nation united in grief. It's surprising, commented *Corriere della Sera* in an editorial, that "anyone in Europe can still refuse to acknowledge the criminal intent of these fundamentalists and the threat they constitute to the moderate Arab world even more than the West." The victims—the editorial went on—died "in the service of a global community that is vulnerable to terrorist attack and that extends from the United States to Israel, passing through Europe." The newspaper also noted that the Italian parliament had put aside its usual divisiveness and solidly expressed its opposition to terrorism. *Corriere della Sera* also noted that withdrawal of Italy's contingent from the American-led Coalition of the Willing in Iraq "would mean a victory for the terrorists."

The Vatican and the Italian Episcopate shared the same view. At the memorial service for the nineteen soldiers on November 18, Cardinal Ruini aligned the Italian bishops with the civil power in supporting the Italian Military Peace Mission in Iraq—so named to dispel any connection with the actual war. Both the ecclesiastical authorities and the politicians spoke of the difference between the American role in Iraq and that of the Italians, between war making and peace making, but also between pacifism and peacekeeping. The United States had launched a military operation that Italy supported while not entirely agreeing with it. Even so, Ruini affirmed that, despite the loss of lives, the Italians could not quit Nasiriyah while they could still be of help to the Iraqis to create a semblance of normality in their country. "We will not run away from the terrorist assassins," the cardinal said in the Basilica of Saint Paul. "On the contrary, we will confront them with courage, energy, and determination."

The president of the Italian episcopate "hopes that Italy will not withdraw its contingent, not because he approves of the American undertaking, but to encourage the involvement of other countries, thus making the pacification of Iraq a truly international effort backed by the United Nations," commented *Corriere della Sera*. This support for Italian participation, the newspaper said, was justified because it was a mission of peace, did in fact have United Nations backing, even if after the fact, and fell under the category of an international peace force, the kind of troops the Holy See had in the past envisioned being sent to world crisis spots. In 1993 Pope John Paul II had spoken of a "humanitarian presence" in Bosnia, and in 1999 of an interposing or separating force in Kosovo. In 2001 the pope had called for a "third force" in the Holy Land as an antiterrorist barrier between Israelis and Palestinians.

The Holy See never changed its view on maintaining an Italian presence in Iraq, but the Italian government eventually did, and Italy's forces were expected to be home by the end of 2006, a goal that was met. A long list of leading cardinals supported the theory that withdrawing Italy's three thousand troops concentrated in the southeast would bring Iraq closer to civil war, and would destroy any hope of interreligious dialogue. The list included Cardinals Angelo Sodano, Carlo Maria Martini, and Dionigi Tettamanzi (Martini's successor as archbishop of Milan), Renato Martino (one of the Church's most outspoken critics of the United States), Tauran, Tarcisio Bertone, Silvestrini, Laghi, and Roberto Tucci (president of Radio Vaticana). "We must not leave Iraq, or there will be chaos," warned Archbishop Filoni, the nuncio in Baghdad. He told an Italian reporter that the situation of Iraqi Christian minorities—the Catholics, Chaldeans, Armenians, and Syrian-Catholics—was increasingly desperate because they were being ignored. "I don't know of a single project that takes the religious minorities into account," he said. "What's going to be the role of the minorities? The Christians account for four percent of the population, but I'm not just thinking of them."

Relations with Washington remained tense. When Saddam Hussein was captured and was shown on television having his teeth examined by an American military doctor, and his hair scrutinized apparently for lice, Cardinal Martino snapped, "I was sorry to see this destroyed man having his teeth checked like a cow. [The Americans] could have spared us that footage." The cardinal accused the Americans of offending human dignity and lacking compassion. For Washington and for many Americans, the idea of Saddam Hussein evoking pity was almost offensive, and betrayed the solidarity required of allies in time of war. Ambassador Nicholson let it be known that he had received hundreds of e-mails from Americans who were angry at Cardinal Martino and the Vatican. But that wasn't the only incident. Vice President Dick Cheney's audience with the pope in January 2004 was noted by omission—or close to it. Cheney's audience was reported in a few lines tucked away on page 5 of *L'Osservatore Romano,* without the customary photo, the least possible attention it could possibly have received.

On June 4, 2004, Bush himself visited the pope. Relations were still awkward and apparently remained so. Condoleezza Rice accompanied Bush to Rome, but not to the Vatican for the papal audience. Her absence was noted, and Tauran discreetly asked Nicholson why the president's national security adviser was not in Bush's party. The ambassador replied that she had stayed behind to work on an important position paper that the president needed for a subsequent meeting.

The Bush administration never understood the Vatican's position on Iraq, but to call it anti-American would be an oversimplification. Neither the pope nor any senior Vatican prelate ever called for the withdrawal of forces from Iraq, and their reason could be called "geo-religious." An editorial in the newspaper *La Stampa* said, "The Vatican was against the war in Iraq all along. But now the problem was different. Withdrawal meant abandoning Iraq to Shiite fundamentalism."

THE BROKEN BRIDGE TO ISLAM

NEGATIVE PUBLICITY

O N MARCH 4, 2003, Europeans learned from the *International Herald Tribune* that the Bush administration's public image expert had resigned. Fourteen months later, the *Financial Times* reported that American efforts to "capture the hearts and minds" of the Arabs had not been successful. Two news items encapsulated the setback to Washington's approach to the Islamic world. True, this was not a failure in the superpower's political or military strategy, but, paradoxically, this failure was more damaging to the American effort. The Bush administration's strategy designed to explain and spread American ideals in the Islamic world had virtually collapsed.

The first to tackle the challenge had been Charlotte Beers, and it was her resignation—for health reasons—that had been reported in the *"Trib."* A Texan with top-level Madison Avenue experience (at J. Walter Thompson and then Ogilvy and Mather, no less), Beers was appointed undersecretary for public diplomacy in 2001 in the immediate aftermath of 9/11. In other words, she was a minister of propaganda. When she was nominated, Colin Powell argued that just as her advertising had made him buy Uncle Ben's rice, she could sell America in the Islamic world.

"Our role is to inform and influence the Muslim population and the Islamic [fundamentalist] movement, and we're doing better in the first effort than the second," Beers told Ennio Caretto of *Corriere della Sera* in an interview published in November 12, 2002. At the time a small hope still remained: the attack on Iraq had not been launched. Condoleezza Rice and Donald Rumsfeld appeared on Al Jazeera television, the Qatar-based Arab satellite network, to extol the virtues of American democracy. In the winter of 2002 Colin Powell gave a wide-ranging interview on MTV. The secretary of state discoursed about everything from the AIDS epidemic to Washington as the capital of a superpower. Shortly afterward the Bush administration launched Radio Sawa, an Arabic-language station broadcasting pop music and news. An Iraqi magazine called the new radio station more dangerous than the Pentagon's missiles.

A few days before her resignation sixty-seven-year-old Beers told the Senate Foreign Relations Committee that the gap between how Americans wanted to be seen and the way they were actually perceived internationally was disastrously wide. In May 2004 Margaret Tutwiler, a veteran State Department official who had been recalled from overseas to run the government's public diplomacy campaign, also resigned after only six months in the post.

For Tutwiler there were no health reasons but the attraction of a less frustrating job at the New York Stock Exchange. Tutwiler must have realized that the American public relations campaign was a battle she could not win when to the difficult task of influencing international public opinion was added the shameful saga of Abu Ghraib, the Iraqi prison where male and female American soldiers had tortured and abused Iraqi prisoners. But Abu Ghraib was the death blow to an effort that was ill conceived from the start. The most ambitious propaganda campaign launched by the United States since the cold war was torpedoed by its own overly optimistic, public relations–oriented, intrinsically ideological approach.

THE GREAT SATAN OR THE GREAT PROTECTOR?

WASHINGTON'S BASIC IDEA was that the Islamic world only needed to be shown the virtues of the American model to adopt it. In his MTV interview Powell rejected Osama bin Laden's characterization of the United States as the "Great Satan" (a label, incidentally, used earlier by Iran's Ayatollah Khomeini). On the contrary, Powell said, America was the Great Protector of the Arab world and of global democracy. This statement gave rise to a joke in European diplomatic circles based on an old anti-American slogan: "Yankee go home—and take me with you." In May 2002 Beers boasted that every important government speech was made available in translation in six languages on the day of delivery, and in twenty languages a few days later. Speaking at the Middle East Institute in Washington, she said her department had organized media tours to the United States for foreign journalists, mainly from Islamic countries. Her public diplomacy office had exposed bin Laden's terror organization to public scrutiny in a four-color publication called *The Terrorism Network,* made available in numerous languages. The booklet was the office's best-selling publication. She said "marvelous photos" of New York's Ground Zero by Joel Meyerowitz were to be put on exhibition in twenty countries. But the Madison Avenue–style campaign revealed a profound ignorance of the Islamic "market" for which it was intended. Beers was skillful at convincing the American consumer, and some Westerners in general, but her efforts to convince "consumers" of a different mentality, culture, and religion revealed the wide gap in her understanding, and one that Beers failed to close.

Beers faced that gap when she went on a mission to Cairo to improve the image of the United States among Egyptian opinion makers and intellectuals. Muhammad Abdel Hadi, a top editor for the newspaper *Al Ahram,* walked out of the meeting frustrated that Beers seemed more interested in talking about vague American values than about specific United States policies. "No matter how hard you try to make them understand, they don't," he complained. The problem, wrote Canadian writer and activist Naomi Klein at the time, was that Beers "believed that America's negative image abroad was a communications problem. But the problem of the United States is not how it's marketed: it's the 'product' itself." Which is why the $62 million spent on launching the Arabic-language television station Al Hurra has proved of no avail in the propaganda war. Samer Shahata, professor of Arab studies at Georgetown University in Washington, was dismissive of the Bush administration's media effort. "You can have all the radio and television stations like Al Hurra that you want, but if the United States policies on Iraq and Palestine remain what they are now they will never win over the hearts and minds of the Arab world," he said.

Karen Hughes, a longtime Bush family adviser, was the next to be appointed undersecretary for public diplomacy in March 2005. Yet it was clear that Washington's approach had not changed, and neither had the effort's effectiveness improved. And, in fact, in the autumn of 2007 she resigned as well, admitting the failure implicitly by saying that she had been given "a work of generations." In the immediate aftermath of 9/11 Bush had received the support and sympathy of virtually the entire world. However, the United States had failed to consolidate that patrimony of solidarity and compassion. The deportation of several hundred al Qaeda and Taliban suspects to Guantánamo had raised questions of legality. The Arab street was enraged by the American double standard in human rights, so it wasn't surprising that the slanderous rumor resurfaced that the attack on the World Trade Center in New York had been the work of Zionist agents hoping to trigger a war against Islam.

In 2002, the increasing American pressure on Iraq was becoming a particular problem for the Vatican, which was greatly concerned about the impact that an attack on Saddam Hussein would have on Christian communities in the Middle East. The United States is considered a Christian country, and it actually is. The U.S. offensive, in alliance with the British, allowed the Islamic fundamentalists to call the conflict a crusade and spin it as a religious war. This viewpoint reduced the space for mediation by the region's more moderate states, and by the Christian minorities who had often been considered useful intermediaries between the West and the Islamic east. Interviewed early in 2002 by *Le Monde,* the French newspaper, King Abdullah of Jordan said, "Bin Laden's strategy is to exploit regional crises to recruit followers and to find justification for his campaign. To fight extremism, we have to end regional conflicts that feed his propaganda. If we add an expedition against Iraq to the existing conflicts in the West Bank and Gaza we will be shooting ourselves in the foot. The West will be even more detested." The young king, himself a target of bin Laden's criticism because of his ties to the West, added, "The international community has to understand one thing: we did not join the United States in fighting terrorism: the United States joined us."

As the Bush administration speeded up its preparations for attacking Saddam Hussein at the end of 2002, bolstering its case for war with false information that Iraq had weapons of mass destruction, the Vatican kept up its efforts to halt the rush to war. Rome publicly warned the nations involved against hasty action, and urged them to rely on the

United Nations weapons inspectors to determine whether Saddam Hussein had actually stockpiled nuclear bombs and chemical and biological weapons. Contrary to Washington's confidence in victory, the Holy See was pessimistic about the outcome, believing that damage was likely to be done to America's credibility. The Vatican's major concern was the impact of the conflict on relations between Muslims and Christian minorities in the Middle East. While the United States formed the "Coalition of the Willing" to back its Iraq policy, the Vatican found itself at the center of a group of countries opposed to the American offensive. The *New York Times* made the point that, like the United States, the Vatican was primarily trying to protect its own interests: The pope was concerned that the conflict would disrupt the delicate coexistence between the various religions in the Middle East. The war, he believed, would blur the distinctions, and indeed the differences, between the Bush empire and the Vatican. In addition, Rome viewed the theory that al Qaeda terrorism and the Palestinian militant attacks against Israel could be eradicated by striking Iraq as illusory, and dangerous.

In the eyes of the Catholic Church the regime of Saddam Hussein, however brutal, was one of the last outposts of secularism in a region increasingly dominated by intolerant religious fundamentalism. Its removal without careful advance preparation, planning, and international involvement carried the danger of sparking religious conflicts between Sunni and Shiite Arabs, and leading to the possible persecution, isolation, and even expulsion of Iraq's non-Islamic communities. So the Vatican countered Washington's anti-Saddam campaign with its own persistent lobbying for peace. Inevitably, though, Rome's evenhanded effort in pressing both sides was seen in Washington as anti-American, and anti-West. "Once communism collapsed, Italy joined the Western alliance, and the Vatican left it," is how Italian General Carlo Jean, a foremost strategist and geopolitical specialist, put it. In addition, the Bush administration's policy of bringing democracy to the Greater Middle East, from Morocco to Pakistan, was seen as equally illusory and liable to create a negative chain reaction. In its efforts to maintain contact with the Islamic world, the Vatican needed to maintain its distance from the American action, and to continue to show a formal respect to the Saddam Hussein regime. The peacemaker pope remained a disturbing element for the Bush administration. Through his spokesman, Ari Fleischer, the president let it be known that he would not be influenced by Pope John Paul II's peace appeals.

"Iraq is a country with an ancient history, in which ecumenism is a daily reality and Christians and Muslims live side by side relatively peacefully," warned Cardinal Crescenzio Sepe, a senior Vatican prelate, in an interview with *La Stampa* on February 26, 2003. "A conflict could change that balance." The cardinal, who as prefect of the Propaganda Fide was responsible for the Church's missionary work, stressed the importance of not linking terrorism with religion, as Islamist extremists had done. He expressed his concern about the Christian communities "in the areas likely to be affected by an eventual conflict. It is dangerous to instrumentalize faith, and that goes for all religions, even Christianity. Unfortunately, the minorities always end up as victims in such tense situations." Sepe's parting shot was that fundamentalism has tended to "distort the pope's pronouncements."

There was recent precedent for this concern that Christian minorities might become targets. The Catholic archbishop of Islamabad and Rawalpindi, Theodore Lobo, recalled that during the American offensive in Afghanistan

> Christians in Pakistan were regarded as Americans and Britons. Unable to attack these two nations, Pakistani protesters attacked us. So on the eve of the Iraq war I called the Islamic journalists and told them: "Remember, our president is Pervez Musharraf, not George Bush." The journalists laughed, but that was what I wanted—to get across the message that to accuse us of being pro-American was ridiculous.

As far as the Vatican was concerned what was valid in Pakistan also applied to Morocco, Egypt, the Palestinians, and, of course, Iraq. The Church's concern extended to Indonesia, the world's largest Islamic country, but also to Nigeria, a country with both Christians and Muslims, and the sub-Saharan region—Malawi, Sudan, Zambia, Kenya, Tanzania. All were—and are—fragile countries vulnerable to the spread of fundamentalism financed by oil-rich Saudi Arabia, and touched by the ripple effect of the Iraq war, the Arab-Israeli conflict, and Bush's unilateralism.

"We mustn't allow a human tragedy to become as well a religious catastrophe . . . War must never be allowed to divide the religions of the world," said Pope John Paul II on March 29, 2003. His audience fully understood his meaning: they were the Catholic bishops of Indonesia on their periodic visit to Rome. Every one of the pope's declarations refuted the Muslim fundamentalist propaganda regarding a new crusade led by Bush. "It's not a conflict between the Christian west and the Islamic east," stated Michel Sabbah, the Latin Patriarch of Jerusalem. "There is a clear distinction between the role of all religions and the political action of one part of the West. This is also due to the efforts of several Muslim personalities." Sabah said that the peace effort had actually resulted in "a union of West and East." But that was wishful thinking. In reality, the situation was worsening. Denominational coexistence had become more complicated. Once the tight control of the Saddam Hussein regime was removed the ghosts of old prejudices would return.

A BRIDGE TO THE ARAB WORLD

THE MAY 2003 issue of *La Civiltà Cattolica* published a detailed account of how the old coexistence was destined to unravel along with everything else in postwar Iraq. Written by Samir Khalil Samir, an Egyptian Jesuit teaching in Beirut, the article said that a low birth rate accounted for some of the slow decline in the Christian population, but the picture had been changing for the past fifty years due to social and cultural shifts in the region following the creation of the state of Israel in 1948. According to Samir Khalil, Christians had been asking for some time "whether they should consider that their space in the Arab world was diminishing and they should be preparing to leave." His own answer was that they should stay.

The real value of Christianity in the Arab world did not lie in numbers. Samir Khalil pointed out the example of Judaism, "a great religion despite the fact that it has barely 16 million followers." Christians needed to shift their thinking from "the numerical problem to a qualitative approach." The Arab Christian tradition had many credits, in his analysis: overall its ability to serve as a bridge between different cultures. But the community felt hemmed in and was suffering from an identity crisis. Christians in the Middle East did not consider themselves Arabs because they tend to confuse Arabism and Islamism. But that ignores the fact that "more than 80 percent of the world's Muslim population is neither Arabs nor Arabized," Samir Khalil wrote. Moreover, the twenty-two countries of the Arab League themselves do not share a common identity, any more than European countries do. The rise of fundamentalism has frightened the Islamic world, forcing it to close in upon itself; in turn, Christians in the Middle East have done the same.

"The Christian community [in the Middle East] is Arab and at the same time something else," Samir Khalil maintained.

> They can't deny that they are Arabs, otherwise they would just be foreigners, expatriates. Throughout history the Christians of the Arab world have been cultural intermediaries between the Arab world and the West—from the Hellenist epoch through the seventeenth century with the Maronites and Europe . . . The Christians are still exercising that same role today, buttressed by a large number of Muslims.

The Christian experience is one of coexistence, alternating periods of collaboration and conflict, and that experience can offer the West "a balanced view of Islam." The Vatican's concern was that the Arab Christians, whose coexistence was already difficult in itself, would be caught in the middle, between the outsider's attempt to "export democracy" to the region and the Arabs' resistance to this influence.

Historically, the role of eastern Catholic communities, Samir Khalil wrote, was to act as

> a bridge. A bridge between Christianity and Islam; a bridge between Islam and Judaism so as to avoid making the Arab-Israeli conflict a religious conflict but to keep it on the political plane; a bridge between the Near East and the West; a bridge between Catholicism and Eastern Orthodoxy; a bridge between the various traditional rites of the East (Syrian, Copt, Armenian, Byzantine, etc.) all of them equally Catholic.

The purpose of a bridge is to "cross from one side to the other," and it presupposes that "there is somebody on the opposite bank, because you can't construct a solid bridge except together. Finally, there is no point in constructing a magnificent bridge if it fails to reach the opposite bank, or if one is not able to communicate in the language of whoever is there, or to be able to offer something that is essential to him." The argument was the antithesis of Washington's "hearts and minds" propaganda that seeks to impose itself—a splendid, costly bridge built from one side and going nowhere.

MUSHARRAF AND THE NEW IRON CURTAIN

WHEN IT CAME to bridges, the Iraq conflict did not so much destroy communication with the Islamic world as further worsen the damage already caused by Islamic fundamentalism, which appears to be determined to destroy moderate Islam. This time the damage was done by a Western attack, militarily strong, but politically controversial. The U.S. attack on Iraq put at risk the solidarity that had sprung up between the United States and other nations following 9/11; it created a scorched earth zone around the regimes that for years had been linked to a violent, extremist, anti–Western version of Islam. The war in Iraq played into the hands of bin Laden's unilaterally declared war. Paradoxically, 9/11 simultaneously divided the Islamic world, united the Western international community, and, contrary to the intentions of the suicide hijackers, weakened the former while strengthening the latter, noted Jack Miles in his study "Religion and American Foreign Policy" in the review *Survival,* published by the International Institute of Strategic Studies (IISS). Unfortunately, eighteen months later, the invasion and occupation of Iraq had the reverse effect, splitting the West and re-uniting the Islamic front, at least temporarily.

The overall effect of the unilateral action of the United States, as so-called moderate Islamist leaders had warned, was to boost the spread of fundamentalism in their respective countries. Following King Abdullah of Jordan, Egyptian President Hosni Mubarak was the next to sound the alarm. On January 23, 2003, *Time* magazine quoted him as saying that if there was one bin Laden to start with, there would be a hundred after the Iraq war. On September 22, 2004, in an address to the United Nations General Assembly, Pakistan strongman Musharraf, Washington's ally in the American-led hunt for bin Laden and the remnants of al Qaeda and the Taliban in the rugged mountainous border area between Pakistan and Afghanistan, spoke of the futility of capturing the terrorist leader and destroying al Qaeda if the root cause of fundamentalist subversion—"the Palestinian tragedy"—was left to fester. The major Western countries must show that they are willing to resolve at the international level disputes that afflict the Islamic world . . . They must act quickly," he warned, before "an iron curtain" descended between the West and the Islamic universe.

Musharraf's use of the historic Churchillian phrase was deliberate and symbolic. Following the Iraq invasion successive polls showed a steady erosion in the image of the United States in the Islamic world and elsewhere. In October 2003 the results of a special survey ordered by the White House revealed the devastating dimensions of America's alienation. A team of thirteen scholars, former ambassadors and former presidential spokesmen coordinated by Edward Djerejian, himself a Middle Eastern specialist and former senior diplomat, spent months touring the Middle East, Europe, and Asia, canvassing the views of Muslims. Their not surprising conclusion: The Iraq war and the Middle East situation had raised the level of hatred against the United States. Arab television stations refused to run spots that spoke of "shared values" between Muslims and Americans. Djerejian described a two-hour program on Al Arabiya television network pointing the finger at "the Americanization of Islam." It was, said Djerejian, their version of the West's view that extremists had taken control of Islam. Moreover, the situation didn't get any better. On June 24, 2005, the results of a Pew Research Center survey were published. The *International Herald Tribune*'s headline pointed out that the image of the United States overseas was worse than China's; and topping the list of anti-American countries were Pakistan and Turkey. Things worsened in 2006 and 2007. Brian Knowlton wrote that "the global image of America has slipped further."

A MOSQUE IN THE VATICAN

THE EMERGENCE OF an Eastern iron curtain constituted a serious threat to religious minorities, and Pope John Paul II intensified his warnings of "a religious catastrophe." The West is essentially "an intruder, an invader," commented the papal nuncio for Kuwait, Bahrain, and Yemen, Archbishop Giuseppe De Andrea.

> It's the same in a secular state like Iraq. But it's surprising that the United States failed to understand this: the Americans were convinced that they would be received as liberators, and the reality has been very different. The West's allies in the Arab world are the two or three percent of the population that forms the political and financial establishment, but that doesn't mean that the countries are allies. Ordinary people believe what they hear in the mosques, and in certain mosques the West is depicted as the land of pornography, music, and corruption, the kingdom of Satan that threatens their identity.

Wahabism, the most conservative Islamic teaching financed by Saudi petrodollars, has steadily grown in influence, leaving little room for reciprocity among religions.

Pope John Paul II had had a personal taste of this attitude some years ago in 1999 when he received then Crown Prince (now King) Abdullah of Saudi Arabia. The pope asked the member of the Saudi royal house whether it would be possible to build a Catholic church in the kingdom. The prince replied that Saudi Arabia was Islam's holy land, and therefore no church would be allowed. When the pope argued that a mosque had been built in Rome, Crown Prince Abdullah replied quickly, "Yes, in Rome. But not inside the Vatican." The story was told by Andreotti, who had arranged the visit. The incident happened sometime before the Iraq conflict, and before the emergence of Islamic terrorism as a major threat. In the space of a few years the situation had worsened. The problem was no longer building a church in Saudi Arabia but saving one's life.

In June 2004 a report on religious freedom by the Church in Suffering organization said Catholics and Protestants were persecuted mainly in Asia, and in some Islamic nations. In Laos, Christianity is labeled as "a foreign imperialist religion." In Nepal, following the decapitation of a dozen Nepalese hostages by Islamic terrorists in Iraq, demonstrators attacked Christian churches as well as mosques because—as one missionary priest explained to *AsiaNews*—"the demonstrators accused the United States of being responsible for the hostages being taken in the first place. To the Nepalese, the United States is a Christian nation, and therefore people turned on all Christians after what had happened to the hostages." In Iraq in August 2004 there were five attacks on Christian churches, causing several deaths, and further attacks occurred in October. "There are people sowing discord between Christians and Muslims so that the terrorists will force us to leave our country, and I hope this will never happen," an Iraqi priest, Father Roufayil, said in an interview with the Italian Catholic newspaper *Avvenire* on August 3.

"THERE IS NO LONGER ROOM FOR US"

THUS AN EXODUS that had been trickling on for decades seemed likely to accelerate. "Back in the twenties of the last century Christians who saw the rise of Arab nationalism, which then seemed a defense against Islamization, began to immigrate because they felt their lives were increasingly at risk in the Middle East," recalls Andrea Riccardi of the Saint Egidio community. Earlier, Muslims, Christians, and Jews had lived together. "The Jews have virtually disappeared from the Islamic world, as a result of the birth of Israel and the spread of Islamic anti-Semitism," Riccardi maintains. "But the Christians had remained as friends of the Islamic world . . . They had a historic function as mediators between the Islamic east and the West."

Since the war and occupation, Iraqi Chaldeans have fled to Syria, Jordan, and to Western countries. "Coexistence seems to be over for the Baghdadi Christians," stated *La Stampa* in a report from the Iraqi capital headlined "Christians escaping: 'There is no longer room for us.'" Iraqi Christians are quoted as saying that wherever they move to in their own country they feel threatened by the Shiite majority. The newspaper said that Christian liquor store owners, tolerated under Saddam Hussein, were now seeing their property attacked because alcohol is banned by Islam. Christian girls were insulted at school because they wore no head covering. But the exodus was also occurring elsewhere. The papal nuncio in Jerusalem pointed out that the Christian community in Israel had dropped to 2 percent. In Iraq it was 3 percent, and little more than that in Egypt and Syria.

The defense of Christians in the Islamic world has always been "a priority for the pope and the Holy See," Riccardi says. "Western countries, however, don't seem to take into account the impact of their decisions on the Christian minorities. Have they become hostages? Are they condemned to emigrate? One thing is certain. The situation of these children of the Near East has never been so dramatic." In September 2004 the British ambassador in Rome, Sir Ivor Roberts, ruffled coalition feathers by declaring in what he thought was a closed conference with Italian and British politicians, bankers, academicians, and journalists, that "if anyone's ready to celebrate the eventual re-election of Bush, it is none other than al Qaeda. Bush is al Qaeda's best recruiting sergeant." The off-the-record comment, quoted in *Corriere della Sera,* is one small indication of the distance between the American "hearts and minds" effort and reality in the rest of the world. The Vatican looked on as its patiently constructed bridges crumbled under the double onslaught from Islamic fundamentalism and American insensitivity.

The errors were not only those of the United States. Consider the silence of moderate Islamists, weakened and intimidated. European and American conservatives have taken advantage of this reticence to push their claim that moderate Islam is nothing more than the fantasy of the West, eager for an interlocutor. "If it is true that not all Muslims are terrorists, it's equally true at this moment that most of the terrorists active in the world are Muslims," wrote Rahman al Rashid, editor of the television station Al Arabiya. The image of the Islamic world was "vile and shameful," commented Alberto Negri in the newspaper *Il Sole 24 Ore,* and moderate and progressive Muslims needed to mobilize, and start by dissociating themselves from Islamic terrorism. Those moderates are the target of Bush's campaign of democratizing the Greater Middle East. But King Abdullah of Jordan adds that intimidating "[t]he majority of moderate and reasonable Muslims is the real objective of the terrorists." The king told *Corriere della Sera* "[t]he entire Islamic

Pius VI and George Washington. They established the first diplomatic contacts between the Holy See and the United States. *(Portraits by P. Batoni, Galleria Sabauda, Turin, and Charles Peale, Historical Society of Pennsylvania, Philadelphia)*

Gaetano Bedini, "the cardinal who hunted heretics." In 1854 he ended his mission to the United States after being threatened by Italian exiles. *(Private collection, Monsignor Salvatore Delciuco, Viterbo)*

MORTE DEL PADRE UGO BASSI
Frate di Garibaldi fucilato dagli Austriaci in Bologna
il 15 Giugno 1849.

Eccomi presso a morte;
Il viver m'è assegnato:
Per troppo amar l'Italia,
Io venni condannato.

Il lamentarsi è vano;
Questo è l'estremo giorno
In cui cadrò di morte
Nell'orrido soggiorno.

    D'un sangue innocente
    Vendetta tremenda
    Dal Cielo discenda
    Sul crudo uccisor.

Tutto lasciar bisogna,
Il sol, le patrie mura,
Il Ciel sereno e limpido,
E andarne in sepoltura.

Cara e diletta Italia,
Di me non ti scordare,
L'ossa la morte mia
Il tuo destin cangiare!

    D'un sangue innocente ec.

Il piombo dell'Austriaco
Mi toglierà la vita,
E trepidante l'anima
Farà di qui partita;

Ma prima di raggiungere
La sempiterna gloria,
Voglio lasciare agli uomini
Di me questa memoria.

    D'un sangue innocente ec.

Speranza della patria,
Giovani entusiasmati,
Crescete e preparatevi
Ad esser soldati.

Alcun sul mio sepolcro
A lacrimar non venga;
Prima d'un pianto inutile
Questa memoria tenga.

    D'un sangue innocente ec.

Chi giace sotto terra
Non può resuscitare;
Bisogna amar l'Italia
Saperla vendicare.

Siate soldati intrepidi
Nell'ora del cimento,
E nella fredda fossa
Io dormirò contento.

    D'un sangue innocente ec.

Addio, gentile Italia,
Addio, fratelli, amici,
Cari parenti, addio...
Sarete un dì felici!

Chi fu la trista causa
Di mia spietata sorte?
Per quattro Giuda perfidi
Subisco questa morte!

    D'un sangue innocente ec.

Sia maledetto il barbaro
Impero tracotante!
D'orribile vendetta
L'ora non è distante!

Morir non mi dispiace,
Chè muoio per il Cielo,
Muoio per predicare
Di Cristo l'Evangelo.

    D'un sangue innocente ec.

Ma già la morte viene,
S'apre l'eterna via,
E prima di spirare
Voglio invocar Maria.

O benedetta Vergine,
Che sì pietosa sei,
Apri l'orecchio angelico
E accogli i voti miei!

    D'un sangue innocente ec.

Così parlò quell'essere
Pieno di patrio amore,
Già, già rapita l'anima
Nel bacio del Signore.

E quando il piombo austriaco
Del cor trovò la via,
Cadde sul suolo esanime,
Gridando: Italia mia!

    D'un sangue innocente ec.

O voi, che dell'intrepido
Invitto sacerdote
Udiste il fato misero
E le dolenti note,

Del generoso martire
Tenete il nome in core,
Se per l'Italia libera
Provate un santo amore.

    D'un sangue innocente
    Vendetta tremenda
    Dal Cielo discenda
    Sul crudo uccisor.

    FINE.

Firenze, Stamperia Salani, Via S. Niccolò 102. 1885 (1)

The execution of "Garibaldi's priest," for which Bedini was said to be responsible.

Ugo Bassi's friend Alessandro Gavazzi, the preacher who confronted Bedini in America, and Cardinal Francesco Satolli, the first apostolic delegate to the Catholic bishops of the United States, photographed in 1895. *(Osservatore Romano photo service, Vatican City)*

The Radio Priest, Charles Coughlin, delivering one of his anti–Roosevelt "sermons" in Cleveland in 1936. *(Bettman / Corbis / Contrasto)*

President Franklin D. Roosevelt delivering one of his historic radio speeches in Washington in June 1942. *(Mondadori Archives)*

Ku Klux Klan members filing into a Baptist church in Whistler, Alabama, in 1956. *(AP)*

Myron Taylor (second from left), Roosevelt's personal representative to the Vatican, with presidential adviser Harry Hopkins, prior to his audience with Pius XII on January 30, 1945. *(Franklin D. Roosevelt Presidential Library)*

Pope Pius XII with Monsignor Giovanni Battista Montini, the substitute secretary of state and the future Pope Paul VI. *(Olycom/Publifoto)*

Harold Tittman, the American diplomat who lived through the Second World War in the confines of the Vatican, and President Harry S. Truman in 1945. *(National Archives and Records Administration at College Park, Maryland* and *Corbis/Contrasto)*

Joseph Kennedy, John F. Kennedy's father.
(Mondadori archives)

Cardinal Francis Spellman in an American combat plane in Tokyo in 1955. *(Mondadori archives)*

Cardinal Francis Spellman, archbishop of New York, prays in St. Patrick's Cathedral. *(E.P.S./Mondadori archives)*

Alcide De Gasperi, the Italian prime minister, in his office in 1949. *(AP)*

Cardinal Spellman with Italian government minister Giulio Andreotti on November 28, 1962. *(Private collection)*

Spellman, "the cardinal of the cold war," visiting U.S. forces in Vietnam, December 19, 1965. *(Mondadori archives)*

Jacqueline Kennedy before her audience with Pope John XXIII at the Vatican on March 11, 1962. *(John F. Kennedy Library, Boston)*

Jacqueline Kennedy during her audience with Pope John XXIII at the Vatican on March 11, 1962. *(Bettman/Corbis/Contrasto)*

President John F. Kennedy visits Pope Paul VI on July 2, 1963. *(Bettman/Corbis/Contrasto)*

Pope John Paul II visiting Paris with, in the foreground, the controversial Archbishop Marcinkus, later implicated in the IOR–Banco Ambrosiano scandal. *(Fabian Cevallos/Corbis Sygma/Contrasto)*

Pope John Paul II and President Reagan meet in Rome on June 7, 1982.
(Bettman/Corbis/Contrasto)

President Reagan, Vatican Secretary of State Cardinal Agostino Casaroli (center), and Papal Nuncio to the United States Monsignor Pio Laghi in the Oval Office in 1983. The United States and the Holy See were about to exchange ambassadors for the first time.
(Official White House photo)

William Wilson, Washington's first ambassador to the Holy See, meets with President Reagan, Papal Nuncio Monsignor Pio Laghi, and Vice President George H. W. Bush at the White House.
(Official White House photo)

President George H.W. Bush and his wife, Barbara, on board Air Force One. Barbara Bush is flanked by Papal Nuncio Pio Laghi and Cardinal Law, archbishop of Boston.
(Official White House photo)

President Bill Clinton and Pope John Paul II in Denver, Colorado, on August 13, 1993.
(USV&WR/Mondadori archives)

President George W. Bush, Secretary of Defense Donald Rumsfeld, and National Security Adviser Condoleezza Rice at the Pentagon press conference announcing the offensive against Osama bin Laden on September 17, 2001, six days after 9/11.
(Reuters/Corbis/Contrasto)

President George W. Bush, his wife, Laura, and their daughter Barbara visit Pope John Paul II at Castel Gandolfo, the papal summer residence in the Alban Hills outside Rome, in July 2001. *(AGI/Mondadori)*

Pope John Paul II meets with Iraqi deputy prime minister Tariq Aziz on the eve of the U.S. invasion of Iraq. *(Olycom)*

Archbishop Jean-Louis Tauran, the Vatican's "minister of foreign affairs," with James Nicholson, the U.S. ambassador to the Holy See. *(Foto Quick)*

Cartoon by Giannelli published in *Corriere della Sera* on February 6, 2003, just before the Iraq war. *(Emilio Giannelli)*

November 18, 2003: Cardinal Camillo Ruini officiating at a funeral service for Italian soldiers killed in Nasiriyah, Iraq. *(Olycam)*

Secretary of State Colin Powell visiting Pope John Paul II, with Ambassador James Nicholson in the foreground. *(Osservatore Romano photo service, Vatican City)*

Kathleen McChesney, the chief investigator into the Catholic pedophile priest scandal. On her left is Archbishop Wilton Gregory, at the time president of the U.S. Conference of Catholic Bishops. *(Getty Images/Laura Ronchi)*

While Cardinal Law (left) celebrated a Requiem Mass for Pope John Paul II on April 11, 2005, Barbara Blaine, pedophile victim, protested in Saint Peter's Square, Rome. *(Alessandro Bianchi/Reuters and Corbis/Contrasto)*

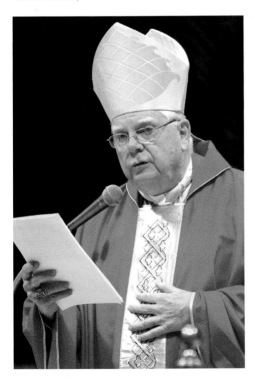

President George W. Bush, Laura Bush, George H. W. Bush, Bill Clinton, and Condoleezza Rice kneeling in Saint Peter's Basilica, with the body of Pope John Paul II lying in state. *(Osservatore Romano photo service, Vatican City)*

Jeb Bush, governor of Florida and brother of President George W. Bush, congratulates Pope Benedict XVI on his election. *(Getty Images / Laura Ronchi)*

President Bush and Francis Rooney (left), U.S. ambassador to the Holy See, meet with Vatican Secretary of State Cardinal Tarcisio Bertone (far right) in Rome on July 9, 2007. *(Osservatore Romano photo service, Vatican City)*

Pope Benedict XVI greets Mary Ann Glendon, U.S. ambassador to the Holy See, at her Diplomatic Credentials Ceremony on February 29, 2008. *(Osservatore Romano photo service, Vatican City)*

community must discredit these terrorists who use our religion . . . Those who commit criminal acts in the name of Islam are not Muslims. The problem is that the silent majority is always on the defensive." The Catholic Church, like moderate Islam, was also on the defensive as the cultural and strategic alienation between Europe and the United States of George W. Bush increased. Even after Bush's reelection in 2004, the president's first European tour promised more than it delivered in terms of improved relations. The United States saw itself as the strong, unchallenged empire of the West, using its military and economic muscle when necessary to reaffirm its hegemony. As for the Vatican, it felt like a moral outpost of a West in decline.

"The West enjoyed two centuries of unchallenged domination, but that is now coming to an end," Cardinal Ruini has said. "Now that the Western world is weakening a clash is always possible, and the challenge is to guide this evolution towards coexistence and collaboration, without any illusions about being able to stop it. It boils down to managing the end of Western hegemony so that the best of our civilization is accepted and made their own by non-Westerners." The Vatican prelate's realistic and somewhat resigned assessment is hardly likely to appeal to a United States convinced of its own strength, an America that Robert Kagan likens to a six-hundred-pound sumo wrestler who keeps pushing until his opponent falls. In contrast to a war in Iraq fought by an Anglophone alliance consisting of the United States, Britain, and Australia, presenting themselves as the sole defenders of democracy, the Church advances a different Western model. The Vatican offers a Western world that extends beyond Europe and the United States to Latin America and Russia on account of their Christian roots. The United States regards such roots as essential qualifications, but not enough.

BUSH'S GOOD SAMARITANS

IN THE WAKE of the American tanks and the marines, the Evangelicals also arrived in Iraq: Christian soldiers for Bush and Protestantism distributing American dollars, medicine, food, and religion. The man behind their mission was Franklin Graham, son of the Evangelical minister Billy Graham, and personal friend of the president. Graham's purpose was plainly stated. Christianity and Islam were as different as light from darkness, he declared. Islam "is a very evil and wicked religion," and for this reason the Iraqi people have to be converted. American humanitarian agencies in Amman and Baghdad collaborated with Graham's organization, Samaritan's Purse. "The way in which preachers have arrived here with the soldiers is not a good thing," complained the Catholic archbishop of Baghdad, Jean Sleiman, to the *Washington Post*. "They think they can convert Muslims, something Christians have not succeeded in doing for the past two thousand years." One community that found the proselytizing unacceptable was American Muslims. They saw it as a not particularly subtle form of cultural colonization. Moreover, Samaritan's Purse distributed money in the name of Christianity and democracy, an association of ideas that did not go down well among the Arabs.

The archbishop of Baghdad was proved right about proselytizing among the Muslims. Samaritan's Purse found little response to its efforts in the Islamic community, which, apart from being tightly closed, hated everything with an American flavor. So Samaritan's Purse shifted its attention to Iraq's Christian minority. "The bishop of Baghdad told me how these Protestants had arrived with the troops, and began to preach to other Christians," wrote the Egyptian Jesuit Samir Khalil Samir. "They had very effective techniques, and they often managed to win over followers who hoped they would get help in emigrating to the United States, or at the very least in receiving support in their daily life in Baghdad." The American missionaries used Arab-speaking preachers to win over the population. In the view of the Catholic Church the Americans were indeed spreading a form of colonial Christianity instead of taking into account the cultural and family traditions of the Arab world: they were not building bridges but Christian cathedrals surrounded by desert.

On December 3, 2004, the gradual process of corrosion in the relations between the Vatican and the United States was again noted by a senior Vatican prelate. This time it was Archbishop Lajolo, the Holy See's minister of foreign affairs, who noted that "the collateral damage from the war against terrorism includes a new Christianophobia in many parts of the world where the political strategy of some Western countries is wrongly seen as determined by Christianity." Ironically, Lajolo made his remarks at a meeting at the Gregorian University in Rome marking twenty years of American-Vatican relations.

Then on December 26, a tsunami cut a disastrous swathe through Indonesia and India, killing in its tidal wave about half a million people. Washington saw that a massive relief effort in the stricken area could repair some of the damage to America's image caused by the Iraq war, and the humanitarian face of the United States was immediately very much in evidence. The Bush administration poured medicine and relief teams into the area, and the president's own father was teamed with former President Bill Clinton to oversee the American aid effort. But in Indonesia, entire Muslim communities were reported to have refused help from Christian aid organizations, whether Catholic or Protestant—an example of the Christianophobia referred to by Archbishop Lajolo. One story told at the time involved the orphans of Banda Aceh, the area hardest hit. According to reports, the government in Jakarta initially accepted the offer of an Evangelical organization World Help to construct orphanages to house some of the thousands of children left without family in the wake of the disaster. The local Muslim community immediately protested that the Evangelical group had an ulterior motive—converting the children to Christianity—and an alarmed government withdrew its acceptance.

According to another version of the same story, World Help had published details on the project on its Web site, describing it as an opportunity to convert the children. The Web site said that thanks to the project, Banda Aceh—in normal times closed to foreigners and to the Gospel—had opened to preaching and converting the children. If the orphans could be placed with Christian children, that might be a base from which to reach the people of Banda Aceh. Nor was this an isolated case. The *New York Times* reported that Sri Lankan Buddhists were enraged when members of a Texas Evangelical congregation, the Antioch Community Church of Waco, tried to convert victims while at the same time giving humanitarian aid and money. The Catholic Relief Services called the episode "immoral." The bridge being built by America was perceived as a trap that could be exploited by Islamic fundamentalists. Everything that came from the rich, corrupt, Christian West was branded as dangerous and harmful. This was an echo of the "intoxication of the West" described by the Iranian intellectual Jalal

Al-e Ahmad in the 1960s: Islamism grew as a timely antidote to it. Now Bush's theology tended to confirm that danger from the West.

Because of the president's strong—and strongly expressed—religious convictions, and the fundamentalist rhetoric of some of his associates, there is the risk that Muslims will fail to distinguish between the reasons for the use of force against Iraq (with veiled threats to Syria and Iran) and the religious language that has been so frequently used in American speeches, commented the IISS review *Survival*. Such an approach was creating a growing value gap between the United States and its more secular European allies. When it comes to values, however, the Vatican is caught between its concern over the harm that a certain type of Christian patriotism exported by the United States can do to Vatican relations with the Islamic world, and the perhaps greater concern that American secularism will combine with European secularism against the Catholic faith.

THE LESS DAMAGING
PRESIDENT

THE VATICAN VERSUS KERRY

THE QUESTION THAT remains hard to answer is why did the Vatican of Pope John Paul II, after strongly opposing the Iraq war, defending the Palestinian cause and the importance of dialogue with Islam, pursuing a multilateral policy in international affairs, and condemning the death penalty, still show an obvious preference for George W. Bush over Democratic candidate John Kerry in the presidential election of 2004? Bush is Protestant, Kerry a Catholic; yet there was no doubt that the Vatican was satisfied with Bush's victory. Or was it with Kerry's defeat? The answer was partly that the American bishops were divided over Kerry. Quite a few had reservations about a liberal Catholic in the White House. For one thing, the senator from Massachusetts was not the model of Catholicism they favored (he was divorced, pro-choice, etc.). For another, and perhaps more important, they were concerned that as president Kerry would put the clock back and distance himself from Rome, just as Kennedy had done. This would have been unnecessary because in one respect the American electorate had progressed: there was no groundswell of animosity against Kerry as a Catholic. This time the rejection came from members of his own faith.

Inside the Vatican, senior prelates had registered favorably Bush's religious approach to politics, his emphasis on family values, his opposition to abortion, stem cell research, and same-sex marriage. It was their calculation that Bush would do less harm to the American Catholic Church than Kerry would. True, Kerry went to Mass on Sundays, but his position on a number of issues had raised the alarm. He had shown symptoms of the cultural relativism frequently denounced by Pope John Paul II as dangerous for the future of the Roman Church. There was also the fact that ever since President Reagan had established relations with the Holy See, the Vatican had had a closer connection with the Republican Party, and the Democrats were viewed in Rome with a certain suspicion. A large number of American Catholics had voted for Reagan.

The Vatican was convinced that having Kerry in the White House would be a source of embarrassment rather than an advantage. The Catholic label was no guarantee that there would be a change in the Iraq war: a Democratic administration would have little leeway to change that situation. The Vatican didn't expect much change in the cultural field—at least not much that the Church would either like or benefit from. On the contrary, Kerry's campaign platform made them suspicious. Writing in *America* magazine on the eve of the 2004 presidential election in the United States, George Weigel, the conservative theologian and biographer of Pope John Paul II, made the point that Catholicism and the GOP were not a natural fit: Republican libertarian views made Catholics uneasy because of their implications for the value of life; and the business sector that supports the party is not as concerned as it should be with social issues. However, the GOP election platform came closer to Catholic values than did the Democratic Party's platform, Weigel maintained. His point supported the Vatican view that of the two candidates Bush would cause fewer problems. The Democrats had become less trustworthy, and more dangerous than the Methodist George Bush, and the Vatican felt it had to defend itself from liberal ideas that were quite distant from Pope John Paul II's orthodoxy.

Interviewed about the same time in *Avvenire,* Weigel, reflecting the same orthodoxy, called Kerry a hostage to the anti-Christian environment. In Weigel's view, John F. Kennedy's old party had changed so profoundly that it could no longer expect the support of American Catholics. The first signs of change dated to 1972, Weigel maintained, when the Democrats began to be identified as "the abortion party." Their "yes" to abortion was a virus that had slowly but inexorably corroded the American Left. In addition, the Democrats had pushed the issue of euthanasia, and the party supports homosexual marriages. The Democrats tend to ignore the teaching of papal encyclicals, from *Cen-*

tesimus Annus to *Evangelium Vitae.* Senator Kerry had voted six times in favor of legislation allowing the barbarous practice of late-term abortion, for all intents and purposes a form of infanticide, Weigel told the Italian Catholic paper. Catholics began to realize that the Methodist president shared their values of freedom and a just society, as opposed to Kerry, whose "ignorance of the teachings of the Church is, to my mind, abysmal," Weigel added.

It was a view that shoved Kerry roughly to the margin, and it was hardly shared by all Catholic voters. But it drew a picture of a liberal Catholic candidate whose views had alienated many Catholics and driven them into the arms of a born-again Christian president. This split was helped by divisions within the American Catholic episcopate, still traumatized by the fallout from the sex scandals, and the views of pundits such as Weigel. Kerry's chances were also undermined by the fact that some priests agreed that he should be denied Communion as a divorced Catholic. If his own coreligionists wouldn't vote for him, then why should non-Catholics? (As it turned out, quite a number did.)

Behind the Democrats loomed the shadow that was even more of an irritant to the Vatican, and that was the shadow of Bill Clinton. "An abyss separated Clinton and Pope John Paul II," stated Paolo Mastrolilli, writing of the cultural and ethical gap between the Vatican and the Clinton White House. As president, Clinton had received the pope in St. Louis with a Polish greeting, "Sto lat I wiecej," or "May you live another hundred years," and in his address he had listed the rights of women as one of the important principles that needed to be reaffirmed. Mastrolilli writes: "In replying the pope recalled the historic Dred Scott decision which originated from Saint Louis, and which opened the way for the Civil War. In the pivotal 1857 Supreme Court decision African-Americans were deemed beyond the scope of constitutional protection. After enormous suffering—the pope went on—the situation was reversed, at least partially."

In his address, the pope stated, "American culture faces a similar time of trial today. Today, the conflict is between a culture that affirms and celebrates life, and a culture that seeks to declare entire groups of human beings—the unborn, the terminally ill, the handicapped, and others considered unuseful—to be outside the boundaries of legal protection."

The pope pleaded with America, the world leader, to affirm a culture of life. In order for these values to be sustained, the nation must continue to honor and revere the family as the basic unit of society.

Mastrolilli detects in the pope's reference to family what he called a "pull at (Clinton's) ears"; the pope's speech was a critique of capitalist materialism, which had intensified following the fall of the Berlin Wall and the end of the Communist empire. The pope also underlined deep doctrinal divergences between Rome and Washington, including their opposing views on the death penalty. In the years following the papal trip the Vatican continued to regard the Democratic Party as the principal exponent of this divergent vision. The Democrats supported the rainbow coalition that was perceived by many in the U.S. Catholic Church as the antithesis of Christian values. In their book *L'Altra America: Kerry e la Nuova Frontiera* (The other America: Kerry and the new frontier) Guido Moltedo and Marilisa Palumbo maintain that the Democratic Party had reached the point where anyone who was even moderately anti-abortion was neither respected nor listened to.

THE ZAPATERO SYNDROME

MEANWHILE IN EUROPE the papacy of John Paul II was experiencing setbacks. In 2004 the Holy See failed in its attempts to persuade the European Union to include in its new draft constitution a reference to the continent's Christian roots. More damaging was the string of secular challenges to the Church following the election in Spain of the Socialist leader Jose Luis Rodriguez Zapatero. There was the danger of contagion when a traditionally Catholic country such as Spain introduced "fast-track" divorce, within a two-month period by common consent. Another danger was the introduction of same-sex marriage, with same-sex couples able to adopt children. And yet a third was the decision that religious studies would no longer be obligatory. The secretary of the Spanish bishops conference, Archbishop Juan Antonio Martínez Camino, also accused the Spanish government of waging a campaign "that seems intended to prepare public opinion to accept euthanasia." All the changes were regarded as acts of war by Rome, which was fearful that the changes would spread to other European countries.

Spain, set on a course of abandoning its centuries-old Catholic roots and becoming "Hollandized" under Zapatero, was a nightmare for the Vatican. The prefect of the Congregation of the Doctrine of the Faith saw the changes in Spain as a disturbing consequence of a continent "condemned to decline." The prefect was Cardinal Joseph Ratzinger; on April 25, 2005, nineteen days after the death of Pope John Paul II, he would become pope as Benedict XVI.

On January 24, 2005, Pope John Paul received the Spanish hierarchy in Rome. Not surprisingly the pontiff used the occasion to give vent to his strong concern. Spain seemed to him to be heading toward dangerous ground. "New generations are growing up in an atmosphere of indifference toward religion, and ignorant of the Christian tradition," he told the Spanish bishops. The pope also noted that "young people are constantly exposed to the temptations of moral permissiveness." In the bishops' report, he saw, he said, "a concern for the very survival of the Church." Moral relativism was "infecting the social structure of the country." Without mentioning Zapatero, the pope said that "religious freedom is being threatened by fomenting disrespect of the clergy, and encouraging faith as a private matter, and opposing its expression in public."

It was a cry of alarm against what the pope regarded as restrictions on freedom of worship. It also helped to explain in retrospect the Vatican's almost public distaste for the Democratic candidate in the American race and his relativist culture: Rome feared a strong transatlantic united front with left-wing European parties—Social Democrat, Labour, Socialist, and formerly Communist. "It's undeniable that the Democrats are becoming like the left-wing European parties" and embracing progressive secularism, Weigel told *Avvenire*. The Vatican seemed clearly to have made a strategic decision to favor Bush. Following Bush's election, Bishop Rino Fisichella, auxiliary of Rome, expressed his satisfaction to the *Corriere della Sera* newspaper thus: "[The Americans] have chosen to vote for fundamental Western values: the central place of the family and of marriage, the sanctity of life, and the need for a democracy to combat terrorism. We must not forget that the Americans were also called upon to vote for a number of referendums on ethical issues: eleven states voted on the question of approving homosexual marriages, and the proposal was defeated in all eleven."

When Andreotti interviewed Colin Powell on relations between the Vatican and the United States, the (by then) former secretary of state replied, "Diplomatic relations with the Holy See are destined to play an increasingly important role. Many of today's main challenges are moral challenges. If you think of the fight against illegal human trafficking, of protecting freedom of worship wherever it is threatened, or of eliminating the scourge of HIV/AIDS, all of this must be faced with moral clarity and the ability to translate that clarity into action."

In the case of Terri Schiavo, the Florida woman who had been in a coma for fifteen years, the Vatican supported Bush's ultimately unsuccessful efforts to avoid the euthanasia decision. The alliance of the White House, American religious groups, and the Vatican, noted Vatican expert Sandro Magister, demonstrated the universality of certain moral issues. The common position of Bush and the pope amplified the case and forced it on the attention of the Democrats, who had still not regrouped following their election defeat. Schiavo was for them a real ethical-religious challenge, and Italian observers in the United States noted a rush toward the center, especially by Hillary Clinton. The parallel thinking between the Bush administration and the Vatican was more poignant because of Pope John Paul's weakness and immobility. The aged pontiff was close to death but still, despite the physical effort, insisting on making public appearances, determined to be a symbol of the sanctity of life. The former ambassador and commentator Sergio Romano found inescapable irony in the fact that many Americans "can support the death sentence and at the same time Terri Schiavo's right to live. They do not consider these two positions contradictory because they have the same religious motivation. They believe that capital punishment is justified in the Bible, and that Terri Schiavo's life is a divine gift that no one has a right to end."

These shared values between Bush's Washington and Wojtyla's Rome took precedence over ecclesiastical concern over the war in Iraq. "The American bishops had been critical of Bush's decision to attack Iraq, but they were subsequently more opposed to John Kerry's liberal politics, which they felt could bring back the permissiveness of the Clinton era," wrote Luigi Accattoli. The Vatican had indeed become obsessed that a kind of "international permissiveness" extending from the United States to Europe would receive a significant boost if a

Democrat were in the White House. In their view, a Democratic president could have launched a series of laws that would dissolve Christian ethics. "Christianophobia" was not exclusive to the Islamic world: it was growing in the West as well, both in the United States and in Europe, the Vatican assumed. The Jesuits had for some time warned that "dogmatic secularism" was putting pressure on Christianity.

Drew Christiansen, the Jesuit editor of the community's magazine *America,* thinks it unusual that the draft of the new European Union constitution should contain no reference to Europe's religious identity, and specifically its Christian identity. Speaking at a United Nations seminar in Barcelona, he attributed this omission to a rationalist aversion toward religion, which is regarded as irrational, and to a lay tradition that believes that there is no place for institutional religion in public life. (In fact, the preamble of the constitution written by the president of the drafting committee, former French president Valéry Giscard d'Estaing, pays tribute to the Age of Reason in Europe.) A similar attitude prevails in the United States, Christiansen said, where the exclusion of believers from politics in democratic societies was an insidious development that needed to be watched. Western dogmatic secularism must not be ignored as a source of Christianophobia. This concern helped explain the attitude of the American Catholic Church hierarchy toward Kerry and the Democrats. The situation of Kennedy's day was in effect reversed. It was not a case of playing down one's religious beliefs, but of defending them against a pathological secularism.

FAITH IS A PRIVATE ISSUE

IN THE 2004 presidential elections the objective of Leonard Leo, who was responsible for the GOP's relations with Catholics, was to persuade them to vote for Bush in even greater numbers than they had backed Reagan twenty years earlier. Private polls had shown that Kerry, the Catholic candidate, was trailing the born-again Christian, George Bush. In 2004 America's Roman Catholics numbered almost 67 million and made up 25 percent of the population. Kerry was not helped by the fact that he was from the city at the center of the pedophile priest scandal. As a senator he knew that many Catholics were against mixing politics and religion. In reality, Kerry spoke very little about his religious faith during the campaign. He wore a small cross round his neck and carried a Bible and a rosary—which was admirable in a Catholic but failed to satisfy Americans seeking firm moral answers. A month before the November 2 election, the *New York Times* warned that Kerry could pay the price for his silence in matters of religion. On stem cell research he had argued in favor of reason and scientific research and against what he called Bush's "ideology of the extreme right." The *Times* noted that in New Hampshire Kerry never uttered the words "religion," "prayer," "conscience," or "God." The paradox of 2004 was that his ostentatious secularism was likely to backfire. The polls began to show that three-quarters of the American public wanted a president "with a strong religious faith." In Ohio, one of the swing states, Kerry was greeted with placards saying VOTE THE BIBLE and CHRISTIANS FOR KERRY. John Green, a professor at the University of Akron, told reporters there were Catholics and moderate Protestants who were not part of the Religious Right, but who still took their faith seriously and were "ready to answer the call."

But Kerry had spoken so rarely about his religious affiliation, let alone his beliefs, that a Pew Research Center poll discovered that only 43 percent of American Catholics even knew that he too was a Catholic. Preelection polls showed Bush leading among Catholics with 45 percent compared to 33 percent for Kerry; and with 63 percent among white Protestants, versus 30 percent for Kerry. The contrast with Kennedy's numbers was striking: the country's first—and so far, only—Catholic president had polled 78 percent among Catholics. Kerry paid the price at the polls for his conviction that a candidate's religious beliefs were "a private matter," and his party paid the price for giving mixed signals on the moral interrogatives that Bush had cleverly made election issues.

KERRY: "A SORT OF CATHOLIC"

THE VATICAN'S MARKED lack of enthusiasm for the Catholic candidate didn't change when, toward the end of the campaign, Kerry began to quote the Scriptures, and reminisce about his days as an altar boy.

Bush remained the decided favorite. Kerry "seems to me to be a Catholic of sorts, considering his position on abortion," was the dry comment of the archbishop of Genoa, Cardinal Tarcisio Bertone, who would go on to be named the Vatican's secretary of state at the end of 2005. Bertone further added, "He doesn't strike me as a consistent Catholic; I don't know that I would actually call him a Catholic." Though the Vatican was officially neutral in the election, the coolness toward Kerry was there for all to see. The impression was that his apparent lack of firmness on moral issues was of greater concern to the Vatican than the unilateralism of the neoconservatives and their theories on preventive war. In Rome, the Church hierarchy realized that they had a problem with Kerry, and perhaps feared a scandal because of his position on abortion, a prelate told *Time* magazine. This time the Vatican was distancing itself from the Catholic candidate, unlike during the John F. Kennedy campaign, when things were the other way around.

A CAMPAIGN AUDIENCE

PRESIDENT BUSH'S STRATEGY was to make his religious convictions a strong campaign weapon, and the White House pressed the Vatican for an audience with the pope as an important set piece of this strategy. The meeting on June 4, 2004, was not easy to arrange. The pope was due to leave for Switzerland to attend a youth congress, and Vatican officials told Ambassador Nicholson that there was no available slot with the pope during the time that Bush would be in Rome. There may also have been some initial reluctance to agree to a meeting while American-occupied Iraq seethed with continuing violence. But that was precisely why Bush wanted his one-on-one with Pope John Paul. The intention was to show 67 million American Catholics that the Vatican might criticize the war and the Iraqi occupation, and condemn the torture of prisoners at Abu Ghraib, but there was still understanding between the Bush administration and the Vatican on human values. As one senior Vatican diplomat who favored the audience put it, "The war is only one chapter in an alliance and a friendship that continues." Bush got his wish, but only after taking the highly unusual step for a president of altering his own schedule to arrive in Rome half a day earlier than had been planned. According to Cardinal Pio Laghi, the White House had bombarded the Vatican with messages requesting a meeting, and Bush had "changed his plans to make the meeting possible."

From a campaign point of view the meeting paid off, even if the president had to sit through a papal rebuke about "deplorable events" that had "troubled the conscience of all." But the pope also referred to the twenty years of diplomatic relations between the Vatican and the United States, and expressed his "esteem" for "the United States representatives to the Holy See," praising their "competence and sensitiveness" in developing bilateral relations.

It was left to the Vatican spokesman, Joachín Navarro-Valls, to state at a subsequent press conference that despite reports of coolness between the pontiff and the president their personal relationship was as good as ever. At the audience, Bush gave John Paul II the American Medal of Freedom, and there was, according to Navarro-Valls, "a convergence of views on the need to involve the United Nations in the normalization process in Iraq." The pope also thanked Bush "for what the president and his administration were doing to defend the family and to promote life," the spokesman said. It was the Vatican's Good Housekeeping seal of approval for Bush's efforts in defense of religion and fighting abortion. Bush's calculation that an audience with the pope would help sway millions of Catholic voters would prove right. The White House had believed that having the support of the pope's moral authority would offset the recriminations and criticisms for the Abu Ghraib debacle, which had come to light five months before the presidential elections.

There was, however, one of those typical incidents that overzealous presidential security agents have a tendency to provoke when traveling abroad. An Associated Press photographer waiting to cover the president's arrival in the Vatican was asked to leave—apparently not too gently—by Secret Service agents. The photographer, Massimo Sambucetti, stood his ground, appealing to a senior officer of the Vatican Swiss Guard, who told the Secret Service they were in his jurisdiction, and he overrode their request.

"BUSH HAS UNITED PROTESTANTS AND CATHOLICS"

GEORGE W. BUSH was the champion of a religious, aggressive majority determined to impose its principles on the federal government, and if necessary the entire world. The fact that as the elections approached, the White House was considering the nomination of a Supreme Court justice, signified that Bush would have an immediate impact on the United States in every aspect from its way of life to its culture. Bush had emerged as a religious as well as a political leader, wrote Dean L. Murphy in the *New York Times.* He was not afraid to talk of God, responsibility, duty, and service; he was not embarrassed to declare that "this country was founded on religious faith," explained Jennifer Granholm, the governor of Michigan. *Avvenire* called him the president who would reunite America.

"The foundations of our civilization" were at stake in the election, wrote Michael Novak in *Avvenire.* In California, despite the presence of a moderate Republican governor in Arnold Schwarzenegger, a stem cell research referendum received a majority vote, but that was the exception that proved the rule, argued Novak. He claimed, "California is the most Mediterranean state, the most pagan, and the least religious, a place where life is not taken too seriously. So it is not surprising that the strong antilife campaign made an impact." But in the rest of the country "the common people" had beaten and humiliated "the establishment," according to Novak, who considered "the people" more religious than their leaders.

Kerry's campaign team blamed their lack of success on a platform that voters found too liberal. They said the Democrats had not known how to speak to the nation, but it was an upset, not a setback. Whatever it was, the failure was noted by the Italian bishops' conference with malicious satisfaction.

Navarro-Valls said the Vatican didn't comment on the results of foreign elections, but behind the formal position of neutrality the Holy See was pleased with the result. On the morning after the election, Ambassador Nicholson hosted an "election breakfast" at the Hotel de Russie in Rome. The satisfaction of the American priests residing in the Vatican verged on enthusiasm for Bush's unfolding victory as the results came in—perhaps not as a victory for Bush as such but for the less flawed of two flawed alternatives. Former Italian Prime Minister Giuliano Amato called Bush's victory the "reaffirmation of a profoundly religious America. A biblical America rooted more in Protestantism than in Catholic ecumenism," and owing something to the traditional militantism of a Mel Gibson, and his film *The Passion of the Christ,* powerful, rough hewn, without the subtleties and the emphasis on forgiveness of religion in the Old Europe.

On February 7, 2005, Condoleezza Rice, by this time secretary of state, visited the Vatican. Her meeting was with her counterpart, Cardinal Angelo Sodano: Pope John Paul was in the Gemelli Clinic being treated for complications following a severe case of influenza. "The Bush administration believes that it owes a great debt to the Holy Father," wrote *La Stampa* commentator Lucia Annunziata. "The President of the United States has visited the pope four times in the past—a record in Vatican-American relations." Rice's mission in Rome was to discuss "values and new roles" that were emerging for the "two heavenly empires," according to Annunziata. Sodano gave the U.S. secretary of state an inscribed medal recalling Europe's Christian roots—a historical reality that the European Union had refused to acknowledge in the draft of its new constitution. The cardinal said smilingly that there was no need to emphasize the Christian roots of the United States. The nomination of John Roberts, a conservative Catholic, as chief justice of the Supreme Court on September 5, 2005, seemed like such a confirmation in itself. That brought the number of Catholic justices in the Supreme Court to four: they would soon become five with the appointment of Associate Justice Joseph Alito—surely another sign of the convergence between Rome and Bush's Washington, which had risen above disagreements over the Iraq war and the differences between Protestants and Catholics, and differing views of the Islamic world to create a communion, a meeting of the minds that was almost instinctive. Both governments, for example, shared a common dislike of Zapatero's Socialist government in Spain, the White House because of Zapatero's decision to withdraw Spanish forces from Iraq, and the Holy See because of the Spanish government's attack on family values and the right to life.

This meeting of minds was the subject of a speech on February 11, 2005, by Cardinal Ruini, who said that the American concept of "civil religion" should serve as a model for Europe. "It seems better able to guarantee the moral foundations and a common vision of the world," he said. For the Americans, "the promotion of democracy becomes a moral imperative in harmony with religious faith." The American model, wrote the radical commentator Giuseppe di Leo, is in complete contrast to "European secularism, particularly as reflected in recent decisions by the Zapatero government." In America the separation of church and state "safeguards religion from state interference"; but in Europe that same separation wishes to "safeguard politics from religious interference." The Vatican, di Leo goes on, seemed persuaded that it needed an alliance with the tough, heroic, self-sufficient American empire to advance its own values, so that the latter would use its military might in the name of Christianity. For its part, the United States hoped to use the Holy See as a kind of parallel United Nations, instead of the real United Nations, which has been considered anti-American.

On April 7, 2005, Bush—in Rome for the conclave to elect a successor to Pope John Paul II—would tell the American cardinals that on such issues as development, relief, and human rights, he trusted Vatican diplomacy more than that of the United Nations. But again, here was an example of how Washington and Rome might share common objectives but could differ over methods. The Church could not and had no desire to weaken the heart of multilateralism, even though the Vatican had been among those calling for United Nations reform.

In any case, Bush seemed to have succeeded in doing what no other president had done: he had united Protestants and Catholics. But even this extraordinary achievement was seen as a mixed blessing by the Vatican because Rome can appear to play a secondary role to a United States that is not only powerful but profoundly religious, and also because of the role that Christian fundamentalism plays in American religiosity. In the past, the Vatican has tried to keep Christian fundamentalism at a distance. The funeral of Pope John Paul II underlined this paradox.

THREE PRESIDENTS
IN SAINT PETER'S SQUARE

A STRATEGIC MOURNING

THE CARDINAL WAS pleasantly surprised. "The President of the United States has ordered a longer period of mourning than in Italy," he said. It was April 2, 2005, Pope John Paul II had been dead just a few hours, and the Vatican had evidence of something senior prelates had long suspected, but now saw in practice: presidents of the United States no longer sent regrets to ceremonies organized by the Holy See.

For the first time, an American president was flying to Rome to be present at the funeral of a pope. In addition, a presidential order had closed all federal offices on the day of the pope's burial, a tribute that had been decided upon earlier, when the pope's condition worsened. President Bush had even appeared on television with his wife, Laura, to express his admiration of the Polish pope, and his gratitude for John Paul II's efforts for world peace.

America's reaction at the institutional level to the pope's death made clear that twenty-six years of Pope John Paul II had weakened, if not cancelled, anti-Catholic prejudice. U.S. presidents were ready to pay fitting tribute to Pope John Paul II, the champion of anticommunism and peace; and that fitting tribute was highlighted by the presence of the president at the funeral. It was a development of epochal proportions. Never before had a president of the United States braved a symbolic lynching by anti-papist sentiment to attend either the election or the funeral of a Roman pontiff. The presence of George Bush, Secretary of State Condoleezza Rice, and two former presidents, George H. W. Bush and Bill Clinton, was seen as more than a diplomatic salute. It was a message to the Holy See, the Catholic world, and the international community that the United States had reassessed upward the importance of the Vatican to American interests.

The high-profile presence was all the more striking compared to the distinguished but low-key official delegations that had been seen at previous funerals. President Jimmy Carter's wife, Rosalynn, headed the group at Pope Paul VI's burial, and then vice president Lyndon B. Johnson represented John F. Kennedy at the funeral of Pope John XXIII. Yet there on April 7, 2005, was the leader of the free world and his two immediate predecessors. It would have been three, but there was no room for former President Jimmy Carter on Air Force One, or at least that was the official story.

THREE PRESIDENTS AND A FUNERAL

THE IMAGE OF the president, his secretary of state, and two former presidents on their knees in front of the dead pontiff in Saint Peter's Basilica provoked no protests back home in the United States. The three leaders spanning five administrations had had their differences with Pope John Paul II over a succession of American military engagements—the first Iraq war, the United States offensive against Slobodan Milosevic's Serbia, and the second conflict against Saddam Hussein that had started two years earlier. The high-level pilgrimage was also seen as a grateful acknowledgment that even in the worst moments of tension with the White House Pope John Paul II had never severed ties with Washington. On the contrary, the pope had provided a kind of moral cover, first when the United States found itself virtually isolated internationally in the aftermath of the launching of the second Iraq war, and again following the reelection of George W. Bush in the 2004 presidential elections.

But the administration's tribute—the flags at half-mast on official buildings, the praise for the dead pope's political as well as moral and ethical legacy—was not solely a genuflection to a historic relationship that was now finished. It was that too, of course, but it also reflected a continuing investment by Bush's America in an alliance with the Holy See, a quality leap in political and diplomatic relations. The Bush administration possibly believed that with the new pontificate there would likely continue to be a meeting of minds on the sanctity of life, abortion, euthanasia, same-sex marriage, and that consensus would compensate for any divergences over Washington's neoconservative unilateralism.

Bill Clinton spoke of the late pope's "mixed legacy," but then Clinton was out of office, and in any case he answered to a different constituency. Bush seemed prepared not to pay heed to the fact that, as the historian Andrea Riccardi put it, "The Catholic Church, instinctively, has never liked empires . . . In reality, the Church considers itself an empire, not in the 'imperial' sense, but in the way Pius XII once explained it, namely in being at home among all people and in not being absorbed by any civilization."

IRAN ACCUSES BUSH OF INFLUENCING THE CONCLAVE

THEREIN LURKED THE hint of fragility in the relationship between the parallel empires. But for the moment, the closeness of the Vatican to Washington was so noticeable that in the days leading up to the conclave the Iranian news agency ISNA alleged that "the large delegation of American leaders in Rome wants to influence the choice of the next papal election . . . Bush's meeting in Rome with the eleven American cardinals on the eve of the pope's funeral gave the president a chance to discuss their strategy in the conclave." The claim was both malicious and wrong, but the Iranians were not the only ones to regard the unusually high level of the American delegation with suspicion. For some Europeans, the timing of the president's meeting with the prelates of the parallel empire on the eve of the papal election was either significant or inappropriate.

But which was it? American intelligence analysts had been thinking about the post-Wojtyla era for some time before the pope's death, and there is no doubt that the White House had its own preferred scenario for how the election of the new pope *should* play out. On December 9, 2004, FBI director Robert Mueller had visited the Vatican, a reminder of the decades-long history of contacts between Rome and the American intelligence and security services; and Bush's meeting with the American cardinals at U.S. Ambassador Mel Sembler's residence, Villa Taverna in the city's Parioli district, fit nicely into this perception of secret contacts. But other than in the James Bond/Godfather context, the idea of Bush trying to influence the vote was a nonstarter. "Bush attended the funeral to pay tribute to Pope John Paul II, and also because he knew the electoral importance of the U.S. Catholic community, and his meeting at the embassy was more his idea than the cardinals'," Thomas Reese, the Jesuit from California who was then editor of *America,* said at the time of the conclave. "It is rumored that the administration did not favor a South American pope, but I'm convinced that the American cardinals will ignore that—if for no other reason than to demonstrate their independence from the White House."

Bush was said to be more certain of the pope he didn't want than the one he did. In his daily diary of the conclave published in *La Repubblica,* Giulio Anselmi reported that

the Spanish daily *La Razon de Madrid* claims that the CIA is trying to influence the electors to vote for the African Cardinal (Francis) Arinze so as to avoid a European pope. Bush wants above all to block any Latin American. The White House would prefer an Italian as the most likely to guarantee a pro-Western papacy; and in this respect the Americans favor (Camillo) Ruini or (Angelo) Scola.

If this was hearsay, there was a widespread belief inside the Bush administration that a pope from Latin America—based on what was known of the likelier candidates—would not be friendly to American multinationals, to capitalism, and to United States interests in general. "There was concern that the Conclave might elect someone hostile to globalism and a free economy," recalled Edward Luttwak of the Center for Strategic and International Studies in Washington. "With Ratzinger, this danger at least has been averted."

On that point the American cardinals needed no convincing. Virtually every one of them was said to have been for Ruini or Ratzinger. The election of the German cardinal testified to a new alliance between conservative Catholics and the American Evangelical Right. Priests such as Don Luigi Giussani, founder of the movement Communion and Liberation, saw the United States as "a contemporary Rome that has the same attraction for Christians as ancient Rome." According to Monsignor Lorenzo Albacete, Communion and Liberation's representative in the United States, "He (Giussani) told me: The United States is a country of ideals, and they are ideals that create fertile ground for the Gospel."

THE CUBE, THE CATHEDRAL, AND THE TRILATERAL

"IF CATHOLICS HAD voted for 'their' candidate, the Catholic John Kerry would now be president. Instead they voted for the Methodist George Bush, believing that he and not their fellow Catholic would best defend the values they believed in." Tom Foley, former Democratic Speaker of the House of Representatives, made this point at a meeting of the Trilateral Commission in Washington just as the cardinals in Rome were gathering to vote for Cardinal Ratzinger as successor to Pope John Paul II. The topic under discussion at this club of distinguished politicians, intellectuals, and industrialists, founded by mega banker David Rockefeller and dedicated to protecting Western values, was the relationship between faith and American politics. It turned out that the alliance of cardinals that elected Ratzinger was thinking along the same lines. "There exists in the world, and particularly in the United States, a movement of Christian renewal that exists outside the framework of specific churches and creates a movement that has to be taken into account," says Cardinal Ruini, president of the Italian bishops' conference and one of Ratzinger's leading backers in the election.

This development, in the cardinal's view, is what has cemented the Vatican under Pope John Paul II first, and continues to do so now under Benedict XVI, and George Bush's America—an America that the cardinal regards as a "model" that responds to "the demand for firm teaching and strong values."

In a long analysis on Pope Benedict and the American neocons published in the French newspaper *Le Monde,* Henri Tincq recalled that the Ratzinger-as-pope scenario first surfaced in the United States at the end of 2004. Tincq does not see this connection as the continuation of the holy alliance between Ronald Reagan and Pope John Paul II of twenty years earlier, but as a result of "a common, pessimistic assessment of the decline of moral values in the West, and the rise of modern laicism with which no compromise is possible." There was no American pressure on the Roman conclave, Tincq wrote. Cardinal Ratzinger's election was the result of "this rejection of any compromise with modernity." Six months earlier, Cardinal Ratzinger, in an interview with *La Repubblica,* had voiced his concern about "laicism transformed into an ideology, which is imposed through politics and which does not give public space to the Catholic or Christian vision."

For Tincq, Ratzinger's election confirmed the new link between "Catholic conservatives and Protestant fundamentalists" over moral values—not coincidentally a key factor in Bush's reelection. The president himself acknowledged the connection at a Catholic prayer breakfast in Washington three days after Pope Benedict's election. Catholics and non-Catholics alike, the president said, should be thankful for the man who sits on the throne of Peter and who speaks with approval of the American model of freedom, which has its roots in moral conviction. Then followed a reference to cultural relativism, one of the new pope's most frequently voiced concerns, and an expression of presidential concern over its prevalence in Europe.

A recent book by George Weigel, who is in the front rank of the so-called theo-conservatives along with Robert Bork and Richard John Neuhaus, is *The Cube and the Cathedral: Europe, America and Politics without God,* in which the cube is La Grande Arche de la Défense, and the cathedral is Notre Dame, both in Paris. The book explores Europe's inability to appreciate its Christian roots. The ultramodern arch stands for Europe's secular humanism and rampant "Christianophobia"; the stunning Gothic cathedral represents the transcendent. The Vatican "cathedral" joined forces with the American "sword" against the "cube," a union forged by Christianity, which incidentally is increasingly the preferred term over Catholicism. France is seen as the cultural core of an indifferent and laicist "Christianophobic" Europe. From the Vatican, Pope Benedict XVI is the man who will "place the emphasis on the neo-conversion of Europe," in Weigel's words. Benedict is "the radical conservative who will surprise you," according to the theologian Michael Novak writing in the Paris *International Herald Tribune.* Novak calls Pope Benedict XVI the right man to fight the war of values in the new millennium.

The presence in Saint Peter's of the top echelon of American leadership was not remarkable to the Roman Curia. "No surprise to me: it was natural," said Ruini at the time. It was the first papal funeral since the death of John Paul I twenty-six years earlier. Before, that is, full diplomatic relations were established between Washington and the Vatican.

ROUGH START FOR THE NEW PONTIFF

MEANWHILE, THE PEDOPHILE priest scandal that had proved seismic for the American Catholic Church on the eve of the Iraq war resurfaced like a wound suddenly reopening when the Vatican assigned Cardinal Bernard Law, latterly of Boston, to officiate at one of the Requiem Masses for Pope John Paul II. In 2004 an angry media campaign had forced Law to resign as archbishop of Boston, and he had gone underground in one of the less publicly well-lit recesses of the Vatican bureaucracy. His archdiocese was still coping with the sordid backwash of his legacy, a huge financial burden and the emotional fallout of the scandal. What might be called Law's boil, in other words, still festered. Thus the American press reacted with renewed anger to his temporary reemergence, blinking, into the limelight.

"Do you think Cardinal Law could actually become pope?" CNN correspondent Jonathan Mann asked Jesuit Father Reese in an interview, without a trace of irony. Not a chance, the Jesuit replied, with a thin, grim smile, perhaps because he was thinking that as a cardinal elector Law was also a candidate, and more unthinkable things had happened in papal elections. There was even a small protest demonstration outside the church where Law celebrated Mass. Barbara Blaine of Chicago and Barbara Dorris of St. Louis were interviewed on American television with the dome of Saint Peter's Basilica as their backdrop. The Vatican, they charged, was "putting salt on an open wound."

There was another reason that Benedict's election had revived the scandal. The press—and particularly the American press—recalled the case of Marcial Maciel Degollado, the Mexican priest who founded the ultraconservative religious order the Legion of Christ. In 1999 Degollado was accused of sexual abuse by eight of his former students (Degollado was by then in his eighties). The case came before Cardinal Ratzinger, then prefect of the Congregation for the Doctrine of the Faith (which some Vatican old-timers still refer to by its historic title as the Holy Office). According to reports he effectively shelved it. But in 2004 he quietly reopened the investigation and sent an investigator to Mexico City to interview Degollado's accusers. Still no immediate action was taken against Degollado, who in any case voluntarily left his post in 2006, following the Vatican's suggestion that he retire to a life of prayer and repentance, and died in January 2008. At the time of Ratzinger's election, however, the new pope's liberal critics cited the case as the shape of things to come on ecclesiastical cases of sex abuse: a failure by the central government of the Church to tackle the scandal and its root causes. Disillusioned progressive American Catholics saw Pope Benedict XVI as a second Wojtyla, and his pontificate as an extension of the Polish pope's narrow, unbending grip on the Catholic world.

If the neoconservatives saw Ratzinger as one of their own, the liberal view was summed up by E. J. Dionne of the *Washington Post* for whom the new pope was a "brilliant and determined" intellectual. Like many neoconservatives in the United States, Dionne had developed a distrust for the Left following "the student protests of the sixties." The pope's cultural approach struck a responsive chord with religious conservatives, even outside the Catholic ranks. The limits of the pope's appeal emerged in a Gallup poll taken in the immediate aftermath of the conclave. Of the 616 American Catholics polled, three-quarters said that in resolving moral issues they relied on the dictates of their own conscience rather than on what the new pope said; only 31 percent declared themselves satisfied with the outcome of the conclave.

Concerned at the profound rift in the Catholic community, the American cardinals tried to counter the media image of a grim pope with assurances that he was not an enemy of modernity. Archbishop Francis George of Chicago said he was sure that Pope Benedict XVI would strengthen the new rules introduced to guard against sexual abuse by priests; his words would prove prophetic.

In July 2005 the pope pronounced the Harry Potter books "a subtle seduction that corrupts young Christians." To many, branding J. K. Rowling's fantasy novels as anti-Christian seemed a bit far-fetched. But the pope also had his defenders. Ernesto Galli della Loggia called him the champion of "a different modernity" in which he still wants to "breathe the past and its values." Conservative media such as the *Washington Times* saw the election as confirmation that "the pendulum of the Church" was swinging to the right. The left-leaning Spanish daily *El País* defined the new pope as "neither a fundamentalist, nor an integralist, but simply a modern reactionary."

Reaction among Muslims was not enthusiastic, and became less so as the new pope's views took shape before the public. On June 20—that is, more than two months after the conclave—the International Islamic Forum for Dialogue complained that Benedict XVI "leaned too far in favor of the Jews." Oriana Fallaci, a writer noted for her hostility toward Islam, saw the papal tilt as a good thing. She felt "less alone when she read Ratzinger's books," she said—in contrast to Wojtyla who was "too soft when it came to the Islamic world."

A NEW RATZINGER "MADE IN CALIFORNIA"

THE VIEW—apprehension in some quarters, reassurance in others—that Pope Benedict XVI's church would remain steady on its current conservative course was reinforced on May 13, when Bishop William Joseph Levada, then the sixty-nine-year-old bishop of San Francisco, was named to the pope's former post as prefect of the Congregation for the Doctrine of the Faith. Levada is a prelate with a gentle manner, but he is well known for his hard-line approach to the American gay liberation movement. In 2000, the Jubilee Year, he tried hard to persuade the Vatican Secretary of State Cardinal Angelo Sodano to force the cancellation of a Gay Pride parade authorized by the city of Rome. To emphasize his point he sent Sodano a videotape of the more exhibitionist and provocative scenes from a similar march in San Francisco. It showed demonstrators satirically—and scantily—costumed as nuns and even as the pope. "You don't know what you're in for," Levada pleaded with Vatican officials. "Stop this before it's too late." *Time* magazine on May 23, 2005, called Levada a practical rather than academic theologian, and someone who mixes diplomacy with his conservatism. But Levada bristles at being described as a conservative. According to *Time,* he dislikes labels altogether. "Every time they try to label me they use secular terms—conservative and liberal—it's not easy for American society to understand the Church."

Still the American episcopate was pleased that the pope had reached across the Atlantic to pick an American for this powerful post in the Vatican Curia. "An American had never filled this post, and certainly not an American from the West Coast," observed Gian Guido Vecchi. Levada, the son of Irish and Portuguese immigrants, reflected the old and new patterns of Catholic immigration in the United States. "America today is undergoing a double osmosis," observes Robert Moynihan, editor of the publication *Inside the Vatican*. "Protestantism is penetrating Latin America financed by private money but with the backing of the United States government. But in the United States Catholicism is growing mainly because of immigrants from Honduras and Mexico. So South America is becoming more Protestant and the United States more Catholic."

But what landed Levada his curial plum was not his ethnic background but the orthodoxy he shares with both the former pontiff and the reigning pontiff. He was a member of the small group that shaped the new catechism; as bishop of Portland, Oregon, he was a strong opponent of euthanasia, even as Oregon became the first state to legalize it; and finally, he made no secret of his hostility toward John Kerry, the "liberal" Catholic presidential candidate. Another important credential was his appointment to the commission established in the wake of the sex abuse turmoil to restore the credibility of the American bishops. In short, he is shaped in the mold of Wojtyla and Ratzinger—and loyally ready to defend his new pope from the derisive label of "God's rottweiler." Levada's reply: "If he's a rottweiler, I'm a cocker spaniel."

But the jokes on Ratzinger's German origin didn't stop, and not all were as good-natured: some plumbed the depths of a residual malice. The British tabloid press, in particular, had a field day with the new pope's teenage membership in the Hitler Youth. The London *Sun*: "From Hitler Youth to PAPA RATZI" to rhyme with "Nazi." As the former head of the Congregation for the Doctrine of the Faith, Ratzinger was also inevitably cast as the Vatican's doctrinal "hard man." And some of the developments in the immediate aftermath of his election did nothing to dispel the skepticism of liberal Catholics. One instance was the departure of Father Reese from the editorship of *America*. Reese had written an editorial on Pope Benedict XVI's appointment that was generally favorable, calling him "Pope John Paul II's closest theological adviser." Reese noted the new pontiff's cultural and moral stature. But the editorial also voiced doubt that the citizens of the new Europe would respond to a Church that distanced itself from a confused and sometimes corrupt culture to preserve the intrinsic purity of a sacred relic. The best hope, he said, was that the Holy Ghost would produce a miracle to break the "stereotypes of the past." To the disappointment of progressive American Catholics, Reese left his post a few days after Pope Benedict XVI's election. Officially, he had resigned following pressure from some American bishops who objected to his nonconformist views. But the rumor was that the objections had originated from the office of the Congregation for the Doctrine of the Faith in March 2005, when Cardinal Ratzinger was still its head.

"THE VATICAN'S ANSWER TO DICK CHENEY"

DURING THE CONCLAVE, Reese was in Rome, seemingly indifferent to the gathering storm. He lived in a room in the Jesuit "headquarters" across from Saint Peter's Square, which also hosted several cardinals summoned to Rome to elect the new pope, including fellow Jesuit Carlo Maria Martini, the former archbishop of Milan, who had come from his retirement home in Jerusalem. Always a regular on American television because he was so outspoken, Reese was a fixture in the blanket network coverage of the papal succession. On April 11, in one of the musty and vaguely mysterious receiving rooms of the Jesuit house, Reese offered his candid view of Vatican-American relations. He expressed sincere, levelheaded support for Pope John Paul II who, he said laughingly, with the exception of his opposition to abortion and same-sex marriage, was too liberal to have ever won an election in the United States. On many issues the pope was actually to the left of John Kerry—against the Iraq war, an opponent of capital punishment, a supporter of the United Nations, and for immigration.

And Pope Benedict XVI? During Pope John Paul II's pontificate the *New York Observer* once described Cardinal Ratzinger as "the Vatican's answer to Dick Cheney." Like the vice president in the Bush administration, Ratzinger was perceived as the pope's gray eminence, a powerful number two man behind the scenes, not too charismatic—more of a great theologian than a political leader, as a pope was expected to be following John Paul II. The new pope was the "Dr. No" of the previous pontificate: no to women in the priesthood, to married priests, to divorce, to birth control. The *Observer* recounted an anecdote in which, following the election a priest in America sends a fellow priest in the Vatican an e-mail message saying: "Avoid the rush. Go at once to Regina Coeli," a reference to the historic Rome jail in Via della Lungara, close to the Holy See.

The comparison with Cheney persisted, and the president's brother Governor Jeb Bush of Florida, in Rome with a United States delegation for Pope Benedict XVI's installation, was asked about it at a press conference at the American ambassador's residence (not the official home of the envoy to the Holy See because Francis Rooney, the Oklahoma businessman, had not yet been named as Washington's new ambassador). "Cheney should be honored to be compared to the pope, and the pope should be honored by the comparison to Cheney," Bush replied to an editorial of the *New York Times* labeling them as "Jurassic archconservatives."

Bush's reply was somewhat disconcerting since it put the new pope on the same level as the controversial vice president. But for the United States the more important issue was the extent to which the new pope intended to continue the transatlantic alliance. The Bush administration was well aware, for example, that Ratzinger was a firm opponent of Turkey's aspirations to join the European Union as a full member, whereas the Bush administration supported Ankara's candidacy. On September 18, 2004, Ratzinger had warned in a lecture that, "Historically and culturally Turkey has little in common with Europe. For this reason it would be a great mistake to integrate it into Europe. It would be better if Turkey were to become a bridge between Europe and the Arab world, or to set up a cultural continent with neighboring Arab countries." Perhaps more directly to the point, Ratzinger was on record as differing from the American and British view of Europe itself. He once expressed his opinion this way: "Europe is not a geographic concept, but a cultural concept, the result of a historical process, sometimes rooted in conflict. The Ottoman Empire was always opposed to Europe."

Even so, the impression among American officials was that Benedict XVI could yet reveal himself to be more pro-Western and even pro-American than his predecessor, and less inclined to differ openly with Bush on foreign policy issues.

REUNITING EUROPE

BUSH'S TRIBUTE TO Pope Benedict on April 19, 2005, as "a man of great wisdom and learning" was a recognition that the new pope was destined to tread the same moral path as his predecessor. But it also seemed like a subtle American hint of what the pope's role should and, by inference, should not be: a sort of tacit invitation to stick to ethical and moral issues in the world and leave the politics to the United States. The choice of the name Benedict by the new pope also sent a dual message. Benedict XV was the pope who branded the First World War as "useless destruction." The other namesake is Saint Benedict, founder of the Western monastic tradition. "I believe that the pope wished to affirm the continuity of the Catholic Church in the long term," declared Jean Delumeau, a leading historian of Christianity. "There was a strong emphasis on Europe in the choice of the new pope." Europe, not Germany: there was some feeling that the choice of a German pope signified the true end of the Second World War. In fact, Benedict's election got a cool reception from institutional Germany where Protestantism competes with Catholicism as it does in the United States.

"There was no groundswell of national pride" in Germany as there had been in Poland following Cardinal Wojtyla's election in 1978, recalled Josef Joffe, editor of the German weekly *Die Zeit*. Robert Moynihan explains that Ratzinger had been a resident of Rome for so long that he was "almost Italian, and in any case was Bavarian." Moynihan, a long-time Ratzinger watcher, says the pope's strategy is to "project the Church as the backbone of Western culture, and the great peacemaker between Protestant, beer-drinking Europe and wine-drinking, Catholic Europe. Ratzinger wants to heal this division." The conflict is not so much between hops and grapes as between two Christianities, with the Vatican becoming more introverted as its efforts to play a role in the European Union continue to be stonewalled.

In this situation Bush's assessment was that Pope Benedict was more likely to immerse himself in outstanding doctrinal issues facing the Church and in the cultural issues of Europe, and not play too great a role in the broader field of international affairs. Thomas Reese points out that Ratzinger supported Pope John Paul II in his opposition to the unilateral conflict against Saddam Hussein, which compounded the problem rather than served as a solution. Reese foresees "continuity in Vatican foreign policy," both in its multilateralism and in its support of the United Nations, with the possibility of "friction" between Washington and Rome over the Middle East, the Palestinian situation, and the UN International Criminal Court (which the Bush administration refuses to recognize, and tries to persuade other countries to do the same).

Pope Benedict's election seemed satisfactory to the Bush administration because the new pontiff's political weight was likely to be less than that of his predecessor who had caused problems for Washington with his interventionist approach to international politics, according to General Carlo Jean, professor of strategic studies at the Luiss University in Rome. Benedict XVI, Jean felt, "will be less engaged politically, focusing on questions of faith and on Europe." Less than a year after Benedict's election, the Vatican's efforts to improve relations with China, which are showing some promise, cast some doubt on those early assessments.

TWO PARALLEL DEMOTIONS

IN REALITY, "no one can tell who Benedict XVI will turn out to be: we only know who Cardinal Ratzinger was," a member of the Bush administration observed confidentially. This thought didn't reassure the White House, but in the Anglo-Saxon mind-set there is the perception that the Vatican is not a major player in geopolitics, but becomes one intermittently, when its influence can be mobilized in the interests of American foreign policy objectives. On the other hand, Washington has grown impatient whenever it has had to take into account the Vatican's activity in an international situation, usually in competition with United States interests. On the Vatican side—although no one would admit it—the United States is perceived as a younger brother: democratic, powerful, above all wealthy, but a neophyte dabbling in the affairs of grown-ups, in other words, politics and diplomacy. A decade of regular contacts and being more or less on the same wavelength has still not removed completely what Lorenzo Ornaghi, rector of the Catholic University in Milan, calls "two gigantic, symmetrical obstacles." Many sectors of the Catholic Church still see the United States not for what it is but through a lens colored either by distrust or by anticapitalist and anticonsumerist prejudice; and America influenced by the opposite prejudice against the Holy See considers the Vatican as irrelevant on the strategic level and intrusive in internal affairs.

The success of works like author Dan Brown's best-selling *The Da Vinci Code* are part of a literary trend that tends to perpetuate the cliché of the Vatican as a nest of plotters and cynics whose legendary secretiveness is used to hide murky activities, and therefore to justify a general revulsion for a clerical institution that would "pollute" the United States with its antiquated obscurantism. It must be said that the generally good relations between the White House and Pope John Paul II and now Benedict XVI have not removed these reservations. Historian Alberto Melloni says, "Saint Peter's Basilica was for George Bush Senior and George W. Bush the new Canossa. They had to come to Rome in order to pay homage to a power that . . . had created problems for them in the form of a media excommunication through Pope John Paul's vibrant speeches against the Iraq war. But that's only a partial explanation."

Melloni maintains that the presence of such an impressive array of world leaders in Saint Peter's on April 7, 2005, was an acknowledgment of the Holy See's success in presenting itself on the world stage as a guarantor of what the historian calls "a planetary communion," of which Pope John Paul II was both the symbol and the creator due to his unique understanding of the mass media. The American leadership, attached to the idea of the strategic and military primacy of the United States, was only ever prepared to accept this reality as a media phenomenon. Members of the establishment close to the Pentagon, such as geopolitical consultant and Center for Strategic and International Associate Edward Luttwak, tend to pigeonhole John Paul II as a somewhat deceptive nine-day wonder, not likely to be repeated, and to predict that as pope Ratzinger will "return to reality," keep the Vatican out of politics, and above all not challenge Washington's strategic thinking.

LUTTWAK: FORGET WOJTYLA

RATZINGER FACED THE enormous challenge of succeeding a pontiff who guided the affairs of the Holy See for almost twenty-seven years, of having lived and worked in his predecessor's shadow, and of having been elected by a conclave influenced by the emotion of John Paul II's long illness and funeral. In its search for faithful and cooperative allies to support its imperial strategy, America looked to Pope Benedict XVI to continue bilateral relations on questions of ethics, but to repudiate Pope John Paul II's policy of involvement in international affairs. For the Church, failing to speak out against United States interests when deemed appropriate means being perceived as pro-Western, which undermines its universal character.

Pope Benedict's first major test of handling an international situation that called for papal reaction was the terrorist bombings in London on July 7, 2005. It is fair to say that it was poorly handled. The initial version of the pope's telegram to the British government—unfortunately made public—called the attacks "anti-Christian." A second version edited by Secretary of State Cardinal Sodano replaced "anti-Christian" with "barbaric acts against humanity." The episode pointed to the delicate balance that the Vatican needs to maintain between its ties to Western culture so dear to Pope Benedict XVI and the Church's wider commitments, including the importance of maintaining relations with moderate elements of the Islamic world. Pierluigi Battista, an Italian journalist, wrote that the Vatican changed the text to avoid "fanning the flames of already serious tension between the Christian world and the Islamic Jihadist movement." The papal message was also bungled on the purely informational level since Britain is officially a multi-cultural and multiethnic society and the victims of the bombings reflected that demographic spread.

The paradox in the Vatican's relations with the United States is that the "parallel empires" can best coexist by emphasizing their differences rather than their similarities—by remaining individually distinct, keeping their distance from each other, and in some instances being in competition and even adversarial. What remains to be seen is whether they have the will and the ability to follow a course that requires patience, time, and action that is not driven by fear but by long-term expectations.

Some Americans would like to forget Pope John Paul II. Luttwak maintains that Wojtyla's pontificate has been "greatly distorted." Certainly, the pope "acted vigorously on Poland, and this had an impact," he says. "But Poland's liberation was the result of the collapse of the Soviet Union, and not the other way around. John Paul II's geopolitical importance has been exaggerated. His real achievements risk being underrated because they were initially overrated." An underlying hostility toward the twenty-seven-year papacy is fueling a strongly critical revision of John Paul II's role in history in which the other parallel empire emerges as the only victor. "The Polish pontiff was an illusion not a political reality," says Luttwak. "He was a media genius who exaggerated the image of papal power. A lot of people think Wojtyla's opposition to the Iraq war was important, but it wasn't: it didn't change anything. Ratzinger's task is to bring the Catholic Church back to earth after this mythification. Benedict XVI will have real impact even though he gives the impression of having less impact."

One senses in these words the antagonism and irritation that many American officials must have felt at Pope John Paul II's public reprimands from the window of his study overlooking Saint Peter's Square, and the pope's "political" initiatives often coming out of nowhere. When Luttwak says, "Pope John Paul II's funeral was his last media operation, and that is why Bush and the others were present, and not out of any sense of devotion," he may be overstating his case for effect, or misrepresenting the facts. But his remarks have to be taken into account. If not quite accurate, they represent a desire on the part of some to restore some distance between the parallel empires. Luttwak points out that

> Bush has never apologized for the war in Iraq, and the reality is that the American empire did not lose against Wojtyla: it won, actually. The United States defeated the pope in the country that mattered most to him: Poland. The United States imported liberal democracy into Poland, whereas Wojtyla wanted his country to be dedicated to the cult of the Virgin Mary. This is the reason for his concealed but strong anti-Americanism. Pope John Paul was an adversary of the United States because he was ambivalent about capitalism. And especially because his Poland, which had been strongly Catholic under the communist regime, was laicized under capitalism and introduced divorce and abortion.

"Italians are interested in what the Holy See does, but in the United States we don't care. There is no Vatican in our geopolitical world," says Luttwak, a hint of satisfaction in his voice. But after two centuries in which the "parallel empires" have come to recognize each other's legitimacy and to understand that they are destined to coexist, and that the one cannot shut out the other even in strategic matters, Luttwak seems merely to be trying to perform an exorcism, endeavoring to make the unbearable and incomprehensible Vatican "Roman empire" disappear along with the passing away of Wojtyla. In this illusory world there is and always will be only one empire, with the Stars and Stripes, bolstered by its military strength, and blessed by God from the outset.

A POPE IN THE WHITE HOUSE

I N APRIL 2008, Pope Benedict XVI visited the United States, thus completing the circle that began with the political pilgrimage to Rome of George W. Bush and the two former presidents. It was the first official visit of a pontiff to the White House after the establishment of full diplomatic relations in 1984. Only John Paul II had been there before, on October 6, 1979. But his meeting with then president Jimmy Carter was, through force of circumstances, an unofficial one.

Twenty-nine years later, Benedict XVI clearly intended his visit to smooth any differences in U.S.-Vatican relations arising from the Iraq war. And above all he wanted to bring closure to the tragedy of the pedophile priests. Upon arriving in the United States, and when in Washington and New York, he repeatedly apologized, and said he was "deeply ashamed" of that scandal—words he reinforced while visiting Australia in July 2008. Simultaneously the pope also sought to soften his own image in the eyes of the American people, who widely viewed the Holy Father as "tough, [as] this inhuman person," according to Pietro Sambi, the apostolic nuncio in Washington. The original invitation had come from Ban Ki-moon, secretary general of the United Nations, for the pope to address the U.N. General Assembly. It was the pope who decided that his first stop on American soil should be Washington. He wanted to underline the pastoral character of his visit, to meet George W. Bush at the White House, and to be in the capital on April 16 for the pontiff's birthday before moving on to New York. To many diplomats the fact that the papal visit coincided with the American presidential campaign at its height added to its significance.

But the actual significance went far beyond that coincidence. Two hundred twenty years after the first contacts between the Vatican and the United States the long and sometimes obstacle-strewn road of their diplomatic and political relations had arrived at a working relationship. Benedict XVI's visit to President Bush meant there was no more room for ambiguity or uncertainty: a reciprocal recognition had been achieved, and a new era was opening between the two "empires." The meeting at the White House in 2008 showed how much things had changed since the tentative initial contacts between Rome and the United States in 1788. In an unusual gesture, the President even went to the airport to welcome the pope not just as a head of State but as a friend. And Giovanni Maria Vian, editor of *L'Osservatore Romano,* the Vatican daily, labeled the trip as a "historic" one.

No longer can the Vatican consider "America" a remote missionary territory. Catholics in the United States exceed 67 million. Today, the Holy See looks upon the United States as a bedrock of Christianity—strong, lively, and wealthy—and as a laboratory of western Catholicism, in contrast to secularized Europe, which is searching for its religious soul. The Bush administration may have been hoping for a less assertive papacy after Benedict XVI's predecessor, John Paul II, but widespread anti-Americanism in the Muslim world and even in a sizeable portion of Europe had rendered the alliance with the Vatican a valuable one for Bush's White House. Francis Rooney, the U.S. ambassador to the Holy See from 2005 to 2007, says "the pope is really important to our country. We need him as an ally now, even more than in 2003"—in other words, when the United States was poised for war with Iraq and the then pontiff tried his best to prevent it.

The war was off the agenda, according to top Vatican diplomats, when George W. Bush met the pope in Rome in June 2007. That way the awkwardness of the president telling the pope what he thought of Pope John Paul's public opposition to the war was avoided. And that way the audience covered shared positions—anti-abortion, anti–gay marriage, and pro-life—and could be described as a success. The frictions of the past would remain in the background.

Well, almost. Some weeks later, Cardinal Jean-Louis Tauran, chosen by Benedict XVI as President of the Council for Interfaith Relations, commented: "I would like to have been a bad prophet when I defined the war against Iraq 'a crime against peace.' Unfortunately, I was not." Then there was what was seen in Washington as a diplomatic snub to Secretary of State Condoleezza Rice, never—it will be recalled—one of the Vatican's favorite interlocutors. In July 2007, Rice requested an urgent meeting with Pope Benedict: the subject of the audience was supposed to be the Middle East. U.S. diplomats in Rome told their Vatican counterparts the secretary would be speaking for Bush himself. But the answer came back: The pope was "on holiday" at his summer residence at Castelgandolfo, the lakeside summer palace in the Alban Hills, south of Rome, where (the Vatican explained) long-standing protocol dictated that he did not receive official visitors, except in very special circumstances. As one cardinal put it: "The Vatican can sometimes be very feminine: we forgive, but we don't forget."

Actually, Rice was able to confer by telephone with Cardinal Tarcisio Bertone, the Vatican secretary of state, who happened to be in Nashville, Tennessee, for the annual meeting of the Knights of Columbus. But Rice's failure to see the pope rankled the administration, taking on a significance beyond the intentions of the Holy See. The old friction over Iraq and the Middle East, it seemed, had resurfaced.

Certainly, the Vatican did not consider the missed audience a snub, and relations between the Holy See and the United States remained steady and excellent in many fields. When it came to Iraq, however, the Vatican believed that the United States was not doing enough to ensure that the safety of religious minorities—including Christians—was guaranteed in the new Iraqi constitution. The papal nuncio had complained to the government in Baghdad. In reply, he had been told that threats and violence against Christians were no more severe than those experienced by other minorities. The Americans were also approached. But they replied that U.S. troops were unable to maintain full control of the territory and had difficulty protecting non-Muslims.

MARY ANN GLENDON, A POST-FEMINIST AMBASSADOR

MEANWHILE, POPE BENEDICT was emerging from the shadow of his predecessor and establishing himself as a key figure in his own right on the international scene. He had been commonly perceived as a transitional pope, but his actions were telling a different story. He had assumed his own stance: a strong, conservative one; but also quite firm and subtle on the Church's relationship with Muslims. He defined his approach as a dialogue between cultures: a broader concept than just that of a dialogue between the two religions. And although on liturgy he dismayed many American liberals—but pleased conservatives—by setting the liturgical clock back and reintroducing the Latin mass, he earned widespread respect among Catholic minorities deeply rooted in Tridentine Mass tradition.

On foreign policy, though the style may have been different, the new pontiff's strategy was not distant from his predecessor's. The Vatican stuck to continuity. The Bush administration, facing growing skepticism at home and opposition abroad, needed an international, credible ally. "The pope has come out of the box. He is confronting the war on terror and extremists of all kinds. He has a global pulpit and is in the middle of the world stage," according to former ambassador Rooney.

To consolidate the dialogue, the Bush administration appointed as Rooney's successor Mary Ann Glendon, already well known and a respected Harvard academic. Described in the Catholic News Agency's profile as a "Catholic lawyer, legal scholar, life and family advocate," she arrived in Rome in February 2008. Her résumé includes ten or so books on subjects ranging from European law and comparative constitutional law, to a study of the modern legal profession, and a history of the Universal Declaration of Human Rights. In addition, she has written numbers of newspaper opinion pieces, in which she expresses strong views against gay marriage, abortion on demand, and "old line '70s feminism."

In 1994, Glendon was appointed by Pope John Paul II to the Pontifical Academy for the Sciences. And in 2004, she was the first woman to become the academy's president. She had also led the twenty-two-member delegation of the Holy See to the U.N. Women's Conference in Beijing in 1995, and served in the Pontifical Council for the Laity. In Rome, she attends meetings organized by former senator Gaetano Rebecchini, founder of the Center for Political Orientation, a think tank connected with conservative Catholic circles.

In short, Glendon was close to the Vatican; even too close, in the view of some. Her appointment raised some doubts in the United

States. "We are appointing someone who has served the Holy See as a diplomat and advisor. Doesn't that seem like a conflict of interest?" mused Steve Bainbridge, a professor of law at UCLA, on his blog. But other prominent academics pointed out that the U.S. government frequently seeks out the services of lawyers who have represented the non-U.S. side of issues; and that while a citizen's religious loyalty and national loyalty sometimes can be inconsistent, they are more often complementary. Thus, one answer could be that the White House wanted to have in Rome an insider able to bring the White House and the pope close together; Bush was eager to please the pontiff.

So far, Benedict XVI's contact with Washington has been indirect and subtle—not openly supportive, but not openly confrontational either. He has followed his own agenda, refusing to be used by anyone. "John Paul II felt challenged by the United States, and in response challenged it," a veteran Vatican diplomat explains. "His style exposed him to the accusation of interference. This pope is more reserved. But he has very solid convictions about America."

PHOTO OPPORTUNITY WITH U.S. MUSLIMS

THOSE WHO EXPECTED a radical change in Benedict XVI's international approach were disappointed. For instance, the White House and the State Department gave every sign of wanting to secure the pope's cooperation in Cuba in the post-Castro era. In 2007, when Fidel Castro seemed close to death, the White House lobbied the Catholic Church to form "a holy alliance" so that together they could restore democracy to the Caribbean island. There were discussions in the Vatican with Cardinal Bertone on the role the Church could play in a post-Castro scenario.

But the Holy See was much more distant, regarding the American perception of how events would unfold—or be made to unfold—in Cuba as too simplistic. The core problem for the Vatican was the delicate balance between the Cuban church community exiled in Florida, and the church in Castro's island.

A similar distance has emerged over relations with Muslims. Most U.S. neoconservatives were enthusiastic at the election of the German pope. They were heartened by his controversial lecture in Regensburg, in September 2006, in which the pope explored the relationship between reason and faith, thereby sparking a wave of hatred among Muslim communities. As Drew Christiansen, editor of *America,* wrote, some analysts "touted Benedict's new, supposedly hard-line position towards Islam. One could often detect neoconservative alliances, with Europeans like Marcello Pera and Americans like George Weigel receiving extensive and favourable attention for publicizing the new pope's alleged toughness on Islam . . . But Benedict didn't share their enthusiasm for finding new enemies."

The Vatican perceived that polemics could turn into a unique opportunity to reset Catholic-Muslim relations; and that beyond outward appearances, the Islamic moderate world was eager to establish a new balance with the Vatican. In fact, there was a shared interest in isolating the extremists.

Sure enough, soon after the Regensburg speech, the leaders of the major Muslim communities in America requested a meeting with the papal nuncio to Washington, Monsignor Pietro Sambi. Their call was unusual in itself. But, even more surprising, they wanted the conversation to end with a photo opportunity—a sign of truce, if not reconciliation.

Why? A reasonable explanation was that in the wake of Pope Benedict's speech American-Islamic leaders had perceived a mounting anti-Muslim wave in the United States. They knew that American Catholic bishops had received thousands of letters and e-mails in support of the pope's controversial lecture and denouncing Islam as a violent religion. The Regensburg polemics were just an opportunity to show the real mood of American public opinion, conditioned by the terrorist attacks of September 11, 2001, the permanent threat of fresh al Qaeda attacks on American soil, and the number of U.S. soldiers killed in Iraq and in Afghanistan by Islamic terrorists.

It was a time when parliaments and Muslim scholars throughout the world were denouncing the pontiff's words, and "clash of civilizations" theorists seemed close to seeing their theories come true. But the Vatican was far from idle. "It is hard to recall (another) crisis in which the Roman Curia responded so rapidly with such concerted action and in such a short period of time," Christiansen declared. "The pope offered expressions of regret, though not apologies . . . Above all, Benedict refused to cancel his visit to Turkey," planned for late November 2006. The flexibility of Cardinal Tarcisio Bertone and the experience of Vatican diplomats transformed the papal journey into a success. Benedict XVI, who as Cardinal Ratzinger had spoken out against Turkey joining the European Union, as pope became an unequivocal advocate of Turkish integration into Europe. In the end, it was quite difficult labelling him as a "hard-liner" on Islam. That was evident in the neocons' disillusioned reactions to the trip. But actually every radical position, among both conservatives and liberals, was destined to be frustrated by the Pope's choices.

What cannot be openly admitted by the Holy See, is that with the end of Bush's second term Rome will have lost a sometimes embarrassing ally in foreign policy, but a combative one on the pro-life agenda. From this point of view, Bush's legacy is a mixed one for the Vatican. The image of the U.S. president confessing in Robert Draper's book *Dead Certain*—"I've got God's shoulder to cry on, and I cry a lot"—reflects Bush's inextricable connection between faith and politics. But it's a reminder that the relations between the Parallel Empires cannot rest only on the dangerous principle of Christianity as just a religion of the West. Such a line of thought proved misleading, and in the end damaging for the United States. But it was damaging for the Vatican as well: the dramatic exodus of Christians from the Middle East is just the first and most visible consequence of Bush's historic mistakes.

ENDNOTES

CHAPTER 1

Page 4: labeled the U.S. Supreme Court: Lexington, "The Papal Court," *The Economist,* January 28, 2006, p. 52.

Page 5: Yet in 1853, the first Vatican: Documents of Cardinals and Officials of the Curia, Bedini, Cardinal Gaetano, Envelope 5A, Vatican Secret Archive.

CHAPTER 2

Page 6: "Not long ago there arrived": Vatican Secretariat of State. "Documents of Cardinals and Officials of the Curia," Bedini, Cardinal Gaetano, Envelope 5A, Vatican Secret Archive.

Page 9: Bedini's visit began in New York: James F. Connelly, *The Visit of Archbishop Gaetano Bedini to the U.S.A., June 1853–February 1854, Analectica Gregoriana,* vol. 109 (Rome: Gregorian University Press, 1960), section B, number 20, pp. 16–17.

Page 11: His mission, warned the *New York Observer*: Connelly, *The Visit of Archbishop Gaetano,* p. 34.

Page 13: the "Know-Nothing" movement: "History of the World: The Story of the United States," part 261, *Corriere della Sera* series, vol. 25, 2005.

Page 13: "Down with Bedini!": Connelly, *The Visit of Archbishop Gaetano,* pp. 98–101.

CHAPTER 3

Page 21: As Thomas Spalding explains: Thomas Spalding, *The Premier See. A History of the Archdiocese of Baltimore, 1789–1989* (Baltimore: John Hopkins University Press, 1989), pp. 1–6.

Page 22: Throughout the colonial period: Ibid., pp. 8–9.

Page 25: Giulio Andreotti, an Italian senator for life: James Nicholson, "USA e Santa Sede: La Lunga Strada," *Libri di 30Giorni,* November 2002, p. 9.

Page 26: "In the eighteenth century, the U.S. mission": Ibid., p. 11.

Page 27: served as an example for Great Britain: Spalding, *The Premier See,* p. 21.

Page 28: "America is considered a land of nonbelievers": Alexis de Tocqueville, *Viaggio in America (1831–1832)* (Milano: Feltrinelli, 1990), p. 180.

Page 29: In spite of their consular rank: Nicholson, "USA e Santa Sede," p. 11, quoting letter to John Forsyth.

Page 29: On June 1, 1847, the Vatican: Connelly, *The Visit of Archbishop Gaetano,* p. 78.

Page 30: "Our government ought to be represented there also": Nicholson, "USA e Santa Sede," p. 13.

Page 30: He said he was pleased: Connelly, *The Visit of Archbishop Gaetano,* p. 78.

Page 31: "But after a while Pius IX asked": Carlo De Luca, "Si svolse in Italiano il primo colloquio tra il Papa e un diplomatico Americano," *L'Osservatore Romano,* April 9–10, 1984, p. 6.

Page 32: James Connelly wrote that: Connelly, *The Visit of Archbishop Gaetano,* p. 83.

CHAPTER 4

Page 33: In James Nicholson's account: Nicholson, "USA e Santa Sede," pp. 16–19.

Page 34: "Black slaves and Roman Catholics are the same": Vatican Secretariat of State: "Documents of Cardinals and Officials of the Curia."

Page 34: Poor pay was the reason: Randal to Secretary of State. L. F. Stock, ed., *United States Ministers to the Papal States,* vol. 1 (Washington, D.C.: Catholic University Press, 1933), p. 255.

Page 35: "an atrocious proclamation": *Storia della Chiesa* XXI/2, Pontificato di Pio IX, p. 661.

Page 36: As a conciliatory gesture: Nicholson, "USA e Santa Sede," p. 19.

Page 37: Following the establishment of an American legation: Ibid., p. 20.

Page 38: Pius IX's suspected sympathy for the South: Connelly, *The Visit of Archbishop Gaetano,* p. 83n.

Page 39: Pius IX was wounded by America's hasty and ill-considered action: L. F. Stock, ed., *United States Ministers to the Papal States,* vol. 1 (Washington, D.C.: Catholic University Press, 1933), p. 429.

Page 40: The American Catholic hierarchy would be free: Gerald Fogarty, *The Vatican and the American Hierarchy from 1878 to 1965* (Washington, D.C.: Michael Glazier Inc., 1985), p. 117.

Page 41: Along with the mosaics and the valuable maps: Cardinal Satolli, *Loyalty to Church and State: The Mind of H. E. Francis Cardinal Satolli* (Baltimore: John Murphy and Company, 1985), pp. 12–15.

Page 44: When Gibbons proposed reciting a prayer: John Tracy Ellis, *The Life of James Cardinal Gibbons,* vol. 2 (Westminister, MD: Christian Classics Inc., 1987), p. 6.

CHAPTER 5

Page 45: The purpose of the dictionary: Review of *Secret Societies in America* (A. Preuss), in *La Civiltà Cattolica,* Year 76, 1925, vol. 1, pp. 335–41.

Page 46: "It's impossible to give you any information": *La Civiltà Cattolica,* Ibid.

Page 46: Already in 1923 the Secretariat of State: *La Civiltà Cattolica,* Year 74, vol. 1, January 1923, pp. 286–87.

Page 49: David Chalmers, in his in-depth study of the Klan: David Chalmers, *Hooded Americanism* (Durham: Duke University Press, 1987), pp. 85–86.

Page 51: William Simmons, another Alabaman: Ibid., p. 113.

Page 52: Archbishop Michael Corrigan of New York wrote: Quoted by Daniela Seresella, *Cattolicesimo italiano e sfida americana* (Brescia: Morcelliana, 2001), p. 126.

Page 52: the *Sacramento Bee* quoted Methodist minister Rev. W. Redburn's complaint: Unpublished texts with Professor J. A. McGowan, Sacramento State College, 1961, p. 19.

Page 53: The Radio Priest, Father Charles Coughlin: Chalmers, *Hooded Americanism,* p. 317.

CHAPTER 6

Page 58: "The Holy Father has welcomed": Cicognani to Spellman, Washington, November 28, 1939. Vatican Archives, AANY, Protocol 231–37.

Page 59: The letter was delivered: Fogarty, *The Vatican and the American Hierarchy,* pp. 262–64.

Page 59: "to gain the pontiff's acceptance": Andrea Tornielli, *Pio XII, il Papa degli Ebrei* (Casale Monferrato: Piemme, 2001), p. 234.

Page 61: On Myron Taylor and Mussolini: Ennio Di Nolfo, *Vaticano e Stati Uniti, 1939–1952: Dalle Carte di Myron C. Taylor* (Milano: Franco Angeli Editore, 1978), p. 16.

Page 62: some German-American bishops were equally soft on the Nazis: Tittman to Secretary Hull, Rome, May 2, 1941. National Archives, 740.0011, European War 1939/10588.

Page 63: "a true gentleman" didn't open other people's mail: Maurizio Molinari, "CIA, miti, segreti, e colpi bassi," *La Stampa,* June 4, 2004, p. 9.

Page 64: the Holy See's profound and detailed knowledge: Sumner Welles, *Time for Decision* (New York: Harper Brothers, 1944), p. 142.

Page 64: Tittman remained as Washington's sole contact in the Vatican: Paul Hoffman, *Oh Vatican!* (New York: Congdon and Weed, 1984), p. 111.

CHAPTER 7

Page 65: well-informed Vatican sources: William C. Bullitt, "The World from Rome," *Life* magazine, September 4, 1944, pp. 94–111.

Page 68: "When Myron Taylor saw Pius XII again": Di Nolfo, *Vaticano e Stati Uniti,* p. 28.

Page 69: On the Soviet regime more a threat than Nazism per Pius XII: Sergio Romano, preface to *Il Vaticano di Pio XII* by Harold H. Tittman Jr. (Milano: Corbaccio, 2005), p. viii.

Page 69: National Committee for a Free Europe: Frances Stonor Saunders, *La Guerra Fredda Culturale* (Roma: Fazi Editore, 2004), p. 118.

Page 70: Myron Taylor took Hopkins to see the pope: Di Nolfo, *Vaticano e Stati Uniti,* p. 415.

Page 71: Myron Taylor wrote to Truman: Ibid., p. 28.

Page 71: When Taylor visited the archbishop of Berlin: Fogarty, *The Vatican and the American Hierarchy,* p. 308.

Page 73: Spellman received a furious letter from Archbishop Montini: Ibid., pp. 330–31.

Page 74: Cardinal Ottaviani . . . visited the United States: Alfredo Ottaviani, *Il Baluardo* (Roma: Ares, 1961), pp. 245–46.

CHAPTER 8

Page 78: "Well, don't expect me to run a country": Roland Flamini, *Pope, Premier, President: The Cold War Summit that Never Was* (New York: Macmillan, 1980), p. 25.

Page 78: former president Truman had joked: Giulio Andreotti, *Gli Usa Visti da Vicino* (Milano: Rizzoli, 1989), pp. 66–67.

Page 78: Of all the messages of congratulations: Flamini, *Pope, Premier, President,* p. 25.

Page 85: On Kennedy and Cardinal Cushing: Andreotti, *Gli Usa Visti da Vicino,* pp. 65–67.

CHAPTER 9

Page 91: "When the archbishop of Krakow was elected pope": "Ma il Papa non si USA," *Limes* I (2000) p. 37.

Page 91: "Andropov called the chief KGB agent": George Weigel, *Witness to Hope* (New York: Cliff Street Books, 1999), p. 260.

Page 93: William Clark . . . recalled that Reagan and the pope: Carl Bernstein, "The Holy Alliance," *Time* magazine, February 24, 1992.

Page 96: "a bad precedent": Kenneth Briggs, "Churches denounce Reagan initiative," *New York Times,* January 11, 1984.

Page 100: "performed important tasks for Wojtyla": Giancarlo Zizola, "Processo al Papa," *Panorama Magazine,* September 26, 1983.

CHAPTER 10

Page 102: "In November 2002, in response to the problem of sexual abuse": Declaration by Kathleen McChesney, United States Conference of Catholic Bishops, Office of Child and Youth Protection, January 6, 2004.

Page 103: the investigation had been conducted by laypeople: McChesney interview with Loretta Brocchi Lee, *Avvenire,* January 8, 2004, p. 4.

Page 103: Geoghan stands out as one of the worst offenders: *Il Regno Fortnightly Review,* Bologna, Documenti 7 (2004).

Page 104: In 1978 the Vatican had written: *Il Regno,* April 1, 2004, p. 233.

Page 107: In the first four months of 2002: *The New Republic,* December 16, 2002.

Page 107: "Law wanted to protect the Church's reputation": Henry Tinq, *Le Monde,* September 24, 2004, p. 5.

Page 108: A former senior Clinton presidential staffer: Conversation with author.

Page 109: Archbishop John Vlazny of Portland, Oregon: Vittorio Zucconi, *La Repubblica,* July 8, 2004, p. 16.

Page 111: "Catholicism weathered the storm": "Il Dio d'America," interview by Emanuele Rebuffini and Gordon Melton, *Avvenire,* March 2, 2005, p. 23.

CHAPTER 11

Page 113: In fact, in recounting the story of the convict: Mike Allen, "Bush Steps Up Efforts for His Faith-based Initiative," *Wall Street Journal Europe,* June 3, 2004, A3.

Page 113: The sole reason that he was in the Oval Office: David From, *The Right Man* (New York: Random House, 2003).

Page 113: Days after the attack, two leading churchmen: Paolo Naso, "I crociati dell'Apocalisse," *Limes* 4 (2002): 101–14.

Page 114: As Bill Keller . . . put it to an Italian writer: Maurizio Molinari, *George Bush e la Missione Americana* (Roma-Bari: Laterza, 2004), pp. 166–68.

Page 114: But as the Italian Protestant historian Paolo Naso recently recalled: Naso, "I crociati dell'Apocalisse," p. 104.

Page 115: On Richard Land: Peter Waldman, "Evangelical Christians Coat U.S. Foreign Policy with an Activist Tinge," *Wall Street Journal,* May 26, 2004, A5.

Page 116: But Horowitz said that the Christian community: Ibid.

Page 117: In 1997 a Baptist review named Michael Horowitz: Ibid.

Page 117: "the notion of America as an antithesis to Europe": Tiziano Bonazzi, *Il Regno-Fortnightly Review*, Attualita Documenti 6 (2004), pp. 18–23.

Page 118: On John Hagee: D. Wagner, "Evangelicals and Israel: Theological Roots of a Political Alliance," *The Christian Century,* November 4, 1998.

Page 119: As pollster Gallup Jr. puts it: Emilio Gentile, "Dio salvi l'America," *Il Sole 24 Ore,* January 11, 2004, p. 29.

Page 121: The undisputed fact is that the 9/11 terrorist attack: Chalmers Johnson, *Le lacrime dell'impero* (Milano: Garzanti, 2004).

Page 122: Novak's response to a critical article in *Civiltà Cattolica:* quoted in *Il Foglio,* January 10, 2004.

Page 122: Bush is the champion of both the Protestant Right: Ron Suskind, "Without a Doubt," *New York Times,* October 17, 2004.

Page 122: he addressed the annual convention of the Knights of Columbus: Alan Coperman, "Bush's Religious Ambiguities," *Washington Post,* September 17, 2004.

Page 122: Bush's collaborators point out: Ibid.

Page 123: "the United States is not only an empire": Geopoliticus, "Perche l'Italia non può usare il Vaticano," *Limes* I (2000): 208.

CHAPTER 12

Page 127: Two days after 9/11: Nicholson, "USA e Santa Sede," pp. 70–71.

Page 128: "The pope is not a pacifist": *Il Foglio,* September 26, 2001, p. 1.

Page 128: In November 2001 about thirty bishops: Giacomo Galeazzi, "Il partito proguerra dei cattolici," *La Stampa,* November 16, 2001, p. 5.

Page 131: Gian Guido Vecchi reported: *Corriere della Sera,* March 26, 2003, p. 16.

Page 132: When the rainbow protest banners: Mimmo Muolo, "Pace senza ipoteche," *Avvenire,* April 2, 2003, p. 31.

Page 134: The strongly pro-American academic: Massimo Teodori, *Benedetti americani* (Milano: Mondadori, 2003), pp. 34–35.

Page 134: "Cardinal Etchegaray's visit to Iraq": Luigi Accattoli, *Corriere della Sera,* March 2, 2003, p. 8.

CHAPTER 13

Page 138: "To delay in taking action after 9/11": Interview with Carlo Rossella in *Panorama Magazine,* February 20, 2003, p. 42.

Page 140: Laghi felt that Bush and Condoleezza Rice: "La Lunga Strada" *30 Giorni* 3 (March 2004): 21.

Page 141: "I had the impression that they had already decided": Interview with John Thavis, Catholic News Service, October 6, 2003.

Page 145: *Corriere della Sera* in an editorial: Stefano Folli, "Il Lutto E L'Illusione," *Corriere della Sera,* November 13, 2003, p. 1.

Page 146: "I don't know of a single project": Gian Guido Vecchi, "Non Lasciamo l'Iraq o Qui Sarà Il Caos," *Corriere della Sera,* November 20, 2003, p. 6.

Page 147: An editorial in . . . *La Stampa:* Luigi La Spina, "Nella Chiesa Prevale Il Realismo," *La Stampa,* April 24, 2004, p. 1.

CHAPTER 14

Page 149: Colin Powell gave a wide-ranging interview on MTV: Carla Power, "Reaching out to Islam," *Newsweek International,* special issue, 2003, p. 41.

Page 153: "'Remember, our president is Pervez Musharraf, not George Bush'": Interview quoted in *Avvenire,* October 2, 2004, p. 14.

Page 154: Michel Sabbah on the peace effort: Interview in *Avvenire,* April 1, 2003, p. 11.

Page 156: Unfortunately, eighteen months later, the invasion and occupation of Iraq: Jack Miles, "Religion and American Foreign Policy," *Survival* 46 (2004): 26.

Page 158: On the growth of Wahabism: Interview with Giorgio Ferrari, *Avvenire,* March 30, 2003.

Page 159: "Back in the twenties of the last century": Andrea Riccardi, *Avvenire,* August 3, 2004, p. 1.

Page 161: Even after Bush's reelection in 2004: Franco Venturini, "Gli Alleati e La Frattura Non Sanata," *Corriere della Sera,* November 6, 2004, p. 1.

Page 161: Cardinal Ruini on the evolution of the Western world: Ruini interviewed by Luigi Accattoli and Massimo Franco in *Corriere della Sera,* March 28, 2004, p. 1.

Page 161: America likened to a sumo wrestler: Mike Steinberger in an interview with Robert Kagan, *Financial Times Weekend,* October 9–10, 2004, p. 2.

Page 163: One story . . . involved the orphans of Banda Aceh: *Avvenire,* January 14, 2005, p. 5.

Page 163: The [World Help] Web site said that thanks to the project: Gabriele Bertinetto, *L'Unita,* January 14, 2004, p. 11.

Page 163: The Catholic Relief Services reacting to attempted conversion of tsunami victims: David Rohde, *International Herald Tribune,* January 24, 2005, p. 7.

Page 163: The bridge being built by America was perceived as a trap: Paolo Mieli, "Come è visto l'occidente dagli islamicí che lo combattono," *Corriere della Sera,* April 30, 2004, p. 43.

Page 164: Such an approach was creating a growing value gap: Dana Allin and Steven Simon, "Bush's World," *Survival* 46, no. 4 (2004–2005): 26.

CHAPTER 15

Page 166: In Weigel's view, John F. Kennedy's old party: Interview in *Avvenire,* October 17, 2004, p. 3.

Page 168: In their book *L'Altra America:* Guido Moltedo and Marilisa Palumbo, *L'Altra America: Kerry e la Nuova Frontiera* (Milano: Rizzoli, 2004), p. 75.

Page 170: When Andreotti interviewed Colin Powell: *30Giorni,* December 2004, p. 12.

Page 170: Italian observers . . . noted a rush toward the center: Massimo Gaggi: "Corsa Dei Democratici Verso Il Centro. Metà Partito Con Repubblicani," *Corriere della Sera,* March 22, 2005, p. 9.

Page 170: The former ambassador and commentator: Sergio Romano letter to *Corriere della Sera,* March 26, 2006, p. 39.

Page 170: "The American bishops had been critical": Marcello Pera and Joseph Ratzinger, *Senza Radici* (Milano: Mondadori, 2004), p. 38.

Page 171: attributed this omission to a rationalist aversion toward religion: Drew Christiansen, *La Civiltà Cattolica,* March 5, 2005, vol. 156, number 3713, pp. 454–55.

Page 175: Bush had emerged as a religious as well as a political leader: Dean E. Murphy, "Can History Save the Democrats," *New York Times,* November 8, 2004, p. 5.

Page 176: Condoleezza Rice . . . visited the Vatican: *La Stampa,* February 8, 2005, p. 7.

Page 177: "It seems better able to guarantee the moral foundations": Guiseppe Di Leo, "L'American way of ethics of Cardinal Ruini," *Il Riformista,* February 8, 2005, p. 4.

Page 177: On Bush visiting Rome for the conclave on April 7, 2005: Filippo Di Giacomo "Prove di alleanza fra Washington e Santa Sede," *Panorama Magazine,* June 2, 2005, p. 76.

CHAPTER 16

Page 180: Bush seemed prepared not to pay heed: Andrea Riccardi, "L'Agenda di Papa Ratzinger," *Quaderni speciali di Limes* (2004): 14.

Page 180: ISNA report on Vatican-Washington relationship: Quoted by Aki Agency, Tehran, April 8, 2005.

Page 180: On December 9, 2004, FBI director Robert Mueller: Apcom news agency, December 9, 2004.

Page 181: In his daily diary of the conclave: Giulio Anselmi, *La Repubblica,* April 8, 2005, p. 11.

Page 182: "If Catholics had voted for 'their' candidate": Tom Foley quoted in Salvatore Carrubba, "USA e Ue separati dai valori," *Il Sole 24 Ore,* April 20, 2005, p. 8.

Page 182: This development, in the cardinal's view: Interview with Luigi Accattoli and Massimo Franco in *Corriere della Sera,* April 29, 2005, p. 9.

Page 183: *The Cube and the Cathedral:* quoted by Salvatore Carrubba in *Il Sole 24 Ore,* April 20, 2005, p. 8.

Page 185: But in 2004 he quietly reopened the investigation: Jason Berry, "A Sign of Hope for Sex Abuse Victims," *International Herald Tribune,* April 25, 2005, p. 8.

Page 185: Still no immediate action was taken against Degollado: *New York Times,* May 22, 2005, p. 11.

Page 185: The limits of the pope's appeal emerged in a Gallup poll: Ennio Caretto, "Smarrimento tra i fedeli USA, solo un terzo è con lui," *Corriere della Sera,* April 21, 2005, p. 14.

Page 186: Ernesto Galli della Loggia on Pope Benedict XVI: *Corriere della Sera,* April 21, 2005, p. 1.

Page 186: The left-leaning Spanish daily: Antonio Elorza, "El Moseoforo De Dios," *El Pais,* May 21, 2005, p. 16.

Page 186: Oriana Fallaci on the pope's leanings: Interview with Tunku Varadarajan, *Wall Street Journal Europe,* June 23, 2005, p. 8.

Page 188: The best hope . . . was that the Holy Ghost: "Benedict XVI" in *America* magazine, May 9, 2005.

Page 189: The *Observer* recounted an anecdote: Terry Goldway, *New York Observer,* April 25, 2005.

Page 189: "Cheney should be honored": ANSA news agency, April 23, 2005.

Page 189: "It would be better if Turkey were to become a bridge": Quoted in "Speciale Papa," *La Padania,* April 20, 2005, p. 8.

Page 190: "There was a strong emphasis on Europe": Daniele Zappalá in an interview in *Avvenire,* April 21, 2005, p. 21.

Page 192: "Saint Peter's Basilica was for George Bush Senior": "L'agenda di Papa Ratzinger: le divisioni di Benedetto XVI," *Quaderni speciali di Limes* (2005): 24.

Page 193: Pierluigi Battista . . . wrote that the Vatican changed the text: "Il Papa e Il Tabù Christiano," *Corriere della Sera,* July 9, 2005, p. 1.

POSTSCRIPT

Page 196: he repeatedly apologized: Ian Fisher and Laurie Goodstein, "Pope, in U.S., Is 'Ashamed' of Pedophile Priests," *New York Times,* April 16, 2008, p. A1.

Page 196: the pope also sought to soften his own image: Ian Fisher and Laurie Goodstein, "Hard-Liner With Soft Touch Reaches Out to U.S. Flock," *New York Times,* March 13, 2008, p. A13.

Page 197: labeled the trip as a "historic" one: Gian Maria Vian, "Un viaggio storico," *L'Osservatore Romano,* April 21–22, 2008, p. 1.

Page 197: "the Pope is really important to our country": Conversation between Massimo Franco and Francis Rooney, December 2007.

Page 197: "I would like to have been a bad prophet": Interview of Cardinal Jean-Louis Tauran by Gianni Cardinale, "Conoscersi per non avere paura," *30Giorni,* July 2007.

Page 199: He defined his approach as: Drew Christiansen, "Benedict XVI: Peacemaker," *America,* July 16–23, 2007, p. 12.

Page 199: "The pope has come out of the box": Conversation between Massimo Franco and Francis Rooney, December 2007.

Page 199: "Catholic lawyer, legal scholar, life and family advocate": "Mary Ann Glendon, New Ambassador To The Holy See?," *Catholic News Agency,* October 26, 2007.

Page 199: Her appointment raised some doubts: Stephen Bainbridge, "Ambassador to the Vatican Glendon," the Stephen Bainbridge Blog, posted November 6, 2007.

Page 200: "John Paul II felt challenged": Conversation between Massimo Franco and an anonymous Vatican official, September 2007.

Page 201: "touted Benedict's new, supposedly hard-line position": Christiansen, "Benedict XVI: Peace Maker," *America,* p. 11.

Page 201: "It is hard to recall (another) crisis": Ibid., p. 13.

BIBLIOGRAPHY

Allin, Dana, and Steven Simon. "Bush's World," *Survival,* Vol 46 n.4, Winter 2004–2005.

Andreotti, Giulio. *Gli USA Visti da Vicino.* Milano: Rizzoli, 1989.

Bernstein, Carl, and Marco Politi. *Sua Santita Giovanni Paolo II e la Storia Segreta del Nostro Tempo.* Milano: Rizzoli, 1996.

Chalmers, David. *Hooded Americanism: The History of the Ku Klux Klan.* Durham, NC: Duke University Press, 1987.

Colombo, Furio. *Il Dio d'America.* Milano: Mondadori, 1981.

Connelly, James F. *The Visit of Archbishop Gaetano Bedini to the United States, June 1853– February 1854.* Roma: Libreria Editrice dell'Università Gregoriana, 1960.

Di Nolfo, Ennio. *Vaticano e State Uniti, 1939–1952: Dalle Carte di Myron Taylor.* Milano: Franco Angeli Editore, 1978.

Ellis, John Tracy. *The Life of James Cardinal Gibbons,* Christian Classics, vol. II, 1987.

Flamini, Roland. *Pope, Premier, President: The Cold War Summit that Never Was.* New York: Macmillan, 1980.

Fogarty, Gerald. *The Vatican and the American Hierarchy from 1878 to 1965.* Washington: Michael Glazier Inc., 1985.

Frum, David. *The Right Man.* New York: Random House, 2003.

Hoffman, Paul. *Oh, Vatican!* New York: Congdon and Weed, 1984.

Johnson, Chalmers. *Le Lacrime dell'Impero.* Milano: Garzanti, 2005.

Mecklin, John M. *The Ku Klux Klan.* New York, 1924. Quoted in David Chalmers, *Hooded Americanism* (Durham, NC.: Duke University Press, 1987).

Molinari, Maurizio. *George Bush e la Missione Americana.* Roma-Bari: Laterza, 2004.

Moltedo, Guido, and Marilisa Palumbo. *L'Altra America: John Kerry e la Nuova Frontiera.* Milano: Rizzoli, 2004.

Nicholson, James. "USA e Santa Sede: La Lunga Strada." *Libri di 30Giorni,* November 2002.

Ottaviani, Alfredo. *Il Baluardo.* Roma: Ares, 1961.

Pera, Marcello, and Joseph Ratzinger. *Senza Radici.* Milano: Mondadori, 2004.

Satolli, Cardinal Francis. *Loyalty to Church and State: The Mind of Francis Cardinal Satolli.* Baltimore: John Murphy and Company, 1895.

Seresella, Daniela. *Cattolicesimo Italiano e Sfida Americana.* Brescia: Morcelliana, 2001.

Spalding, Thomas. *The Premier See: A History of the Archdiocese of Baltimore, 1789–1989.* Baltimore: Johns Hopkins University Press, 1989.

Stonor Saunders, Francis. *La Guerra Fredda Culturale.* Roma: Fazi Editore, 2004.

Teodori, Massimo. *Benedetti Americani.* Milano: Mondadori, 2003.

Tittman, Harold, Jr. *Il Vaticano di Pio XII.* Milano: Corbaccio, 2005.

Tocqueville, Alexis de. *Viaggio in America (1831–1832).* Milano: Feltrinelli, 1990.

Tornielli, Andrea. *Pio XII, il Papa degli Ebrei.* Casale Monferrato: Piemme, 2001.

Weigel, George. *Witness to Hope.* New York: Cliff Street Books, 1999.

Welles, Sumner. *Time for Decision.* New York: Harper Brothers, 1944.

Also, material from the Vatican Archives, *Spogli di Cardinali e Officiali di Curia*; the National Archives of the United States. Also cited, *Corriere della Sera, La Stampa, Avvenire, Limes, 30Giorni,* and other publications.

INDEX

ABOUT THE AUTHOR

Massimo Franco is political analyst for *Corriere della Sera,* the leading Italian daily, where he writes a daily column. He has written a best-selling Italian-language biography of former Italian prime minister Giulio Andreotti and a volume on the failure of U.S. intelligence after the 9/11 terrorist attacks, and he regularly covers the relationship between the Vatican and Italian politics. In the 1980s Franco was a visiting scholar in the department of political sciences at the University of California, Berkeley, where his research focus was interest groups and electoral campaigns. He is a member of the International Institute for Strategic Studies (IISS) of London.